Praise for *The Catholic Catalogue*

"Putting the richness of Catholic liturgy and life on full display, Melissa Musick and Anna Keating show us that Christianity is constituted by keeping habits, performing practices, and embodying the traditions of the Church. This book will be useful to Catholics, indeed to all Christians, looking for ways to make their faith practical. At one point, this remarkable mother-and-daughter team quote Thomas Aquinas, who reminds us, 'The things we love tell us what we are.' *The Catholic Catalogue* instructs us in the virtue of love and thus helps to make us what we are called to be: disciples."

—Stanley Hauerwas, professor, Duke Divinity School

"It is written that faith without works is dead; one could not ask for a better guide to a lively life of faith. *The Catholic Catalogue* offers ritual recipes for the everyday and extraordinary moments alike; presenting often-neglected wonders from two thousand years of tradition in precisely the form we need them today. Every domestic church should have one."

—Nathan Schneider, author of *God in Proof: The Story of a Search from the Ancients to the Internet*

"From St. Polycarp's martyrdom to prayerful room blessings, *The Catholic Catalogue* offers a smart, modern look at the varied aspects of our faith tradition. Through personal stories and well-researched history, Musick and Keating not only describe the building blocks for a Catholic household but demonstrate why, for so many, the Catholic Church feels like home."

—Kerry Weber, managing editor for *America* and author of *Mercy in the City*

MELISSA MUSICK & ANNA KEATING

*The* CATHOLIC
CATALOGUE

A FIELD GUIDE TO THE DAILY ACTS
THAT MAKE UP A CATHOLIC LIFE

I

IMAGE

New York

All rights reserved.

Published in the United States by Image, an imprint of the Crown Publishing Group, a division of Penguin Random House LLC, New York.
www.crownpublishing.com

IMAGE is a registered trademark and the "I" colophon is a trademark of Penguin Random House LLC.

Library of Congress Cataloging-in-Publication data is available upon request.

ISBN 978-1-101-90317-9
eBook ISBN 978-1-101-90318-6

Printed in the United States of America

Permission acknowledgments can be found on p. 417.

*Text illustrations by Chau Nguyen*
*Cover design by Jessie Sayward Bright*
*Cover illustration by Jeannie Phan*

10 9 8 7 6 5 4 3 2 1

First Edition

*For Martin,*

*and for our children,*

*for whom this was a life before it was a book*

*and*

*For Geoffrey*

# Contents

~~~~~~~~~~~~~~~~~~~~~~~~

## Summer Ordinary Time 227

## Autumn Ordinary Time 258

## Part Three: SEASONS OF LIFE

## Childhood to Adolescence 300

~~~~~~~~~~~~~~~~~~~~~~~~~~~~~~~~~~~~~

Birds aren't known by what they feel or think. They're known by habits and habitats, by diet and coloration. Tree-clinging birds do just that; they cling to trees. So field guides to birds are arranged by areas of identification that might help you find, say, a Bohemian Waxwing or a Western Tanager.

We've written a field guide to the daily acts that make up a Catholic life, for Catholics, like birds, can be identified by habits and habitat, by diet and coloration. Like bird life, our life can be identified by its practices. Some of ours are going to Mass on Sundays and holy days of obligation; saying certain prayers at certain times of the day; making our confessions; fasting during Lent and feasting during Easter; and wearing the white baptismal garment, the religious medal, the alb, or the clerical collar.

Before all else Catholicism is a life, a life that moves through cycles and seasons. That's why this book, this field guide, is divided into sections organized around these times and seasons—of the Church year, of human life—and the elements—smells and bells, religious signs and symbols, fasting and feasting, gathering and processing, baptizing and burying—that mark us as Catholics.

Some of us grew up celebrating St. Lucy's Day with breakfast in bed, or cooking minestrone soup on the Memorial of St. Joseph the Worker, but many of us did not. Many of these cultural practices have been lost. Perhaps you grew up Catholic but you're not sure what it means to *be* Catholic. Maybe you want to know more about your faith and its practices. Perhaps you are considering joining the Church, or you just joined and you're unsure of how to keep track of feast days and name days and maybe wondering why they even matter. Maybe you'd like to know what a wake is and how it differs from a funeral. Maybe you're curious about what it means to keep Lent.

Maybe you'd like a book to give to non-Catholic friends and family who have questions about the flock of which you are a part. If so, this book is for you.

If you've ever used a field guide, or a cookbook, you know that it doesn't have to be read in order from front to back. Probably you'll start with what interests you most. In a field guide to birds, it might be identifying the little bird with the red crest you saw this morning. In that case, you'll start with your geographical area and then go on to characteristics of birds in that region. In a cookbook, you'll probably go to the section that meets your needs. If you're planning to make a birthday cake, you'll turn to pastries. Use this book in the same way. If you wonder why Catholics use incense and holy oil, go to "Smells and Bells." If you've heard of the Advent wreath but you don't know how to pray around it, go to "Advent." If you're going to be a godparent or will be attending an infant baptism for the first time, go to "Childhood and Adolescence."

People usually pick field guides because they are interested in a subject. Often, a cursory glance becomes a study, and the casual glance at birds outside the window progresses to a walk in the forest with a pair of binoculars. That's our hope with this guide, too. Start anywhere you like, with any practice that catches your attention or speaks to your heart. This book is an opportunity to discover, or re-discover, the sounds and sensations of being Catholic. We pray the life will draw you in and delight you, and fill your days with its riches.

Melissa Musick
June 9, 2015, Memorial of St. Ephrem the Syrian,
deacon and Doctor of the Church

# Part One

# SMELLS AND BELLS

# WHAT WE KEEP: THE VENERATION OF HOLY RELICS

And so we afterwards took up his bones which are now
more valuable than precious stones and finer than refined
gold, and laid them in a suitable place.

–FROM AN EYEWITNESS ACCOUNT OF
THE MARTYRDOM OF ST. POLYCARP, AD 155

Catholicism is all about what we keep: communion with God and the saints, communion with one another, communion with our beloved dead. In the Church, there is a way of keeping this communion that is centered on the veneration of *relics*. The word "relic" is from a Latin word, *reliquiae*, which means *remains*. *First-class relics* are the material remains of the bodies of canonized and beatified saints. A relic of this sort might be a piece of one of the saint's bones, though, in some cases, the entire body of a saint is preserved. *Second-class relics* are objects, such as a piece of clothing that touched the saints' bodies, or instruments used by the saints during their lifetime. An example of this is the writing desk at which St. Thérèse of Lisieux wrote *The Story of a Soul*. *Third-class relics* are objects, such as a piece of cloth, that have touched a first-class relic.

Venerating relics is part of the rich devotional life of the Church. Relics, like icons, are doorways into the divine. And, like icons, they can seem odd to Westerners, until we learn more about the ancient practice. As we reflect on the holy life of the saint whose relic we honor, we are drawn closer into the Christ to whom the saints have given their lives. The idea of relics may be new to you, and keeping relics may be a new practice, but it is grounded in simple human needs.

You may have a picture of a dead parent or grandparent or child or close friend. You may keep the picture in a special place in your house or in a locket you wear close to your heart. My husband carries his late father's wallet. I carry my late mother's billfold. These are daily objects for daily use, so we are prompted to remember our loved ones daily. You want to remember a person who was, and is, important to you, who taught you how to live, who showed you the pathways of faith. This is not worship, but it is right respect and honor.

Our very recent ancestors in the nineteenth and early twentieth centuries commonly kept locks of hair. Christians found comfort in the soft hair and its assurance that the dead who once lived in this world will live forever in Christ. They are hidden from our sight, but we cherish the reminders of their mortal and eternal lives.

We *venerate*, or honor, relics, but we don't worship them. We worship God alone. Theologians distinguish these two truths using the Greek words *latria* and *dulia*. *Latria* refers to the worship owed to God, and only God: Father, Son, and Holy Spirit. *Dulia* refers to the veneration, or honor, we owe to the saints. You probably know the word "venerate" best from the Good Friday liturgy, when we are invited to come forward during the service to kiss or kneel before the cross. We do not worship the cross; we worship the One who hung upon it. But we do honor the cross as the instrument of our salvation.

### THE MARTYRDOM OF POLYCARP

Relics have been venerated from the earliest days of the Church. The first documented case of Christians gathering the remains of a martyred saint and keeping those remains for veneration comes from the middle of the second century and the martyrdom of St. Polycarp, the bishop of Smyrna, who was burned at the stake in AD 155.

Polycarp was consecrated a bishop by the apostle John, who died around the turn of the second century. Polycarp was beloved of his people and revered as a living link to the apostles. An eyewitness to Polycarp's death recorded what he saw and heard for his fellow Christians. The writer describes Polycarp as the flames consume him:

> The fire took on the shape of a hollow chamber, like a ship's sail when the wind fills it, and formed a wall round about the martyr's figure; and there he was in the centre of it, not like a human being in flames but like a loaf baking in the oven, or like a gold or silver ingot being refined in a furnace. And we became aware of a delicious fragrance, like the odour of incense or other precious gums. As the bones and ashes grew cool enough to be gathered up, the faithful took them and laid them in a suitable place.

The writer describes the saint's remains as "more valuable than precious stones and finer than refined gold."

## VERONICA'S VEIL

Polycarp's martyrdom marks the earliest known account of the harvesting and keeping of relics for veneration, but it may not be the earliest instance of such devotional practices. Recall the story of St. Veronica, whose name is related to the Latin phrase *vera icona*, that is, *true icon*, or *true image*. Catholics are familiar with the story of Veronica wiping Jesus's bruised and bleeding face as he walked to the cross. Though this story is not recounted in Scripture, it has long been held as worthy of remembrance by the faithful and is part of the Stations of the Cross. Until 1600, the cloth, or "Veronica's Veil," was kept inside the old St. Peter's Basilica in Rome.

When the new St. Peter's was constructed under Pope Julius II, the cloth was lost, or, at least, it was considered lost. It turns out that for hundreds of years the cloth has been kept in a Capuchin church in Manoppello, in the Abruzzo region of Italy. The cloth measures 17 by 24 centimeters, and it bears the life-sized image of a human face. The cloth is finely woven and the face is finely featured. But scientists doing microscopic examinations of the image can find no trace of paint. Indeed, the fabric is byssus, a costly fabric made from weaving the threads a certain kind of sea mussel, a bivalve mollusk, makes, found on the ocean floor. The threads must be harvested from the sea during the month of May. There is at least one known living byssus weaver, a woman from the island of Sant'Antioco. She has seen the cloth in Manoppello and agrees that it is indeed byssus. She agrees that the cloth, though it can be dyed, will not hold paint.

The image seen on the cloth is that of a bearded man whose right cheek is swollen. His beard is partially ripped out. Fresh wounds can be seen on his forehead and lips. His nose appears to be broken. He looks like a man who has been beaten. The pupils of his eyes are black, and, though no scientist has found traces of paint, it does appear that the cloth around the eyes has been scorched, as if something or someone had heated the threads to a high temperature. Scholars who have studied both this cloth and the Shroud of Turin say the image on one matches the image on the other. It is the same man.

John described Jesus's empty tomb in his Gospel. He writes of Peter and "the other disciple," running to the tomb after hearing Mary Magdalene's startling news that she had found it empty. The "other disciple" arrives first but does not go in. He waits for Peter. But the "other disciple" does look into the tomb and sees "the burial cloths there." (Note the use of the plural.) John writes,

> When Simon Peter arrived after him, he went into the tomb and saw the burial cloths there, and the cloth that had covered his head, not with the burial cloths but rolled up in a separate place (JOHN 20:6-7).

The Vatican takes no official position on the relic and its authenticity, but the Capuchins and citizens of Manoppello believe the cloth in their village church is "the cloth that had covered his head." They do not worship this cloth, and if it were found to be unrelated to Christ's death and burial, it would not shake their faith in Christ. Still, they venerate the cloth as a link to Christ, and the Church encourages the veneration as a reminder of Christ's suffering. Pope Benedict XVI visited the shrine and prayed there in September of 2006.

In the stories of relics kept and venerated throughout the ages it is important to note what is kept. Property is not venerated. Currency is not venerated. Gold and jewels are not venerated. What is venerated is some link, some connection to a saint. The value lies not in the relic itself, but in the holiness of the one to whom it belonged in life, and often the relic is kept in a central place where the whole community can see and appreciate it.

Some find the harvesting and keeping of relics by the Church distasteful, but think about what we often strive to keep after a loved one dies: money and houses and jewelry. Heirs fight over such things. Families are torn apart by squabbles over inheritance. Is it more distasteful to keep the fingernail of a saint than to keep Mom's money market account?

What we choose to keep tells us what matters to us. Consider what you have that reminds you of the dead. Why does it remind you of that person, and how do you use that object in your life? I still have my grandmother's pancake griddle. I've used it regularly for almost forty years, and I always think of her when I take it down from its hook. Though my grandmother is not a canonized saint, she taught me what it means to follow Christ. I am reminded of her teaching whenever I use a tool she used and respected. Maybe you have kept something that should be given away, either to a family member or to someone in the community who has need of it. We live in an age of hoarding, of getting and keeping long past our ability to store or use or enjoy an item. As we reflect on relics, perhaps we should clean out some closets and give away what belongs to another, keeping only those things that bring goodness into every aspect of our lives.

# 2

〰〰〰〰〰〰〰〰〰〰

## HOLY WATER AND THE SIGN
## OF THE CROSS

*Let us then not be ashamed to confess the Crucified. Be
the cross our seal, made with boldness by our
fingers on our brow.*

−ST. CYRIL OF JERUSALEM, FOURTH CENTURY

When my son was a baby I enrolled him in a Parent's-Morning-Out program at a local Presbyterian church. A few mornings a week he'd play with other two-year-olds, sing songs, and read stories. But his favorite thing about the program was that it took place in a building full of water fountains. Before drop-off and after pickup, he'd stop at a water fountain, pull up a step stool, and take a sip.

One day, he dipped his hand in the water fountain and made the sign of the cross. With great concentration he drew his right hand from his forehead to his breast, then from his left shoulder to his right shoulder, mimicking the gesture he'd witnessed at table and church.

I smiled as I watched him as he was lost in the rhythm of this ancient gesture and delighted by an excuse to play in the water. I felt both happy and self-conscious, as the other parents—none of whom were Catholic—watched us as they walked by. I looked at my sweet boy, now soaked with water, and told him not to do it again, that water fountains were only for drinking. Like any good two-year-old he asked me why, and not knowing how to answer him, I let it drop.

After that it became a ritual. He would bless himself with water from the water fountain, *every time* I took him to Parent's-Morning-Out. Unlike his mother, he was not ashamed.

## THE SIGN OF THE CROSS

Christianity is a *way* (Acts 9:2). It's a series of practices, both physical and spiritual, aimed at what Servant of God Dorothy Day once called "a revolution of the heart, a revolution which has to start with each one of us." Catholicism isn't an ideology or a philosophy. It is a religion: a lifetime of small acts, performed over and over again until they become an integral part of one's life.

Pope Benedict XVI once wrote, "The most basic Christian gesture in prayer is and always will be the Sign of the Cross." You don't have to be educated or literate to perform this simple act, nor do you need to be educated or literate to understand it. Like all ritual gestures, it speaks without words. To make the sign of the cross is to say yes to God, yes to the Blessed Trinity, yes to the passion of Christ and the forgiveness of sin. The sign of the cross is a reaffirmation of one's Baptism, a rejection of evil, and a way of "putting on Christ" (Galatians 3:27).

As early as the second century Tertullian writes that Christians marked the four points of the cross on their bodies. He writes: "In all our travels and movements, in all our coming in and going out, in putting on our shoes, at the bath, at the table, in lighting our candles, in lying down, in sitting down, whatever task occupies us, we mark our forehead with the sign of the cross." The sign of the cross is still used by Orthodox, Eastern, and Latin Rite Catholics as well as by some Anglicans, Lutherans, and Methodists.

The first Christians traced the sign of the cross with a thumb on their foreheads. The early martyrs crossed themselves in this way before going to their deaths.

At Mass, before the Gospel is read, Catholics all around the world trace the sign of the cross with their right thumb over their forehead, mouth, and chest, praying silently that the Word of God might be always on their minds, on their lips, and in their hearts.

The cross was first traced on my children's foreheads shortly after they were born. Within a couple of hours of their birth they had been marked as members of the Body of Christ by their parents and grandparents, and by the Eucharistic ministers who came to the hospital to bring us Holy Communion. When my daughter was born, she and I were the only people in the room when an elderly lay minister came to bring us the Eucharist. He entered the room and addressed my newborn daughter and myself as "Sisters in Christ."

The cross would be traced on my children's foreheads again at their baptism, and it will be traced again at their Confirmation.

At Mass we make the sign of the cross for our children when they are too little to know how, but also when we want to give them a blessing. And as they continue to grow they also learn how to make the sign of the cross for themselves, crossing their upper bodies before and after prayer, and when genuflecting before the Eucharist.

## HOW TO MAKE THE SIGN OF THE CROSS

Different Christians make the sign of the cross in different ways. In the Latin Rite, we trace the outline of the cross over our upper body with our right hand, palm open. (The five fingers of the hand symbolize the five wounds of Christ.)

This can be done silently or with the words "In the name of the Father (touch forehead), and of the Son, (touch lower chest or stomach) and of the Holy Spirit (left shoulder and then right shoulder)." Some people kiss their fingers after making the sign of the cross as an additional act of reverence or devotion. Crossing one's upper body in this way is an abbreviated form of a full body, head to toe blessing, which also occurred in the early Church.

When the sign of the cross is accompanied with the prayer, "In the name of the Father and of the Son and of the Holy Spirit" it concludes with "amen," a word that means "yes" or "it is so." In saying "amen" we say yes to God, yes to the loving community of the Trinity, yes to the Incarnation, yes to taking up the cross, and yes to loving unto death. We also say yes to the fundamental reality of who we are: redeemed sinners.

In the Eastern Rite, the sign of the cross is made with the first three fingers of the right hand joined at the fingertips. These fingers represent the Trinity. The remaining two fingers are pressed against the palm, to represent the unity of Jesus's human and divine natures.

In both the Latin and Eastern Rites, the sign of the cross can be made with or without holy water. Fonts of holy water, water that has been blessed by a priest, are placed at the entrances of Catholic churches. Before walking in and out of church on Sunday, Catholics dip their fingers in water and bless themselves, thus recalling their baptism and echoing the Jewish custom of ritually cleansing one's hands before prayer.

## LIVING IN BODIES

When you stop to think about it, making the sign of the cross is a profound and scandalous act. Why would Christians want to recall, again and again, the broken and lifeless body of their God, and the instrument of torture used to execute him? Perhaps because the cross is a sign of God's love for us—God's radical solidarity with us—and at the resurrection, his triumph over sin and death. Dostoevsky writes of a man looking at an image of Christ on the cross and saying, "Beauty will save the world."

I remember as a teenager sometimes wishing for a disincarnate, less bodily Christianity. I wanted to belong to a church that was less ancient, more modern, less strange. I worried when my parents made the sign of the cross in mixed company that people would think they were superstitious, or uneducated fools. I wanted God to be a private matter. I wanted him to live in my heart, not on my head. Being Catholic was embarrassingly bodily, and I knew that public expressions of religion, like the sign of the cross, were considered poor taste. As I've grown, I'm more grateful that the Church tells us that bodies matter. From the beginning, Christianity was more than a system of thought; it was a set of practices. Eventually I came to accept that those practices had formed me, and whether I liked it or not, I was Catholic in my bones.

Still, I made the sign of the cross for almost three decades before I fully appreciated its meaning. It took a two-year-old crossing himself in a public water fountain to show me. As I watched my son, lost in the rhythm of this ancient gesture, I saw how through faith we are all children of God in Christ Jesus (Galatians 3:26). I saw how the cross of Christ transfigures ugliness, undoes inequality, and relieves dread. "For all of you who were baptized into Christ have clothed yourselves with Christ. There is neither Jew nor Gentile, there is neither slave nor free person, there is not male nor female; for you are all one in Christ Jesus" (Galatians 3:28).

# 3

# PALLS, VESTMENTS, LINENS, AND HABITS

My dear children, you have become a new creation, and
have clothed yourselves in Christ.

—FROM THE ROMAN CATHOLIC RITE OF BAPTISM

Watching family and friends lay the funeral pall (the cloth laid over a casket before the procession into the church for the funeral Mass) is to observe a markedly domestic practice. They lift and place the pall like a bedspread or a tablecloth, smoothing the top, straightening the sides, and ironing out wrinkles with their hands. And, almost always, there is the final smoothing near where the dead person's head lies in the casket. This is an instinctive act: tucking someone into bed, pulling the covers tight, the last touch to face or hair, the final words in the darkness.

The word "pall" is from the Latin word *pallium*, meaning "cloak." Since the reforms of the Second Vatican Council, the cloth is usually white. The color white reminds us of the white baptismal garment. The baptismal gown is at the root of all Catholic vesture, or ritual clothing. It is the garment we all share in common, and with which, lay or ordained, we are all vested.

All the baptized receive, in the words of the rite, "the white garment [which is] the outward sign of [our] Christian dignity." But some in the Church—all the ordained and some vowed religious—wear additional clothing as a sign of their calling and station.

The word "vestments" is from a Latin word *vestitus*, that means, simply, "clothing." Through the centuries it has come to mean a certain type of ecclesiastical clothing. Because the twenty-first century is fairly casual in terms of dress, seeing vestments (or vesture, as it is sometimes called) can make us uneasy. Yet most of us know the effect of a particular kind of formal dress: the graduation gown, the doctor's white coat, the pilot's uniform, or the judge's robe. Each of these denotes a station and a set of duties and responsibilities. The clothing speaks of skills mastered and the obligation to use those skills for good.

The clothing that is worn affects its wearers as much as it does those of us who meet people clothed in the vesture of their offices. Donning the robe reminds a judge of her duty to put personal preferences and opinions aside and decide a case based solely on the applicable law. Putting on the firefighter's helmet is a reminder of the pledge to put one's own life at risk in order to save others. A surgeon dressed in flip-flops and shorts and wearing a cartoon T-shirt might be skilled and careful, but that look does not convey professionalism in the same way that a crisp white coat does.

Liturgical vestments (clothing worn during religious services) have an ancient history for both Jews and Christians. Exodus 28 details the rules for priestly vestments to be worn in the Jerusalem Temple. Scripture commands that "sacred vestments" be made "for the glorious adornment of your brother Aaron . . . to consecrate him as priest" (Exodus 28:2-3). The elements of the vestments include: "a breastpiece, an ephod [a sleeveless garment made of purple cloth, with various elaborate embellishments, to be worn by the priest], a robe, a brocade tunic, a turban, and a sash" (Exodus 28:4). They are to be made of "gold, violet, purple, and scarlet yarn and fine linen" (Exodus 28:5).

In the Church, vestments owe more stylistically to Rome than to Jerusalem, but they serve the same dual purpose: they bring the liturgical celebrant into the background, while bringing his role, or station, into the foreground. It is not "Father Frank's Mass." The Mass is an action of the Church, by the Church, for the life of the world. Parish members noting Father's penchant for seasonal bow ties or his well (or poorly) tailored suits would find it harder to have him disappear into the rite.

I once asked a wise priest how he gets through presiding at the funeral of a beloved family member or friend. He said, "I do the same thing I do before any Mass; I remind myself that this is not about me." And that's the purpose of vestments as well, to remind the wearer that it's not about him. As Theodore Klauser writes in *A Short History of the Western Liturgy*, our vestments had their origin in the fourth-century Roman courts of the emperor Constantine, where they were taken from imperial dress befitting various imperial offices, but they have been, in Klauser's words, "spiritualized." He writes,

> Hence, none of us today when we see a bishop complete with mitre, pallium, pastoral staff, ring and bishop's shoes, accompanied by lights and incense and presiding from a canopied throne, has the feeling that here we have a dignitary who is caught up in worldly affairs. On the contrary, in the course of a process which has gone on for centuries the insignia and privileges which were once the symbol of secular power have been so transformed that they now suppress the individuality of the human person who temporarily holds the office and brings to the forefront of our attention the spiritual nature of the high office he holds.

The elements of liturgical attire that are most familiar to us since the reforms of the Second Vatican Council are the **alb**, the **stole**, the **chasuble**, and the **dalmatic**.

The alb is the garment common to all ordained and instituted ministers of any rank. It is a white gown ("albus" is a Latin adjective, meaning "white") and it reminds us of the white baptismal gown worn by everyone who has been received into a Christian church. The alb is customarily tied at the waist with a **cincture**, or rope belt.

When worn by a priest, the stole goes on over the alb like a scarf. Its two rectangular ends hang down below the knees. In ancient Rome, a stole functioned the same way a police officer's badge does today, as a sign of office. But it also served as a work cloth for slaves, who might use it to polish items or wipe sweat from their faces. It is a sign both of office and of the work a priest is called to do. The stole will customarily be worn in the colors proper to the liturgical season.

If a deacon wears a stole, he drapes it over his left shoulder and across his chest, diagonally, like a sash. This style was first mandated in 633 by the Council of Toledo and continues to be the norm for a deacon's stole.

The priest wears the chasuble over the alb and the stole. The chasuble is a loose, sleeveless, almost poncho-like garment, with a hole for the neck and a wide, circular shape. It helps to remember that the word "chasuble" comes from the Latin word *casula*, which means "little house." Some see in the chasuble a reflection of the seamless garment Jesus wore to his crucifixion. As with the stole, the color of the chasuble clergy wears customarily reflects the color of the liturgical season.

The dalmatic is a vestment worn only by deacons. It is worn over the alb and the stole. The dalmatic is a form of ordinary clothing from the ancient Roman province of Dalmatia. It is a knee-length (though it can be longer) garment made with sleeves and slit down the sides. Until the ninth century, when the chasuble was introduced for priests, both priests and deacons wore the dalmatic. Like the stole and the chasuble, the color of the dalmatic a deacon wears reflects the liturgical season or a given feast.

The liturgical colors are white, red, green, purple, and rose.

**White** is used during Easter and Christmas; the Solemnity of the Most Holy Trinity; celebrations of the Lord other than of his passion, celebrations of the Blessed Virgin Mary, of the Holy Angels, and of saints who were not martyrs; the Solemnity of All Saints (November 1) and the Solemnity of the Nativity of St. John the Baptist (June 24); and the Feast of St. John the Evangelist (December 27), the Feast of the Chair of St. Peter (February 22), and the Feast of the Conversion of St. Paul (January 25).

**Red** is used on Palm Sunday and Good Friday, on Pentecost Sunday, on celebrations of the Lord's passion, on the "birthday" feast days of apostles and evangelists, and on celebrations of martyr saints.

**Green** is used in Ordinary Time.

**Purple** is used in Advent and Lent. It may also be worn for funerals.

**Rose** may be used, where it is the practice, on Gaudete Sunday (Third Sunday of Advent) and on Laetare Sunday (Fourth Sunday of Lent).

There is liturgical dress, and then, according to the Code of Canon Law, canon 284, there is also appropriate dress for priests and deacons outside of the liturgy:

> Clerics are to wear suitable ecclesiastical garb according to the norms issued by the conference of bishops and according to legitimate local custom.

That means priests in the United States might, according to the customs of their diocese or order, wear black pants, black shirt, and a white collar (familiarly known as "clericals") or the ankle-length black tunic called a cassock. In some dioceses in the United States, deacons wear black pants, gray shirts, and white clerical collars. The concern is for modest dress and for visibility. It may seem odd to speak of modesty and visibility in the same sentence, but daily clerical dress falls under the same category as liturgical vesture in that it brings the role forward while causing the individual within the role to fade.

Ordained or vowed religious life is not an hourly job; one is always fulfilling one's calling. During the persecutions of Ugandan Christians under the reign of Idi Amin, between 1971 and 1979, those going to their deaths needed to see the shepherds among them. For those people the clerical collar was a sign of hope. When the Carmelite Sisters of Compiègne were condemned to death as traitors in July 1794, during the French Revolution, they fashioned makeshift habits out of rags to wear as they were carried through the streets on the way to the guillotine. As they mounted the scaffold, they renewed their monastic vows, asked permission of their superior to die, and began singing "Veni, Creator Spiritus" ("Come Holy Spirit"), their hymn of profession. Though the individuals were not necessarily recognizable, the crowds could see that these were vowed religious sisters going to their deaths.

Most religious orders for men and women have a distinctive garb, or dress. The habit often has its origins in the time in which the order was founded. For instance, the Franciscan habit is based on the dress of the poor in the time of their founder, St. Francis. The habit is a plain brown tunic, tied with a rope belt. The tunic had a hood for protection against the weather, and there are sandals for the feet. For many orders of women religious, the traditional habit was the dress customarily worn by widows in the time of their founding. When Blessed Teresa of Calcutta founded her order, she wrote of her desire that each sister "become Indian-minded." To this end, she adopted an Indian sari for all the Missionaries of Charity. Not all religious wear habits. Their distinctive sign, they say, should be found in their works. Many will simply wear a cross that is particular to their order and calling. Others contend that they need to be recognizable to those in need and that the habit is a helpful, and constant, reminder of their calling.

There is a set of traditional prayers for a priest to say before, and as, he vests. Though it is no longer required that these prayers be used, neither is it forbidden. Here is the prayer for washing hands before vesting:

> Give virtue to my hands, O Lord, that being cleansed from
> all stain I might serve you with purity of mind and body.

When we consider the clothing of the Church, let us consider how we present and conduct ourselves. Is there virtue in our hands? Are we recognizable as Christians by our words and deeds? Are we modest and dignified? Can we be identified as leaven and salt and light in the world? During the Rite of Baptism we pray that we will bring the dignity of what our white garments symbolize "unstained into the everlasting life of heaven." May that be our prayer as well.

## 4

~~~~~~~~~~~~~~~~~~~~

# HOLY OILS AND INCENSE

His head is anointed with the unction of sacred chrism, that
the baptized person may understand that in his person a
kingdom and a priestly mystery have met.

–JOHN THE DEACON (C. 500)


For we are the aroma of Christ for God.

–2 CORINTHIANS 2:15A


## HOLY OILS

Each time one of my children was baptized, the **chrism** rubbed into
my son or daughter's head seemed to soak into the baby's scalp. I remember sitting and nursing the newly baptized child as the scent of
balsam rose and enveloped us. The scent lasted for days, "the aroma
of Christ for God" in my arms and at my breast. I am reminded of
those sweet days every time I smell the blessed mixture of olive oil
and balsam that is chrism. I am reminded of those sweet days every
time another child or adult is anointed and baptized and given the
true name we share, as members of "a chosen race, a royal priesthood, a holy nation" (1 Peter 2:9).

Catholicism is an incarnational life. Because Christ became a
man, fully human and like us in all things but sin, our flesh is made
holy. Human flesh is of God and something we share with God. So
Catholics worship God with their bodies as well as with their hearts
and minds. Smells and tastes and movement and song are all part of
our worship and our daily life.

One of the ancient fleshly practices of Catholicism is anointing with oil. It has its roots in Jewish tradition. Israelite kings were anointed with oil (1 Samuel 10:1; 2 Kings 9:3). Israelite priests were anointed with oil (Leviticus 8:30). We know that baptized Christians were anointed with chrism from at least the third century. In *The Apostolic Tradition of Hippolytus* (c. 215), Christians are instructed in the rite of baptism:

> And afterward, when he comes up out of the water he shall be anointed by the presbyter [from the Greek word *presbyteros,* meaning, simply, priest] with the Oil of Thanksgiving, saying: "I anoint you with holy oil in the name of Jesus Christ."

Hippolytus calls chrism "the oil of thanksgiving." Psalm 45:8 calls it "the oil of gladness." Such oil is not a salve or a liniment of the kind we use for sprains or other injuries. It is closer to perfumed oil, the oil we might smooth on our bodies before a date or a night out. It is an oil of celebration, and it is used in other liturgical celebrations in addition to baptism: Confirmation, priests' and bishops' ordinations, and for the dedication of churches and altars. St. John Chrysostom calls it "myrrh," which was one of the gifts offered to the infant Christ, and he writes, "The myrrh is for the bride, the oil for the athlete."

Chrysostom gets at the truth of our Catholic life; we are called to different tasks at different times, and we have oils for these various times. The **Oil of Catechumens** is used, as the name suggests, to anoint catechumens (someone who is undergoing instruction for the purpose of being received into the Church) before baptism. (It is also used to anoint infants before baptism.) The purpose is to strengthen those who are about to go down into the blessed waters. The prayer is that the anointed will be granted "wisdom to understand the Gospel more deeply . . . and strength to accept the challenges of Christian life."

This reminds us of Chrysostom's understanding of some holy oil as like the oil that is rubbed on an athlete's body before a contest. The oil is to loosen and warm muscles, getting them ready for work.

We also anoint the sick and the dying with the **Oil of the Sick**.

This anointing reminds us that because we share in the suffering of Christ, as a given of the human condition, our suffering is holy. The prayer for this anointing asks for healing "in body, in soul, and in spirit," and deliverance "from every affliction." The Oil of the Sick is a powerful antidote to other ills with which we are beset. Materialists seek only healing of the body. Spiritualists seek only healing for the mind. The Church knows that we are body and spirit, and that all aspects of our natures matter. The Church also knows that we can meet death with hope and can rejoice in a healing that may take place here or beyond our sight.

These oils are blessed by the bishop of each diocese during Holy Week and are distributed to each parish. Sometimes the oils are stored in a boxlike structure called an ambry. Each type of oil is in a separate container marked for its particular use.

"Incense" comes from the Latin word *incendere,* which means "to burn." When I was a campus minister for Catholic students at a local college, my husband and I hosted Thursday night community suppers in our home. I often cooked big pots of clam sauce. The recipe called for many cloves of garlic, minced and sautéed. One student told me, "Even if I were blindfolded, I could find your house. I could smell where to go." Sense memories take us places. We step into a house on Thanksgiving and the smells of cinnamon and cloves, of roasting onions and simmering gravy take us to every Thanksgiving feast of our lives. We open up the closet of a dead family member to clean it out and we are overcome by familiar odors of cologne or perfume and that particular something, the smell that evokes a whole person, a way of being, a history, a life.

For ancient Jews and Christians, and for us, thousands of years later, incense is the odor and the sign of prayer. Smoke always rises heavenward. In Psalm 141, the psalmist prays,

> Let my prayer be incense before you;
> my uplifted hands an evening offering (PSALM 141:2).

God instructs Moses to build a special altar for burning incense (Exodus 30:1-10). God tells Moses,

On it Aaron shall burn fragrant incense. Morning after morning, when he prepares the lamps, and again in the evening twilight, when he lights the lamps, he shall burn incense. Throughout your generations this shall be the regular incense offering before the Lord (EXODUS 30:7-8).

When the magi come to Bethlehem to pay homage to the infant Christ, one of the gifts they brought was frankincense, or incense. Frankincense is dried sap, or resin, from Boswellia trees that grow in the Middle Eastern deserts of Oman and Yemen, and in the African deserts of Somalia and Ethiopia. Lots of elements can be used to make incense, but when we speak of liturgical incense, think of frankincense rather than, say, sandalwood.

The tradition of using incense in worship comes to Christianity from "our elder brothers in faith," the Jews. In Catholic worship, incense may be used to honor sacred objects such as the Gospel book, the altar, and the Precious Body and Precious Blood after the consecration. It is also used to honor human beings, living and dead. Incense is traditionally a part of evening prayer, "the twilight, when he lights the lamps," as referenced in Exodus.

If you are interested in reading more about the value of incense in worship, get a copy of *Sacred Signs* by Romano Guardini. Here's Guardini on the "free and objectless" beauty of incense. He compares it to the "waste" of costly oil Mary pours on Jesus at Bethany shortly before his crucifixion:

> The offering of incense is like Mary's anointing at Bethany. It is as free and objectless as beauty. It burns and is consumed like love that lasts through death. And the arid soul still takes his stand and asks the same question: What is the good of it?

> It is the offering of a sweet savor which Scripture itself tells us is the prayers of the Saints. . . . Like pure prayer it has in view no object but its own; it asks nothing for itself. It rises like the Gloria at the end of a psalm in adoration and thanksgiving to God for his great glory.

## 5

~~~~~~~~~~~~~~~~~~~~~~~~~~~~

# MAKING AND PRAYING
# WITH CANDLES

I have three candles here on the table which I disentangle
from the plants and light when visitors come. . . . The flames
move light over everyone's skin, draw light to the surface
of the faces of my friends.

–ANNIE DILLARD, *Holy the Firm*

Catholics have a sacramental worldview. We believe that material things, properly used, can be vehicles of grace. Catholic liturgies include candles, music, art, water, wine, bread, oil, incense, vestments, and, in some parts of the world, even dancing, because it is believed that material realities can strengthen our spiritual relationship with God. God the Father may be pure spirit, but God the Son was incarnate, and we live in bodies and experience reality through them.

So while it isn't necessary to light a candle in order to say a blessing at a meal, for example, it can be helpful, increasing in us a sense of attentiveness, gratitude, or reverence.

We use candles for both practical and mystical reasons. During the Mass, candles are used for beauty and illumination, but a lighted candle also represents Christ, as Jesus said in John 8:12, "I am the light of the world. Whoever follows me will not walk in darkness, but will have the light of life." The candle's flame thus represents Jesus, the light no darkness can extinguish. Some people see a light shining in the darkness as a sign of hope, others as a sign of love, as a candle produces light by giving of itself.

Many Catholic churches have banks of votive candles, usually placed before statues or icons, where people can kneel and pray at any time of day. These burning candles become a visible reminder of the prayers of the community rising up to God. Instead of "I'll pray for you," someone might say, "I'll light a candle."

Candles are used during the celebration of the Mass, and vigil lights are often kept burning near the tabernacle (where the Eucharist is kept) as a sign of Christ's presence. At the Easter Vigil the Church gathers in the darkness and kindles a fire from which a candle is lit. The priest or deacon then blesses the candle, which symbolizes the risen Christ, the Morning Star. Catholics also pray with candles in the home during the season of Advent as they prepare for Christmas, or during Lent when they prepare for Easter.

Candles welcome us into the world and accompany our departure from it. Catholics receive a candle at their baptism, and they light a candle placed before a crucifix before receiving the sacrament of the anointing of the sick or viaticum, also known as last rites.

For official liturgies, the Church prefers that the candles be made of pure beeswax. Bees have often been praised by poets, naturalists, and theologians for pollinating flowering plants, as well as for producing honey and wax. St. Benedict, whose feast is on July 11, is the patron saint of beekeepers. Pope Pius XII in his 1948 address to beekeepers said, "Have not bees been sung in the poetry, sacred no less than profane, of all times?"

At the Easter Vigil bees are mentioned in the Exsultet, or Easter Proclamation: "On this, your night of grace, O holy Father, / accept this candle, a solemn offering, / the work of bees and of your servants' hands. / . . . a flame divided but undimmed, a pillar of fire that glows to honor God. For it is fed by the melting wax, which the mother bee brought forth."

For a long time no one knew exactly how bees reproduced, so the pure wax extracted by bees from flowers also came to symbolize the pure flesh of Christ, untainted by sin. Moreover, Catholics saw in beeswax candles a way of honoring both the work of human hands and the wonder of creation.

A good time to try lighting a candle as an aid to prayer might be before blessing and sharing a meal in your home. Notice how lighting a candle quiets the room, draws everyone's attention, and helps people put aside the work and worries of the day before saying a blessing over the meal. Social scientists have found that engaging in rituals like lighting a candle or saying a blessing before eating, because they make us more mindful, actually make the food taste better.

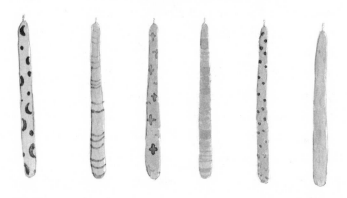

Making or decorating beeswax candles for use in your home is a fun activity to do on your own or with children. The German art supply company Stockmar sells tapered beeswax candles as well as colored sheets of beeswax for decorating them. You can create shapes out of the beeswax sheets and then, using the warmth of your hands, affix the colored beeswax to the tapered candles. A box of candles and a box of beeswax sheets would make an excellent gift for a child or friend who enjoys making beautiful things or working with their hands.

If you want to make your own candles, you can also purchase beeswax sheets and wax-coated candle wicks. To create a candle, simply roll the sheets of beeswax over the wicks and use your fingers to create a smooth seam. Finally, trim the end of wick that will be lit to half an inch.

After making your candles, use them at dinner, give them as gifts, or place them on a home altar, shrine, or in a prayer corner. School-age children enjoy getting to light a candle. Children learn with their senses, and every child reacts powerfully to light and darkness. After lighting the candle a child or adult could lead the family in a simple table blessing such as, "Bless us, O Lord, and these thy gifts, which we are about to receive from thy bounty, through Christ our Lord. Amen."

Or the doxology, which can be sung:

Praise God, from whom all blessings flow;
Praise Him, all creatures here below;
Praise him above, ye heavenly host;
Praise Father, Son, and Holy Ghost. Amen.

Or this one from a New Zealand Prayer Book: "Jesus of the wedding feast, of breakfast by the lake, bless this food we have prepared for you and all our friends. Be with us now and at all our meals, give us appetite and joy in eating together. Blessed be God in our daily bread. Amen."

In a world illuminated by electric light, candles might seem like yet another outmoded technology. And yet, by candlelight we see differently, and remember what we too often forget, the beauty of the world, and the wildness of God's presence among us.

## 6

~~~~~~~~~~~~~~~~~~~~~~~~~~~~

# MEDALS AND SCAPULARS

The special quality of beauty in crafts is that it is a beauty
of intimacy. . . . People place their pictures high up on walls,
but they place their objects for everyday use close to them
and take them in their hands.

—SŌOETSU YANAGI, *The Unknown Craftsman*

Every culture has talismans, objects that carry weight and import
for the ones who wear them. The word "talisman" comes from the
ancient Greek *telesma*, a word meaning "ritual," and it has an equiva-
lent in Spanish, French, Italian, Modern Greek, and Arabic. Some say
a talisman has magic powers, but we know it is not magic but meaning that gives the talisman its significance. The talisman itself is a
sign that points to a reality, and it is that reality which gives meaning.

Talismans are objects that tie us to our deepest and truest selves.
We may toss out shoes with abandon and donate old clothing, but it
is the rare person who tosses a mother's wedding ring or a father's
service medal or a grandparent's Bible.

Religious medals are talismans, too. The power of a religious
medal lies not in the medal itself, but in its reminder of the power
of Jesus Christ and the example of his saints in our lives. Wearing a
cross is a reminder of the One who set us free and at what cost. Wearing one's baptismal saint or Confirmation saint on a chain serves as
a reminder of all to which our names call us. Medals connect us to

our baptism and its promises, those we make and, more important, those God makes to us. In baptism, God names us children, sons and daughters. As children, we are heirs to the kingdom of heaven, and wearing a medal or scapular (two small pieces of cloth bearing a devotional image and connected by two strips of ribbon) can be a daily reminder of our true names and natures.

Wearing a medal is an ancient Christian practice. We know there are second-century medals bearing the images of Sts. Peter and Paul. We have a record from the fourth-century saint Zeno of Verona of the practice of giving religious medals to the newly baptized. By the Middle Ages, pilgrims began wearing medals marking the sacred shrines they visited.

In the sixteenth century, Pope Pius V began the practice, kept to this day, of blessing religious medals. This blessing is meant to link us more closely to the reality to which the medals point: not the image of Christ stamped in bronze, but Christ himself; not the image of the cross etched in silver, but the cross itself.

That's what makes blessed religious medals (which can be blessed by any priest or deacon) sacramentals in the eyes of the Church. Sacramentals are sacred signs instituted by the Church to prepare us to receive the fruit of the sacraments and to sanctify different circumstances of our lives. Notice the word "sign." A sign telling you that you are entering Pittsburgh is not itself Pittsburgh. The sign points to the reality that is the city. And so it is with sacramentals. They point the way to the real thing.

Are religious medals worth buying and giving and wearing? If a practice has persisted for almost two thousand years, certainly people have found it both useful and meaningful. Religious medals are available at every Catholic book and gift store. Consider giving a newly baptized or confirmed Catholic a medal bearing the image of his or her patron.

Scapulars are very much like medals in use and practice, but they are more commonly worn under one's clothes. From the Latin word *scapula*, meaning "shoulder," the scapular is part of a monk's traditional garment. It is a wool garment worn over the tunic to protect it from dirt and grime. The scapular stretches across the shoulders and comes down in front, almost like an apron. When laypeople wear scapulars, they take a very abbreviated form of the garment: two small squares of wool, attached to each other by ribbons, and placed so that one square lies against the chest and the other against the back of the wearer.

Most of us have the experience of dressing in a particular manner for work or sport. Athletes know that a certain way of thinking goes along with putting on shoulder pads or running shoes, with donning a helmet or slipping in a mouth guard. Businesspeople know the power of a suit and doctors of a white coat. Firefighters trust in the protection of their uniforms and police in the authority of theirs. In the same way, a scapular is meant to remind the wearer of the work before her, the task to which she is set. The scapular is a constant reminder, placed against the skin, against the heart, that the wearer belongs to Christ and is, wherever the day leads, to do the work of Christ in the world.

Like medals, scapulars are to be blessed by a priest or deacon. (Some scapulars are signs of Third Order lay membership in a religious order, that is, those who live according to the rule of a religious community and unite themselves to it in prayer and works of mercy, but who continue to work and live outside the monastery or convent. These scapulars are reserved to those Third Order members.) The best-known scapular is the brown, or Carmelite, scapular of Our Lady, but there are also scapulars particular to the Benedictines, the Dominicans, and the Norbertines.

Reading this blessing for medals and scapulars may help you understand how, through the quality of intimacy of "everyday use," they become a means of drawing us closer to God,

> May almighty God bless with his gentle kindness and give
> you the vision of his saving wisdom. Amen.

May he continue to nourish you with the teaching of faith and enable you to remain steadfast in doing what is right. Amen.

May he turn your steps always toward him and lead you along the pathway of peace and charity. Amen.

# 7

# MAKING AND BLESSING A HOME, HOSPITALITY, AND CHRIST ROOMS

We are so "full" of ourselves that there is no room left for
God. And that means there is no room for others either, for
children, for the poor, for the stranger.
—POPE BENEDICT XVI, CHRISTMAS EVE MESSAGE, 2012

Catholics—young or old, married or single, rich or poor—are called to lives of hospitality. Whether you live in a house, an apartment, or in a single room, this chapter is for you.

We are sometimes tempted to say, "I'll host guests when I have more room/enough plates/more money/a nicer place/a remodeled kitchen." Along with being single, being poor, or living in modest quarters can be used as an excuse for not practicing hospitality. Hospitality, we say, will come with the house, or the nicer house, or the marriage. But hospitality, which is what a home is meant to provide, is established in the Old Testament as a sacred duty (Deuteronomy 10:18-19). In his letter to the Ephesians, St. Ignatius of Antioch tells them that Christ is present in guests. We recall that Christ began his earthly life as a guest in, not a house, but a stable. So, even though we are surrounded by showrooms and magazines that tout a lifestyle that we may never attain, Catholics are called to hospitality, which is a life.

## BLESSING YOUR HOME

Whether you have just moved in or have lived in the same place for years, blessing your home is the first step in rightly ordering your home, because it dedicates the house, and anyone who lives in it, to God's service. You've probably spent some time deciding on placement of the couch or bed. Take as much time and figure out where the crucifix or icon will be placed. Gather, with all the members of the household or with friends from your parish, and pray:

> *Leader*: Peace with this house and with all who live here.
> Blessed be the name of the Lord
> *All respond*: Now and for ever. Or, Amen.

Choose a reading such as one of these: Luke 10:5-9; Luke 10:38-42; Luke 19:1-9; Genesis 18:1-10.

Walk from room to room, blessing each room and sprinkling it with holy water (which you can get from your parish). We encourage you to sing while you walk, something simple and familiar. It helps to sing the same verse or antiphon over and over until everyone knows the words, so that even the timid singers will feel emboldened to join in. "Praise God from Whom All Blessings Flow" is a good choice.

Here are some prayers from various Christian traditions, Lutheran and Episcopalian, as well as Roman Catholic. Adapt these to your situation.

### Prayer at the Entrance
O God, protect our going out and our coming in;
let us share the hospitality of this home with all who visit us,
that those who enter here may know your love and peace.
Grant this through Christ our Lord.

Amen.

### Prayer in the Living Room
O God, give your blessing to all who share this room,
that we may be knit together in companionship.
Grant this through Christ our Lord.

Amen.

### Prayer in the Kitchen
O God, you fill the hungry with good things.
Send your blessing on us, as we work in this kitchen,
and make us ever thankful for our daily bread.
Grant this through Christ our Lord.

Amen.

### Prayer in the Dining Room
Blessed are you, Lord of heaven and earth,
for you give us food and drink to sustain our lives
and make the heart glad.

Help us be grateful for all your mercies,
and mindful of the needs of others.
Grant this through Christ our Lord.

Amen.

### Prayer in the Bedroom(s)
Protect us, Lord, as we stay awake;
watch over us as we sleep,
that awake, we may keep watch with Christ,
and asleep, rest in his peace.
Grant this through Christ our Lord.

Amen.

### Prayer in the Bathroom
Blessed are you, Lord God of all creation.
You give us water for refreshment.
May this be a place of cleansing and health that we might
serve you all our days.

Amen.

Gather again where the cross or icon is to be hung. Let every person present kiss or reverence the sacred object before it is hung. Join in a final prayer:

*Leader:* Be our shelter, Lord, when we are at home,
our companion when we are away,
and our welcome guest when we return.
And at last receive us into the dwelling place
you have prepared for us in your Father's house,
where you live for ever and ever.
*All make the sign of the cross as they say Amen.*

## HOUSEWARMING GIFTS

If you are invited to bless a person's or family's house, you may want to bring a gift. One Jewish custom is to bring salt and bread. The origins of the custom are unknown, but it is probably tied to a prayer that the house will never know hunger or want, and it is so entrenched in Judaism that salt and bread are supposed to be the first gifts brought into a home. You might bring a candle, that the light of Christ might always fill the house. Or perhaps you could bring a bottle of wine that there might be celebrations and rejoicing. Another good gift is a plant for the garden or the windowsill, another sign of vigorous life. Don't concentrate on the cost of the gift but on its meaning.

## CHRIST ROOMS

Pray about the demands and possibilities of hospitality. Pray about the ways God wants you to use your living space. In her 1945 essay, "Room for Christ," Dorothy Day writes of the need for those of us who have homes to offer a room to those who are homeless. She writes that in the early Church, "in every house then a room was kept ready for any stranger who might ask for shelter." It makes us wonder about the rudeness of the people of Bethlehem. Couldn't the innkeepers who turned her away see that Mary was tired and heavily pregnant, and in need? Day reminds us that the tired and the weary, those in need, are still among us, and that every one of them bears the image and likeness of God. To welcome a stranger, she says, is to welcome the Christ.

The stranger who has a claim on a room in your home might be a nephew or niece in trouble, or one fleeing trouble at home. It might be an elderly parent or a brother or sister who has lost a job. It might be a friend who has no family nearby and needs a place to recuperate from surgery. At various times, and for various reasons, the stranger with a claim on a place in your home is a spouse or a child, struggling with illness and disability.

My husband and I cared for my elderly mother in our home for the last eight years of her life. It was a blessing to be allowed to care for her, but it was also the hardest work I have ever done. Though she was the woman who bore and raised me, age and illness and, finally, dementia, made her a stranger to me at times. So I do not want to suggest that the hospitality to which Christ calls us is anything other than the cross. The objections of the citizens of Bethlehem are my own: "We have no room." We have no more time or patience or money or strength. My patience and strength *did* fail, and I found that there was no more room in my heart. I learned, slowly and reluctantly, to ask for help, and in the help of others I found room.

Dorothy Day is far down the road to sainthood, and most of us have not even stepped onto the path. But we can begin to practice hospitality and ask God to help us grow in hospitality. Just begin. Throw a party. Ask a neighbor over for coffee. Say hello over the fence or in the lobby. Invite guests to dinner (even if it is cheese sandwiches on chipped and mismatched plates), and try saying yes when a friend asks you to put up people they know but you don't. You will wind up with extra dirty laundry, but you may also wind up with new friends, or, at least, some interesting stories. Get used to saying yes, sometimes even when your first impulse is to say no, and see where God leads you. But understand that welcoming children and your ill or elderly relatives, is radical hospitality, as well. Practicing charity when you share a place with housemates can be radical hospitality, too. Sometimes the "stranger" is a member of your family. Sometimes the "stranger" is your roommate or friend.

~~~~~~~~~~~~~~~

# 8

# SACRED SPACE AND CHURCH ARCHITECTURE

Next to the Blessed Sacrament itself, your neighbor is the
holiest object presented to your senses.

–C. S. LEWIS, *The Weight of Glory*

## THE CHURCH AS THE BODY OF CHRIST

When we think of sacred space we might think of a Gothic cathedral like the Cathedral of Notre Dame in Paris, with its dramatic vaults, Corinthian columns, and rose windows. Beautiful art and architecture play an important role in our tradition because beauty is an attribute of God.

And yet, it is equally important to remember that the Mass can be, and often is, celebrated everywhere: in basements; on beaches; in prisons, shopping malls, and slums.

How can these secular spaces be considered sacred, that is, set apart, or made holy? Jesus said, "Where two or three are gathered together in my name, there am I in the midst of them" (Matthew 18:20). When the liturgy is celebrated, God is not in some faraway place. He is in our midst. He is present in the Blessed Sacrament, present in the Word, and present among the assembly, that is, the Mystical Body of Christ. So part of what makes a space sacred is the use to which it is put.

When Chaldean Christians in Iraq fled the Islamic State of Iraq and Syria, they had to leave their ancient churches behind. But even in exile, there is sacred space. Because of the indwelling of the Holy Spirit, the people of God *are* the dwelling place of the Lord. They are the holy temple. They are the Church. So the assembly itself is part of what makes sacred space sacred. The other part, of course, is the Eucharist, because Jesus is fully present in the breaking of the bread.

## THE CHURCH AS BUILDING

The word "church" can refer to God's people, but it can also refer to the building in which people gather for common prayer, to hear the word of God, and to receive the sacraments.

Because Christ's presence is realized in the church (in the Eucharist, in the assembly, in the Word of God), the structure itself is seen as the house of God on earth. Thus, the building is set aside for the celebration of divine mysteries and formally dedicated to God. In Catholicism, only people and churches are anointed with chrism, or holy oil. When an altar is dedicated it is anointed with oil, incensed, and finally lit with candles. The prayer of dedication reads in part, "Make this altar a place  of communion and peace so that those who share in the body and blood of your Son may be filled with the His Spirit and grow in your life and love."

In the early Church, Mass was celebrated, by necessity, in people's homes. Typically, a wall was removed to make space for a large gathering of people, and a baptismal font would be in a separate building. (The practice of a separate baptistery continues in some churches to this day, like St. John Lateran in Rome.) When Christians were no longer a persecuted minority, they outgrew these house churches and started constructing formal buildings, or basilicas, which were designed to help encourage reverence and an encounter with the divine.

Mass can be said anywhere, yet some spaces are more conducive to liturgical celebrations than others. The acoustics of a space, the quality of light, the possibility of procession, the presence of sacred art, can either hinder or support the liturgical life of a community. Spaces shape us, just as we shape them.

Even people who are not religious often seek out beautiful churches as places for quiet reflection, because beauty is healing. When the University Medical Center of Princeton redesigned its rooms to make them more beautiful, patients requested 30 percent less pain medication and recovered more quickly. Even if we never visit one of the great monasteries or cathedrals, it is reassuring to know that such repositories of beauty exist, and that in them there are monks and nuns chanting and pilgrims praying for the salvation of the world.

Catholics have a sacramental worldview. We believe that material things, rightly used, can be vehicles of grace. So we often praise God with our senses, with smells and bells. Patrons donate flowers for the altar, everyone puts money in the collection basket to pay for the incense, and if you're lucky, a trained musician stands up to sing.

The Catholic Church has long been a patron of the arts. Pope Benedict XVI once called a Baroque church "a unique kind of fortissimo of joy, an Alleluia in visual form." When a woodworker builds an altar for his parish, or an iconographer paints an icon for her church, these are acts of love and adoration. Love for the people of God who will gather within these walls, and adoration, insofar as the art itself aims to make the invisible God more visible. As Dana Gioia once wrote, "Dante and Hopkins, Mozart and Palestrina, Michelangelo and El Greco, Bramante and Gaudí, have brought more souls to God than all the preachers of Texas." This is because at its best sacred art and architecture preach the Gospel without words.

## NOTABLE ASPECTS OF CHURCH ARCHITECTURE AND DESIGN

Different church buildings serve different functions. Some, called martyria, were built over relics, or over the tomb of a martyr, like St. Peter's in Rome. Others, often called shrine churches, were built so that pilgrims could commemorate an important moment in the life of Christ. The Church of the Holy Sepulchre, for example, was built on the spot where Jesus was crucified.

Some of the ornate interiors of Catholic, Orthodox, and Byzantine churches were originally intended to be experienced as visions of heaven. For example, in St. Paul's Outside-the-Walls, Jesus is seen seated on a throne surrounded by heavenly beings (as he is depicted in Scripture, in the book of Revelation).

Similarly, many Gothic churches incorporate garden imagery, vines, leaves, or flowers carved in stone, to suggest a return to the Garden of Eden, and with it, a state of grace.

Some churches have cross-shaped or cruciform interiors, housing the worshipers within the fundamental symbol of Christianity.

Jesus lived in the Roman Empire, so many of the churches built in the first few centuries of Christianity incorporate Roman architectural elements, reinterpreting them in light of the Gospel. For example, in the Roman world, a triumphal arch was used to mark the ceremonial entry of a leader into a city after a military campaign. This same arch was used at the entrance of churches to signify the victorious entry of Christ and his followers into heaven.

Catholic Church architecture varies from age to age, and from place to place. Spanish missionaries to the United States and Mexico didn't build Gothic cathedrals. They built churches in the local style, using regional materials. As a result, Mission-style churches have smooth adobe walls made out of clay, sand, and straw.

Similarly, Catholic churches in China often feature curved rooflines and tiled roofs, echoing traditional Chinese architecture and design. The unique cultural heritage of a people should be expressed in their places of worship, so not all churches look alike. The small Catholic chapel on the Pine Ridge Native American Reservation in

South Dakota has Lakota figures in its stained-glass windows and both Lakota and Christian symbolism in its wall hangings and art.

## THE EXPERIENCE OF ART AND SPACE

However humble or ornate, churches should be beautiful. As the theologian Hans Urs von Balthasar wrote, "Before the beautiful—no not really *before* but *within* the beautiful—the whole person quivers. He not only finds the beautiful moving; rather he experiences himself as being moved and possessed by it."

Some of my most formative experiences of common prayer and worship occurred in the Shove Memorial Chapel on the Colorado College campus. My mother was the campus minister for Catholics at the college when I was a teenager, and I would sometimes join her students in the side chapel for Evening Prayer or Mass. Shove Chapel, a nondenominational chapel, was designed by the architect John Gray in the Norman Romanesque style, and its limestone walls, round arches, and tall ceilings evoke an eleventh- or twelfth-century cathedral.

When my mind would wander, as it often did, during the silence of evening Mass, I would watch the frankincense burning on charcoal briquettes at the back of the chapel, the fragrant smoke rising along with our prayers. I would gaze at the carved stone walls, the painted ceiling, and stained-glass windows. I would close my eyes and listen to the ancient chants and hymns, sung without accompaniment, echoing off the chapel's limestone walls. The seating in the chapel was split down the middle, so we faced one another as in choir stalls. I would glance at the faces of the people around me. We knew one another. The community was small.

The beauty of the space and the sense of belonging I experienced there has stayed with me. Perhaps as you read this description a beautiful church you once visited or prayed in appears in your mind.

As Christians we believe that having access to beauty, truth, or goodness should not be the exclusive privilege of the wealthy few, or of students at an expensive liberal arts school. Beautiful churches should be for everyone, because God is the author of beauty.

What's more, beautiful liturgical spaces speak to the dignity of those assembled. A poor laborer, who lives in a dangerous or run-down neighborhood, might nevertheless play the piano in a beautiful cathedral. At church, he has his dignity. There, the rich and the poor drink from a common cup.

In the liturgical calendar we recognize the importance of certain church buildings. All Catholics have a parish church, but the entire Roman Catholic world also shares a single church: the Basilica of St. John the Baptist (or St. John Lateran) in Rome. On November 9 Catholics celebrate the birthday of this fourth-century basilica (a word that means "a building for a king"). St. John Lateran is the home church of all Catholics because it is the home church of the Bishop of Rome. Tradition holds that the high altar is built over a simple wooden table on which the apostle Peter celebrated the Eucharist, and that the church was dedicated in the year 324.

Likewise, on November 18 Catholics celebrate the Dedication of the Basilicas of Sts. Peter and Paul, Apostles. These churches were built in Rome over the ground where St. Peter and St. Paul were martyred. St. Peter's Basilica is the better known of the two, because it is the church the whole world associates with the pope and the Vatican. St. Peter's was consecrated in 329. St. Paul's (sometimes called St. Paul's Outside-the-Walls) was consecrated in 324.

I visited these churches, as well as the Basilica of St. Francis of Assisi, when I traveled to Rome for World Youth Day in 2000. As an American teenager, I was awed by the frescoes, but what moved me most of all were the pilgrims who walked beside me in these lavishly scaled buildings. Some of them wore sandals made of recycled tires and carried pieces of cardboard on which to sleep. Many had come from poor countries, at great sacrifice, and it struck me that these were their churches. The paintings of Giotto and Michelangelo weren't locked away in the vault of a wealthy collector. They were on the walls of public buildings, where millions of pilgrims knelt, and continue to kneel, in prayer.

# 9

# PROCESSIONS

What is a procession? A journey, distilled.

-JANET SCHLICHTING

Catholicism is an embodied tradition. We bow and bend. We touch and kiss. We bathe and anoint. We stand upright and lie prostrate. We eat and drink. We light candles and fill the air with fragrant smoke. We sing and keep silence. We sit still and we get up to journey.

Journeying is in our bones. Jesus meets his disciples on a mountain in Galilee after the resurrection (Matthew 28:16-20). They gather, but they don't stay. Jesus sends them out into "all nations." According to the tradition, Peter went to Rome, Andrew went to Greece, Thomas went to India, Matthew went to Ethiopia, Simon the Zealot went to Persia, James (son of Alpheus) and Matthias went to Syria, and Philip went to Asia Minor. They all died far from home. Only James (son of Zebedee) died in Palestine (Acts 12:2). Leaving home to journey in faith is woven into the fabric of the Church.

We are called to journey in faith. One of the ways we make that journey is in processions. The journey in faith may not be to a foreign country. We may go to the house of a neighbor or to a street corner or into our own heart, but the Church knows that we need practice for all these journeys. We practice in processions.

## PROCESSIONS

Most of us have experienced processions by walking with fellow parishioners on Palm Sunday or on the Feast of Corpus Christi. But processions are also a good way to mark feast days and fast days in the home, a good way to declare the domestic space for Christ. You don't have to be elaborate. Mark the end of the Church year by giving everyone a paper crown to wear (which you can buy or make) and process through the house and yard, if it isn't too cold, singing a well-known hymn like "To Jesus Christ, Our Sovereign King." If there are children who don't yet read, they can join in on the rousing, and easily learned, chorus: "Christ Jesus, Victor! Christ Jesus, Ruler! Christ Jesus, Lord and Redeemer!" And that's basically all you need: people to process, a reason to do so, and a song to sing.

Imagine how this simple formula can be adapted to other days in other seasons. Bring in the Advent wreath (or, if it is too unwieldy, the candles to the wreath) in procession singing, "O Come, O Come Emmanuel." If you have children, take advantage of their natural need to move, and make your family prayer on the First Sunday of Advent, and days yet to come, a walking prayer. Let the children hold candles (thick pillar candles, with a sturdy base), or a small vial of holy water for blessing the wreath.

In Mexico the Mass at midnight on Christmas Eve is called the "Mass of the Rooster," because it is believed that the rooster, first among all the animals in the stable where Jesus was born, leapt to the roof and proclaimed his birth. In England it is said that bees swarm and buzz a hymn of praise to Christ on that night, and throughout Europe we hear the stories of cattle kneeling in their stalls in homage to the Christ Child at midnight on Christmas Eve. Find these stories and read them during Advent. Then perhaps your early Christmas morning procession could include children taking the parts of animals from the manger scene. Process through the house, carrying candles and the figure of the baby Jesus and singing a carol like "O Come, All Ye Faithful," or "Joy to the World." End at the crèche, where baby Jesus is placed reverently in his crib, as all, humans and animals, kneel in worship.

A Lenten procession could incorporate a shorter form of the Stations of the Cross, with just a brief description of the action at each station and a period of silence before moving on. You might choose not to sing during Lent, leaving the singing until Easter, but don't forget the candles. In every season we are proclaiming Jesus Christ, the Light of the World.

Any Easter procession should include candles and water and flowers and some delicious Easter bread or cake. At Easter the procession can often take place outside. If you have a backyard shrine to Mary, make the procession to the statue of the Virgin and decorate it with flowers. "Be Joyful, Mary" is an Easter hymn that is easy to learn to sing. Sing, or say, a favorite "Alleluia" over and over again as you process. Maybe the procession could precede the Easter egg hunt and lead to the starting point for the race to the eggs.

These processions can be adapted for name days and birthdays, too. To the traditional "Happy Birthday to You," add this verse, or one like it, "Happy Birthday to you, to Jesus be true. May God's richest blessings be always with you." Or "May the Good Lord bless you. May the Good Lord bless you. May the Lord bless and keep you, in all that you do." For name days, see if you can find a hymn for that particular saint. If not, "For All the Saints" is a good choice.

Will there be spilt water and dripped candle wax and people bumping into one another and forgotten verses or mixed-up words or general silliness? Probably. A lot depends on the sizes and ages of the children in your household. Most Americans will be uncomfortable the first time they take part in a domestic procession. We are taught to be observers, an audience, for the trained musicians who sing and the trained dancers who move. But singing and moving are human traits and human gifts, as well as human needs. A Jesuit priest, Father Carl Dehne, cautioned me at my oldest son's baptism that we should not worry when holy celebrations are marked by "amiable confusion." He meant that we are not actors and that our lives in Christ are not performances. We are people and should be at peace with the limits of age and maturity and human nature. The important thing is to join in prayer and praise, and to keep doing it.

# 10

# HOW TO DO
# EUCHARISTIC ADORATION

Mystery is a great embarrassment to the modern mind.

—FLANNERY O'CONNOR

It is difficult to be present in the moment. We are often full of worries about the past and preoccupied with how to arrange our lives so that they will go better in the future. What a challenge and gift it is to be in the moment, with God, and to open our heart like a book. Eucharistic adoration is one way of opening our heart to God.

Eucharistic adoration is the practice of reverencing, praying, or meditating in the presence of the consecrated bread of the Eucharist, of being in the adoring gaze of God and trying to return that gaze.

"Eucharist" is a Greek word meaning "thanksgiving." To be human is to give thanks. "Adoration" is derived from a Latin word describing the reverence, awe, and wonder due to God alone.

Many saints who are known primarily for acts of charity, such as Francis of Assisi, Elizabeth Ann Seton, Katharine Drexel, and Damien of Molokai, practiced Eucharistic adoration. Eucharistic adoration helped them be in the present moment and see in the person before them the face of Christ. Blessed Teresa of Calcutta spent an uninterrupted hour, or Holy Hour, every day before the Blessed Sacrament. She said that this time spent with Jesus helped her and her fellow Missionaries of Charity to become more loving and compassionate to the poorest of the poor.

## HISTORY OF THE EUCHARIST

Catholics, and many non-Catholics as well, believe that Jesus is fully present, body, blood, soul, and divinity, in the Blessed Sacrament. Christians have believed in the Real Presence of Jesus in the Eucharist since apostolic times. In fact, when Christ told his followers that they should literally eat his flesh and drink his blood, the teaching was so off-putting that, according to John's Gospel, many of them withdrew after hearing it and no longer followed him (John 6:66). Jesus says, "Unless you eat the flesh of the Son of Man, and drink his blood, you do not have life within you" (John 6:53). Seeing his followers reject Him because of this difficult teaching Jesus asks the twelve apostles, " 'Do you also want to leave?' Simon Peter answered him, 'Master, to whom shall we go? You have the words of eternal life' " (John 6:67- 68).

Christians have been consuming the Eucharist, the body and blood of Christ, in the form of bread and wine, since the first century. And yet, it is a mystery we may never fully grasp. As C. S. Lewis writes, "The command, after all, was Take, eat: not Take, understand."

Nevertheless, Catholics believe the words of Jesus at the Last Supper, when he said, "This is my body," and "This is my blood." We take and eat.

## COMMUNAL PRACTICE AND PRIVATE DEVOTION

In the early Church, consecrated Hosts were reserved in churches, monasteries, and convents for the sick and dying and all those who were unable to attend Mass. Justin Martyr, who died in AD 165, wrote of the practice of setting aside Hosts to be taken to the homes of absent members: "Everyone participates in [the elements] over which thanks has been given; and they are sent through the deacons to those who are not present." The practice of reserving the Eucharist was also discussed at the Council of Nicaea in 325. Over time, because people were aware of Jesus's presence in the Eucharist, they began to reverence or pray before the consecrated Host, which was often kept in a small box or chrismal for this purpose. Depictions of this receptacle can be seen in second- and third-century frescoes.

All Catholics adore Jesus present in the Eucharist during Mass. This occurs when the congregation kneels and the priest elevates the Blessed Sacrament, when we genuflect before the tabernacle (where the consecrated Host is reserved), as well as when we bow before receiving Holy Communion.

In addition to this communal adoration of Jesus, many people desire to sit or kneel quietly in the presence of God. Anyone can do eucharistic adoration. All are welcome.

Some churches have times of the week reserved for exposition of the Blessed Sacrament. The chapel is usually quiet and dark, and the consecrated Host is placed on the altar for adoration. Sometimes it is in a monstrance (a special vessel for holding the consecrated Host). There may be a few songs, hymns, or readings at the beginning of the service, but then the church is silent and people can come and go as they please.

Many parishes have a Blessed Sacrament chapel, a space for quiet contemplation. These parishes may offer perpetual adoration, in which people sign up for different hours of the day so that someone is always in the presence of God in the Eucharist.

Sitting in silence is one of the gifts of adoration. As the prophet Elijah discovered in the cave, sometimes God speaks to us in the silence. Sitting in silence before the Eucharist develops in us a sense of wonder and awareness at the miracle of our lives. As Blessed Teresa of Calcutta said, "When you look at the crucifix, you understand how much Jesus loved you then. When you look at the Sacred Host you understand how much Jesus loves you now."

At times, it may be difficult to quiet one's thoughts and be still. Silence can be uncomfortable, and the present moment can be painful. We may be acutely aware of our own unworthiness, doubt, or sin. If the silence is difficult there are many things one can "do" during eucharistic adoration: ask for forgiveness, forgive those who have hurt you, pray for those who are sick or in need, pray the psalms, pray the words of a favorite saint, meditate on a passage of Scripture, talk to God, or pray the Jesus Prayer, "Lord Jesus, Christ, son of the living God, have mercy on me, a sinner." Or pray the words of the father of the sick son in Mark, "I do believe, help my unbelief" (Mark 9: 24).

Then, after that, try just being still. Bow, or kneel, or sit quietly. Listen: to your heartbeat, your breathing, the settling of the church building, the sounds outside, and the voice of God when it comes, as Elijah heard it: "after the fire, a light silent sound" or as older translations have it, "a still, small voice."

## PRAYERS FOR EUCHARISTIC ADORATION

### The Jesus Prayer
Lord Jesus, Christ, son of God, have mercy on me, a sinner.

### The Anima Christi
Soul of Christ, sanctify me. Body of Christ, save me. Blood of Christ, inebriate me. Water from the side of Christ, wash me. Passion of Christ, strengthen me. O good Jesus, hear me. Within your wounds hide me. Permit me not to be separated from you. From the malicious enemy defend me. In the hour of my death call me. And bid me come to you, that with your saints I may praise you forever and ever. Amen.

### Adore Te Devote
I adore you devoutly, Godhead unseen, who truly lies hidden under these sacramental forms. My soul surrenders itself to you without reserve, for in contemplating you it is completely overwhelmed. . . .
—THOMAS AQUINAS (1225–1274)

# 11

# DAILY PRAYER AND CHRISTIAN MEDITATION

*Frequently, only silence can express my prayer.*

−ST. THÉRÈSE OF LISIEUX

It's difficult to have a meaningful relationship with anyone if you never spend time together. When you are the mother of a newborn, it's often hard to explain to others what you "did" all day. Simply holding, feeding, or soothing your baby doesn't square with our understanding of activity. We like things that can be easily measured or crossed off a list. I remember wishing there were a kiss counter on my newborn's head when he was sick so I could at least have a sense of accomplishment at the end of the day. And yet spending time with your baby, heart to heart, skin to skin, is precisely what you are supposed to be doing after he is born. It is the foundation for your life together, which is to follow.

In the hecticness of daily life, being present to the other is hard to achieve. But we need to spend time with one another if we want to have close bonds. Simone Weil writes, "The love of our neighbor in all its fullness simply means being able to say to him, 'What are you going through?'"

Prayer, among other things, is a way of spending time with God. It is a means of creating the conditions for the possibility of encountering His love. In daily prayer, Catholics meditate on God's Word, speak with Him honestly, and open their hearts to receive His grace.

As St. Thomas Aquinas tells us, the *telos*, or "goal," of the Christian life is friendship with God. We long for this. But we cannot achieve this union as a result of our own efforts or striving. Catholics believe that this friendship with God is given as a gift of divine grace. In Mark, after the incident with the rich man Jesus's disciples ask him, "'Then who can be saved?' Jesus looked at them and said, 'For human beings it is impossible, but not for God. All things are possible for God'" (Mark 10:26-27).

So often we want to retain the illusion of control. We attempt to white-knuckle it through the storms of life, pretending not to need anyone, thinking of ourselves as wholly autonomous, capable of achieving fulfillment by means of our own efforts at self-improvement or self-reproach. In this mind-set, it is difficult for us to receive correction or assistance. In this closed stance, we are less open to relationship with others, and less open to relationship with God.

One goal of daily prayer is to set aside purposeful activity, and the illusion of complete control, and spend time alone with God. When we stray from the discipline of daily prayer we are less aware of God's presence in our lives, and too often we fall into patterns of self-destruction and sin. As a wise priest once told me, "The only sin is not letting God love you." But how can we be open to God's love if we don't spend time with Him in prayer, meditation, or contemplation? Many Catholics find a private practice of silence and meditation somewhat intuitive, as there are many periods of silent contemplation in the Mass.

Prayer, meditation, and contemplation are ancient practices dating to the earliest days of the Church. As early as the year 270, St. Anthony the Abbot withdrew from the world and devoted his life to silence, meditation, and prayer. Because meditation is often associated with Hinduism and Buddhism, many Catholics are hesitant about using the term, but a Christian who meditates is not trying to tap into some vague cosmic reality or void. Christian meditation is focused on the person of Jesus. As Thomas Merton writes, "The true end of Christian meditation is therefore practically the same as the end of liturgical prayer and the reception of the sacraments: a deeper union by grace and charity with the Incarnate Word who is the only Mediator between God and man, Jesus Christ."

The goal of Christian prayer and meditation is to open ourselves to friendship with God. The early Church fathers spoke in even more dramatic terms, arguing that the goal of Christian existence was *theosis*, or "divinization." An intimacy so complete that we are, at the end of our lives, subsumed into God's being, or divinized, existing forever in His presence. But how is this possible when God is everything that we are not? God is infinite. We are finite. God is all good. We are sinful. God is hidden, and we experience reality through our senses. If God is beyond all our modes of apprehension how then do we approach Him?

Jesus is the bridge between God and man. Christ humbled himself in the Incarnation to share in our humanity. By receiving the sacraments and meditating on the life of Christ in Scripture, Catholics pray that they might be made holy and, by God's grace, come to share in His divinity. As a Roman Catholic priest prays when he is preparing the Eucharistic table, "By the mystery of this water and wine may we come to share in the divinity of Christ who humbled himself to share in our humanity." Or as St. Clement of Alexandria wrote in the first century, "He who listens to the Lord, and follows the prophecy given by Him, will be formed perfectly in the likeness of the teacher."

We long for our hearts to become like God's heart. This takes time, practice, and devotion. For Catholics, conversion isn't a one-time event; it's a lifelong process. As C. S. Lewis writes in *Mere Christianity*,

> [God] shows much more of Himself to some people than
> to others—not because He has favourites, but because it is
> impossible for Him to show Himself to a man whose whole

mind and character are in the wrong condition. Just as sunlight, though it has no favourites, cannot be reflected in a dusty mirror as clearly as a clean one.

As we progress in virtue and prayer we enter more deeply into the mystery of God. Spending time with God in prayer and meditation is one way of opening our hearts to receive His mercy and grace.

## DAILY PRAYER

Some Catholics make time for prayer first thing in the morning. Some pray the Angelus at noon. Still others use their commute as their prayer time. It may be helpful to pray at the same time and place every day so that it becomes a habit.

On the days when I am home with my kids, and I can get them to nap at the same time, I like to make this my prayer time. I sit on my back porch with a cup of tea and the readings of the day.

## *LECTIO DIVINA*

A common form of daily Catholic prayer, practiced by many non-Catholics as well, is called *Lectio Divina*, which is Latin for "divine reading." The practice of *Lectio Divina* has its roots in Origen in the third century. He taught the practice to St. Ambrose, who, in turn, taught it to St. Augustine. It was adopted as a monastic practice by St. Benedict in the sixth century. Here is the basic outline:

1. To begin, take a moment, silence yourself, and be aware of God's presence.

2. Ask God to be with you. For example, silently pray, **"Come, Holy Spirit." Or make an Act of Spiritual Communion.** Pray the words of St. Alphonsus Liguori:

   My Jesus, I believe that You are present in the Blessed Sacrament. I love you above all things, and I desire to receive you into my soul. Since I cannot now receive you sacramentally, come at least spiritually into my heart. As though you have already come, I embrace you and unite myself entirely to you; never permit me to be separated from you. Amen.

3. Next, read the Scripture readings of the day, which can be found online at the USCCB website, for example, from the Laudate app, in your church bulletin, or in publications like *The Magnificat*. Catholics believe that the Holy Spirit inspired the authors of the Bible, many of whom also knew Jesus. So reading Scripture is one way of allowing God to speak to us.

   Read the readings slowly, and as many times as needed. Meditate and reflect on them. What stands out? What applies to your life at this moment? What is Jesus trying to say?

4. Finally, **pray**. Speak openly and from the heart. Give praise, express gratitude, offer petitions for your needs, pray intercessions for the needs of others, or ask for guidance. As St. Paul writes, "Have no anxiety at all, but in everything, by prayer and petition, with thanksgiving, make your requests known to God" (Philippians 4:6).

5. The final step is to **sit in silent contemplation**. Some people sit for one minute, some for five, some for twenty. If it helps, set a timer. You may spend the whole time struggling to quiet your mind. Try not to judge the prayer. Don't give

up, or give in to despair. Gently bring your attention back to the task at hand—opening your heart to God. For, "We do not know how to pray as we ought, but the Spirit itself intercedes with inexpressible groanings" (Romans 8:26). God honors our intention. Just keep showing up.

Sitting in silence is an act of moving into the hidden God, not with perfect understanding, but with faith seeking understanding. As the Trappist monk Thomas Merton writes in *Thoughts in Solitude*:

> The fact that I think I am following your will does not mean that I am actually doing so. But I believe that the desire to please you does in fact please you. And I hope I have that desire in all that I am doing. I hope that I will never do anything apart from that desire. And I know that if I do this you will lead me by the right road, though I may know nothing about it. Therefore I will trust you always though I may seem to be lost and in the shadow of death. I will not fear, for you are ever with me, and you will never leave me to face my perils alone.

Some find that silent prayer can be a kind of practice for death, as it entails surrender. At its best it is an encounter between the soul and its Creator.

Having a daily meditation or prayer practice is good for your health, and it is proven to make people more compassionate. A recent study in the *Journal of Psychological Science* found that 50 percent of people who participated in daily meditation for eight weeks gave up their seat on a bus to a person in obvious pain. Of those who did not meditate, only 16 percent offered their seat.

## OTHER FORMS OF DAILY PRAYER AND CHRISTIAN MEDITATION

St. Clare of Assisi and the Franciscans use a more visual form of daily prayer. It involves gazing upon a religious object such as a cross, a practice that can facilitate meditation. The goal is silent concentration and awareness, as we contemplate the image. The concluding prayer is asking God to give us the grace to imitate Jesus, that is, to make a gift of our life on behalf of others.

In the Orthodox and Eastern Catholic Churches, meditation can take the form of repeating a sacred word, such as "Jesus," or a short prayer, such as the Jesus Prayer: "Lord Jesus Christ, Son of God, have mercy on me a sinner." Repeating a sacred word or short prayer can be helpful when the mind wanders. It is a way of gently returning one's attention to the work at hand. One Catholic who struggled with silent meditation told me that when her mind wandered to her to-do list, she repeatedly told herself, "Nowhere to be, nothing to achieve. Jesus. Jesus. Jesus."

## PRAY THE PSALMS

Jesus prayed the psalms, and Pope Benedict XVI called them "a school of prayer." The psalms are an ancient form of Jewish prayer. There are 150 psalms, and because they are short, if you pray one psalm daily you will soon internalize them and learn them by heart. Many Catholics get a book of psalms and commit to praying one a day. The psalms give us the words when we lack them. They teach us to cry out to God honestly, offering praise and complaint, and they always remind us of His faithfulness. The psalmist tells us that God's faithfulness persists, even when we cannot perceive it.

1. Before you read the psalm say: "O Lord, open my lips, and my mouth shall declare your praise."
2. Read the psalm. If possible, read it aloud. Notice the structure: Rejoice, repent, request. What are you grateful for? What sin do you need to turn away from? Finally, offer prayers for yourself and for the world.
3. Conclude with a Glory be: "Glory be to the Father, and to the Son, and to the Holy Spirit, as it was in the beginning, is now, and ever shall be, world without end. Amen."

## 12

## TABLE PRAYERS

> If the only prayer you ever say in your life is
> thank you, it will be enough.
>
> —MEISTER ECKHART

When I first started working as a teacher, I taught homeless adults working to earn their GEDs. My classes began hectically, with students talking, rustling papers, and looking to find a seat. It was a struggle to get everyone focused so that we could begin.

My second teaching position was much different from the first. It was at a private high school where classes began with prayer. I'd never experienced this before, as I'd gone to public school.

It was fascinating to me, how the daily ritual of praying before class would quiet the room and focus our attention without anyone having to say, "Be quiet." I would walk into the room while everyone was talking, then we would stand for a moment, until everyone was silent. Next we would say a short prayer, such as Psalm 19:

"Let the words of my mouth, and the meditations of my heart, be acceptable in thy sight, O Lord, my strength, and my redeemer."

This simple rite quieted the class and restored a sense of dignity to the work at hand. It helped me, too, to gather myself before we began.

These days, my attention is more divided than ever. I am forever misplacing my phone, forgetting the baby's pacifier or a form my child needs for school. It's tempting to be always distracted, always in a rush. When I'm living in this mind-set, even eating becomes simply an act of refueling. My body needs calories, so I cut up an apple or make a sandwich and eat it in front of the computer as I work.

But when I am eating with my children, I always remember to pause and pray. For one thing, if I forget, my three-year-old will remind me, saying, "Mama, we haven't prayed."

Ron Lieber writes in his book *The Opposite of Spoiled* that only 44 percent of Americans report saying grace on a daily basis. American children are not accustomed to having to pause and reflect. Praying before meals teaches patience and gratitude. It helps children to develop an appreciation of what they do have, which in turn makes it easier for them to become contented adults who will make wise choices. Someone who has learned how to wait, and to be grateful for what they have, will be less willing to overspend, for example.

When we say grace before a meal, we put aside the sense of our own importance, the distractedness and the busyness that so defines our present age, and thank God for His mercy. We remember, for a moment, that we are human beings. We are more than the payers of bills, the burners of calories, or the fixers of leaky faucets. We are mothers and fathers, brothers and sisters. We are beloved of God. We need to pause and remember. We need to pause and give thanks.

Historically, Christians have prayed before and after meals, a practice we inherited from Judaism. The *Book of Blessings* puts it this way:

> Christians, whether alone or with companions at table, say grace before and after meals to thank God for his goodness in providing their daily food. As they gather at table and see in the food they share a sign of God's blessings on them, Christians should be mindful of the poor, who lack even the

bare minimum of food that those at table may have in abundance (1030–31).

## PRAYING AT TABLE

Catholics eating alone, or with co-workers at a restaurant, might choose to pray a silent prayer (Matthew 6:6) of thanksgiving for their food, which "God has given and human hands have made."

At home, some Catholics like to alternate between unstructured prayers and memorized prayers, which everyone can easily say in unison. Grace before meals can be as simple as holding hands, bowing heads, and saying, "Thank you, God."

## PRAYER BEFORE AND AFTER MEALS

After making the sign of the cross, the classic Catholic prayer we say before meals is:

> Bless us, O Lord, and these thy gifts, which we are about to receive from thy bounty, through Christ our Lord. Amen.

Traditionally, there was also a prayer at the end of meals, though it has mostly fallen out of use.

For example, after making the sign of the cross all say:

> We give thee thanks for all thy benefits, almighty God, who lives and reigns forever. [And may the souls of the faithful departed through the mercy of God rest in peace.] Amen.

## PRAYER AT BREAKFAST

> O Lord, shine your love on us, and gladden all our days. Let your loveliness shine on us, and bless the work we do, bless the work of our hands. Amen.

## SHORT TABLE BLESSINGS

After making the sign of the cross we say:

"The eyes of all look to you, you give them food in due time. You open wide your hand to feed all living things." —PSALM 145:15-16

"The Lord bless us and keep us." Amen.

"The Lord's face shine upon us and be gracious to us." Amen.

"Lord look upon us with kindness and give us peace." Amen.

"May God bless our meal and grant us a compassionate and understanding heart toward one another." —MOUNT ST. MARY'S ABBEY

"We give you thanks, almighty God, for all your blessings; you live and reign for ever and ever. Amen."

"Lord, send out your spirit, and renew the face of the earth." —PSALM 104:30

"To all else thou hast given us, O Lord, we ask but one thing more. Give us grateful hearts. Amen." —GEORGE HERBERT

"O God our Father, be thou the unseen guest at our table and fill our hearts with your love. Amen."

"Come, Lord Jesus, be our guest and let these gifts to us be blessed." —LUTHERAN PRAYER

## SUNG PRAYERS

Consider a sung prayer like the **Doxology:**

Praise God, from whom all blessings flow;
praise him, all creatures here below;
praise him above, ye heavenly host;
praise Father, Son, and Holy Ghost. Amen.

This version of the **Doxology** is sung to the same tune:

Be present at our table, Lord;
Be here and everywhere adored;

Thy creatures bless and grant that we
May feast in paradise with Thee.

Or sing the **Trisagion** before meals. *Trisagion* is a Greek word meaning "the Three Holy." It goes like this:

Holy God, holy mighty God, holy Immortal One, have mercy on us. Give praise to the Father, and to the Son, and to the Holy Spirit. Holy God. Holy mighty God, holy Immortal One, have mercy on us.

~~~~~~~~~~~~~~~~~~~~~~~~~~~~~

# ORDERING TIME

~~~~~~~~~~~~~~~~~~~~~~~~~~~~~

# 13

~~~~~~~~~~~~~~~~~~~~~~~~~~~~~~~~~~~~~

## THE DAY: MORNING, NOON, EVENING, AND NIGHT PRAYER

God then separated the light from the darkness. God called
the light "day," and the darkness he called "night." Evening
came, and morning followed—the first day.

–GENESIS 1:4-5

Time given to Christ is never time lost, but is rather time gained
so that our relationships and indeed our whole life may
become more profoundly human.

–ST. JOHN PAUL II

Christians believe that God, who created the universe and everything in it, also created the divisions between light and darkness that
we call "day" and "night." And if God saw fit to mark time and distinguish different periods of time, so must we. One of the ways the
Church divides the day and the night is with times of prayer. These
prayers are anchored by the psalms, and the psalms for each time of
prayer are suited for particular needs. Why is it so upsetting to hear
the phone ring past midnight, when a ringing phone at noon causes
no immediate alarm? There is something about the darkness—some
sense that everyone we love should be inside, asleep in our beds and
so, we hope, safe—that makes the sound of a phone ringing late at
night sound like an alarm or a siren sounding danger, while a phone
ringing at noon sounds like a telemarketer or a friend wanting to

borrow your truck. The Church recognizes and addresses the various needs of the day in its prayer.

We call this daily cycle of prayer the Liturgy of the Hours. (You may also have heard it called the breviary.) "Hours" does not signify the length of the prayer, but its use at a particular time, or hour, each day and night. In its full form the Liturgy of the Hours consists of eight specific times for prayer. (If you divide a twenty-four-hour day by eight, you'll get prayer every three hours.) Since the Christian day, like the Jewish day, begins at sunset, let's begin there.

The Liturgy of the Hours was traditionally made up of the following hours: **Vespers**, prayed around six in the evening, when we need lights to read or see; **Compline**, around nine, before going to bed; **Matins** (also called Vigils, Nocturns, or the Night Office), at midnight; **Lauds** at three; **Prime** at six; **Terce** at midmorning, around nine; **Sext** at midday, or noon; and **None** at midafternoon, around three. Current practice has seven hours: the Office of Readings, Morning Prayer, Daytime Prayer at midmorning, midday, and midafternoon, Evening Prayer, and Night Prayer. Some religious communities pray all the hours; every religious community prays some of the hours. The same is true for priests. The laity are also called to pray each day, but most laypeople who pray the Liturgy of the Hours commit to two, three, or four of the hours—usually Vespers (Evening Prayer) or Compline (Night Prayer), Prime (Morning Prayer), and, sometimes, Sext (Noon Prayer). We'll devote most of this chapter to Evening Prayer, Night Prayer, and Morning Prayer.

Dividing the day through prayer reminds us that all time belongs to God. The night is not the realm of the wicked; it is under God's sovereignty. Our workday doesn't belong to the company. It, too, is under the sovereignty of God. Dividing the day with prayer reminds us that we are more than the cleaners of messes, the uncloggers of toilets, the payers of bills, the diggers of holes: we are the sons and daughters of God. We can call upon God and listen for God's voice and sing God's praise with the angels and saints.

The structure of Evening Prayer, Night Prayer, and Morning Prayer is similar:

> the sign of the cross
> hymn
> psalm
> Scripture reading
> Gospel canticle
> intercessions
> Our Father

## EVENING PRAYER OR VESPERS

One way to think of Vespers is that it, like Night Prayer and Morning Prayer, is a "hinge moment." A door swings open on its hinges to reveal whatever is waiting on the other side. So, too, dusk opens on to night, bedtime opens on to the unconsciousness and lack of control that is sleep, and dawn opens on to light and a new day. Each of these hinge moments has its needs and hopes and fears. At Vespers, the close of the workday, we are aware of the ways we have sinned, of all the wrong that we have done and all the good that we have left undone. There is often weariness and a certain sadness at the fading of the light.

So Vespers may begin with lighting a candle as we make the sign of the cross. Then there's the hymn—and here's one, easy to learn and sing—that speaks to the truth that Jesus Christ is "the light no darkness can extinguish." (If you can't track down the plainsong tune, you can sing this to the tune of "Praise God from Whom All Blessings Flow.")

*O radiant Light, O sun divine*
*Of God the Father's deathless face,*
*O image of the light sublime*
*That fills the heav'nly dwelling place.*

*Lord Jesus Christ, as daylight fades,*
*As shine the lights of eventide,*
*We praise the Father with the Son,*
*The Spirit blest and with them one.*

*O Son of God, the source of life,*
*Praise is your due by night and day;*
*Unsullied lips must raise the strain*
*Of your proclaimed and splendid name.*

TEXT: PHOS HILARON,
TRANSLATOR: WILLIAM G. STOREY;
MELODY: JESU, DULCIS MEMORIA, TRADITIONAL
GREGORIAN PLAINSONG, L.M.

The major hours—evening, night, and morning—each also has an assigned Gospel canticle or song from Scripture. At Vespers we sing the Magnificat, or Canticle of Mary (Luke 1:46b-55.) There are many settings of this canticle. Here's one that can be sung to the tune of "Amazing Grace," or any common meter tune.

*My soul proclaims the Lord my God. My spirit sings His praise.*
*God looks on me, and lifts me up. And gladness fills my days.*
*All nations now will share my joy; God's gifts he has outpoured.*
*His little one God has made great. I magnify the Lord.*
*For those who love God's holy name, His mercy will not die.*
*God's strong right arm puts down the proud, and lifts the lowly*
     *high.*
*God fills the hungry with good things; the rich he sends away.*
*The promise made to Abraham is filled with endless day.*

TEXT: SR. ANNE CARTER, RSCJ,
TUNE: NEW BRITAIN

We bring our Evening Prayer to a close with our petitions, asking God for help and strength, for healing and forgiveness. Then, we close as Jesus taught, asking that, whatever our hopes, God's will might be done.

## NIGHT PRAYER

Night Prayer is as quiet as bedtime. Think about your childhood, the childhoods of your children. What do children need at bedtime? They need consistency and repetition—this blanket and no other, that song and no other. Keep that in mind at Night Prayer and strive for simplicity and prayers learned by heart. The Church understands Night Prayer as children do, that the loss of consciousness and control is a little death. It can be frightening, which is why we adults so often anesthetize ourselves with alcohol, drugs, or television. Consider this verse from the Celtic tradition:

> *I lie in my bed*
> *As I would lie in my grave,*
> *Thine arm about my neck,*
> *Thou Son of Mary victorious.*

Begin with the sign of the cross, and these words: May the all-powerful God grant us a restful night and a peaceful death.

If you want to sing a hymn, consider one of the most beautiful hymns from the English tradition, "Abide with Me."

Then sing, or say Psalm 131, followed by the Canticle (Song) of Simeon (Luke 2:29-32).

The day ends as it begins, with the sign of the cross.

At night, all children want their mothers. So our final hymn is to Mary. People are sometimes nervous about learning to chant, but the Salve Regina (Hail, Holy Queen) is not hard, either to learn or to sing.

## MORNING PRAYER

Morning Prayer is all about assumptions: Who owns the day? To whom do I belong? To whom do I owe my time and allegiance? If I rise "the boss of this house and this day," that will orient the rest of the day in a particular way. If I rise giving thanks to God for keeping me safe through the night and waking me to another day, that will orient the rest of the day in a quite different way. Are my children possessions or gifts? Is my breakfast mine by right or is it a gift? Morning Prayer is all about opening our eyes and seeing rightly.

It begins, as all our prayer begins, with the Sign of the Cross.

"Praise God from Whom All Blessings Flow," or another familiar hymn of praise, is a good way to begin the day.

There are several psalms the Church sings at Morning Prayer. Perhaps the most representative of the hour is Psalm 63, as it speaks of a right ordering of our relationship with God, as well as a longing for God that persists even in our sleep, all through the night.

If you cannot read the daily Scripture in the evening, at Vespers, read it now.

The morning Gospel canticle is the Canticle of Zechariah (Luke 1:68-79). Here's a common meter doubled (C.M.D.) version that can be sung to "O Little Town of Bethlehem," or "Forest Green," or "Ave Verum Corpus," or almost 200 hundred other tunes.

> *Blest be the God of Israel, the ever-living Lord,*
> *Who comes in pow'r to save His own, His people Israel.*
> *For Israel you now raise, Salvation's tow'r on high*
> *In David's house, who reigned as king, and servant of the Lord.*
>
> *Through holy prophets did He speak His word in days of old,*
> *That he would save us from our foes, and all who bear us ill.*
> *On Sinai He gave to us His covenant of love:*
> *So with us now He keeps His word, in love that knows no end.*
>
> *Of old He swore His solemn oath, to father Abraham:*
> *From Him a mighty race should spring, one blest for evermore.*
> *He swore to set His people free, from fear of every foe,*
> *That we might serve Him all our days, in goodness, love, and*
> *peace.*

*O tiny child, your name shall be, the prophet of the Lord;*
*The way of God you shall prepare, to make His coming known.*
*You shall proclaim to Israel, salvation's dawning day,*
*When God shall wipe away our sins, in His redeeming love.*

*The rising Sun shall shine on us, to bring the light of day*
*To all who sit in darkest night, and shadow of the grave.*
*Our footsteps God shall safely guide, to walk the ways of peace;*
*His name forever more be blessed, who lives and loves and*
*saves.*

TEXT: JAMES D. QUINN, S.J., TUNE: FOREST GREEN

Singing God's praise, hearing of God's faithfulness in Scripture: All this gives us the courage to bring our prayers to God. We pray our petitions and close with the prayer Jesus taught us, the Our Father (Matthew 6:9-13).

~~~~~~~~~~~~~~~~~~~~~~~~~~~~~~~~~~~~~~~~~~~~~~~~~~~

# 14

# THE WEEK: KEEPING FRIDAY, SATURDAY, AND SUNDAY

I have prepared a precious crown in my treasure house, and
its name is Week, and within it a jewel that far outshines
all others, and its name is Sabbath.

–THE BABYLONIAN TALMUD

Days are intuitive: light is followed by darkness, which is followed
by light, as long as we live. Call it a day, or whatever you like; it is the
most natural way to divide time. But the week is a gift to us from the
Jews (Exodus 31:17). The Jewish week is patterned on God's own acts
of creation, followed by a day of rest (Genesis 2:1-3). When the Romans conquered the Jews, they saw that their week, with a full day of
rest, was a good way of marking time within the larger framework of
months and years, so they adopted it. They adopted the week, but they
changed the way the days within it were named. In the Jewish calendar only one day, the Sabbath, has a name. And just as the Church
counts weeks between seasons (the Sundays between the Baptism of
the Lord and Ash Wednesday are numbered, not named, as are the
Sundays between Pentecost and the First Sunday of Advent), so, too,
are the other days of the Jewish week numbered, "second day," "third
day," and so on.

English speakers use Roman names for three of the days: Sunday
(Sun's day), Monday (Moon's day), and Saturday (Saturn's day). The

remaining four days of the week are named after Norse gods: Tuesday (Tiw's day), Wednesday (Woden's day), Thursday (Thor's day), and Friday (Freya's day).

For Catholics, three days of the week—Friday, Saturday, and Sunday—have special meaning. Jesus Christ was crucified on a Friday afternoon, the day of preparation for the Sabbath, which begins at sundown. Christians, from the early days of the Church, have kept Friday as a day of fasting and abstinence from meat. Many people say that the Friday fast disappeared with the reforms of the Second Vatican Council, but this is technically untrue. If you check canons 1249–1253, you will find the exhortation to keep the fast, as well as to keep the day, in a particular way, by prayer and works of mercy. If anything is to blame for the disappearance of the Friday fast, it is the way the pace of our lives fractures and dissolves time, erasing the healthy boundaries between light and darkness, work and rest, feasting and fasting. Sports events and parties and movies that debut on Friday and "getting a head start on the weekend"—these are not going away. How, then, can we keep the day?

## THE FRIDAY FAST

Fasting has long been understood as a proper way to mark Christ's passion. Think about the events that led from the Garden of Eden to Gethsemane: Adam and Eve refused to hear and obey God's word regarding the tree of life. They ate what was not theirs to eat. Fasting, then, is a way of acknowledging that there are holy boundaries around our lives and our behaviors. Not every bit of food within our sight and reach is good for us to take. And that understanding has special relevance for our society, in which we never seem to stop eating.

Some Catholics are quietly abstemious throughout the day on Friday, eating little, or fasting from all food, until dinner that evening. By doing so they both keep the fast and are free to join with their friends and families at dinner parties and other events. Others refrain from meat on Fridays, which allows them to have dinner with friends, just with a vegetarian menu. Given the rise of vegetarian and vegan options, at home and in restaurants, and given the desire of many Catholics to eat in a way that is more respectful of the earth and its resources, abstaining from meat is something you can do without drawing attention to yourself.

## THE SABBATH

In the early Christian Church, Saturday remained the Jewish Sabbath, a day of rest. It still is, though most of us ignore it and its particular place within the week. Saturday, the Sabbath, was and is the seventh day of the week, the one on which, according to the Scriptures, God rested from the work of creation (Exodus 20:8-11). In the Ten Commandments, recorded in Deuteronomy 5:6-21, a second reason is given for keeping the Sabbath rest. It reminds the Hebrews that they were once slaves in Egypt, slaves brought out into freedom by God. So the Sabbath rest is kept both in imitation of God and in honor of the freedom God alone can give. Slaves can never rest. Only free men and women can rest.

Jesus kept the Sabbath. We know very little about his personal life, but we know about his observance of the Sabbath from the Gospels. He kept the Sabbath in life and in death, rising from the dead only after the Sabbath had ended. In the fourth century, Gregory of Nyssa, bishop and saint, sought to keep both the Sabbath and the Lord's Day (the name Christians early on gave to Sunday) holy. He called them "sisters," and said that the Sabbath is the "crown of creation," while the Lord's Day is the "crown of the new creation."

Very few twenty-first-century Western Christians keep the Sabbath. But it is our loss that we have entered into a new kind of slavery—the slavery of instant access and a workday that never ends—by rejecting the Sabbath rest that both God the Father and God the Son gave us and themselves kept. Reclaiming the Sabbath is surely one of the most countercultural things we can do.

## THE LORD'S DAY

Christians often speak of Sunday as the Sabbath, but it is historically known as the Lord's Day. In the Roman Empire in which the Church was born, Sunday was a workday, as it is for Jews and Christian Sabbatarians today. So Christians would have put in a full day's work and then gathered to worship. Sunday, or the Lord's Day, is the day for liturgy, a Greek word that means "public work." It is the day set aside to gather for the Eucharist, from another Greek word meaning "thanksgiving."

But, if possible, this thanksgiving should not be limited to an hour or so at the parish. Because Sunday, or the Lord's Day, celebrates the resurrection, the dawning of a new creation and the ushering in of the kingdom of God, the whole day should have a festive air. Those of us who are invited at Mass to partake of the heavenly banquet should bring that sense of joy into the whole day. This is a day for feasting at home, for setting a welcome table and inviting guests to dine with you. If there is ever a day for a tablecloth or flowers or candles on the table, it is Sunday, when we anticipate life eternal.

Perhaps you can go and share a meal with someone in a nursing home. One of the dreams of Sunday, and of life in the kingdom, is that no one should be alone, abandoned, or forgotten. That's why many Catholics volunteer at the local soup kitchen on Sundays, or make visits to sick friends or homebound parishioners. Notice that all of this involves work, but not work directed toward making money or earning a promotion. This work is an outgrowth, a natural extension of the liturgy. It is worship carried over and permeating every hour of the day.

Many people have to work on Saturday and Sunday. Whatever your schedule, try to find ways, even small ones, to make these days stand out from the rest. Maybe Saturday will be the day you paint your toenails or take a nap or phone a friend for a long visit. Maybe it will be the day you take a bike ride or go bowling or have a beer with a friend. Do something that reminds you of your freedom in Christ.

If you have to work on Sunday, check around. There are probably Vigil Masses on Saturday afternoon or evening, or Masses on Sunday evening. You can get to Mass even if you have to work. And take comfort in knowing that you are doing what the first Christians did in going to worship after or before work.

If you want to try a Sunday feast, remember what your grandmother told you: "Many hands make light work." Prepare the main dish and ask your guests to pitch in and bring wine and side dishes. Keep it simple. You're not auditioning for a cooking show. You're celebrating the Lord's Day.

# 15

# THE MONTH: TIME PUNCTUATED BY HOLY DAYS

*Blessed feast of blessed martyrs,*
*holy women, holy men,*
*with affection's recollections*
*greet we your return again.*

-FROM A TWELFTH-CENTURY LATIN HYMN

Like the day, the month is an intuitive cycle. The moon waxes and wanes in a period lasting 29 1/2 days. Consider that our months last anywhere from 28 to 31 days, and you'll understand how the length of a month is based on the phases of the moon, from new moon to new moon. If you track the phases of the moon, you'll see that the four lunar phases divide almost exactly into four seven-day weeks.

Like the earth, our lives are lived in cycles. We are born, we grow, we age, and we die. Spring comes and the earth blossoms. Summer comes and the harvest ripens. Fall comes and the plants begin to wither. Winter comes and the earth sleeps in darkness.

The moon is dark, and then a sliver of light appears. The light grows brighter and brighter until the moon is a full round orb in the night sky. Then the light disappears.

The sun rises and light fills the day. Evening comes, and the light fades. Night falls and all is dark until the sun rises again.

The Hebrews marked the beginning of each new month by the

moment when the first sliver of lunar light, following the new moon, could be glimpsed in the evening sky.

> From new moon to new moon,
> and from Sabbath to Sabbath,
> All flesh shall come to worship
> before me, says the Lord (ISAIAH 66:23).

The Hebrews gave precedence to one month before all others (Exodus 13:3-10). It was the month of Abib, or "the month of ripe grain." It fell near the vernal equinox (equinox means "equal night," because the day and the night are of equal length on this day. In the Southern Hemisphere, this day is called the autumnal equinox). It is, to this day, the time when the festival of Passover, the holiest days in the Hebrew calendar, begins, on the tenth of this "month of ripe grain." In second-century Asia Minor evidence shows that Christians celebrated Easter Sunday on whatever day the Passover began.

Later, Rome declared that the season of Easter must always begin on a Sunday, but the feast is still near the time of Passover and is, like Passover, determined by the lunar cycle. Easter always begins on the first Sunday following the first full moon after the vernal/autumnal equinox. What if the first full moon comes on the equinox? Then Easter will begin on the following Sunday. So Easter can begin as early as March 22 and as late as April 25.

The Jewish calendar may powerfully influence our own liturgical calendar, but the English names of the months are all from Roman/Latin sources. January (Janus), March (Mars), May (Maia), and June (Juno) are named for Roman deities. February comes from a Latin word, februa, which means "to cleanse." (It's interesting that Lent most often begins in February.) April is from the Latin word aperio, which means "to open," like a bud. July is named in honor of Julius Caesar (100–44 BC), who is credited with the development of the Julian calendar. August is named after the grandnephew of Julius Caesar, Augustus Caesar (63 BC–AD 14). By September, a certain naming weariness seems to have set in, for the rest of the months are named after their position in the early Roman calendar: September comes from the Latin word septem, meaning "seven," because it was the seventh month. And so it goes, with October through December named eight (*octo*) through ten (*decem*).

Within the framework of the month, time, in addition to being divided into days and weeks, is marked by the remembrances of saints and of particular days devoted to Jesus Christ. We call these remembrances and celebrations solemnities, feasts, and memorials. (Though most of us just use "feast" as an all-encompassing term.) Solemnities rank with Sundays as days of importance for Catholics to gather and worship at Mass. Here's a list of solemnities that are holy days of obligation for the United States Catholic Church (canon 1246):

> January 1, the Solemnity of Mary, Mother of God
>
> Thursday of the Sixth Week of Easter, the Solemnity of the Ascension
>
> August 15, the Solemnity of the Assumption of the Blessed Virgin Mary
>
> November 1, the Solemnity of All Saints
>
> December 8, the Solemnity of the Immaculate Conception
>
> December 25, the Solemnity of the Nativity of Our Lord Jesus Christ

Whenever January 1, the Solemnity of Mary, Mother of God; or August 15, the Solemnity of the Assumption; or November 1, the Solemnity of All Saints falls on a Saturday or on a Monday, you don't have to attend a Mass in addition to the Sunday Mass, though you are certainly free, and encouraged, to do so.

Other solemnities that are not holy days of obligation (often because they fall on a Sunday, which is always a holy day of obligation) include the Epiphany of the Lord; Joseph, Husband of Mary; Holy Trinity; the Body and Blood of Christ (Corpus Christi); the Sacred Heart; the Birth of John the Baptist; Peter and Paul, Apostles; the Annunciation of the Lord; and Christ the King. If you look on a church calendar and see a day marked with an *S*, you know it is a solemnity.

Just below solemnities in terms of importance are feasts. Most of the apostles have feast days. Some saints get more than one, like John the Baptist, whose birth is a solemnity and whose beheading is a feast; or St. Paul, who shares a solemnity with St. Peter, but who has a separate feast day for his conversion. St. Peter has a separate feast for the Chair of Peter, honoring him as the first pope. St. Mary, who is honored with solemnities, is also honored with feasts, such as the one celebrating her birth. The archangels have a feast day, and so does a building, St. John Lateran, which is the parish church for the whole Roman Catholic world; as well as an inanimate object, the cross, on the Feast of the Exaltation of the Holy Cross. Some events in the life of Christ, like his Presentation in the Temple, are feasts. The first deacon, Lawrence, is honored on the feast of his martyrdom. If you're looking at a church calendar, look for an *F* to let you know the day in question is a feast. One of the things you'll notice is that feast days usually honor saints (or angels or buildings or objects) that truly have universal appeal.

Memorials are next in rank and include most of the saints. By celebrating memorials, particular religious communities, nations, or ethnic groups can honor saints who are of particular interest to them while the universal Church is not required to join in. St. Kateri Tekakwitha, a Native American saint, for example, probably has more devotees in North America than in Vietnam; whereas St. Stanislaus probably has more devotees in Poland than in Peru. One of the ways to tell if a saint is more locally or more universally known is by the marking on the calendar. *M* signifies what is called "an obligatory memorial," one that is kept by the entire Church. A lowercase *m* signifies a day that certainly may be kept, but it is not incumbent on the entire Church to recognize or keep that memorial.

The month, with its solemnities, feasts, and memorials, gives us all sorts of ways to enter into the mystery and the wonder that is God. There are saints who were vain, others who were humble, saints who had criminal pasts, and others who were known for their scrupulousness from childhood. There are saints who loved to dance and feast, and saints who remained silent and ate very little. Saints can be either converts or Catholic born; they may be people who persecuted Christians or people who were persecuted for being Christian. There were learned saints and illiterate saints. No one tries to keep every feast or memorial. But do try to learn about your name saint or a saint whose life has significance for your own. Find ways to keep those days and rejoice in the good, and varied, company we have on our journey to God.

# ADVENT

∿∿∿∿∿∿∿∿∿∿∿∿∿

# 16

# THE FEAST OF OUR LADY OF GUADALUPE

*The most astonishing thing about miracles is that they happen.*

–G. K. CHESTERTON

The Feast of Our Lady of Guadalupe (December 12), patroness of the Americas and the unborn, falls four days after the Feast of the Immaculate Conception (December 8) and three days after the Memorial of Blessed Juan Diego (December 9). Within a five-day period we have three wonderful reminders of Mary. The celebration of Our Lady of Guadalupe marks the second appearance of Our Lady to Juan Diego, and it stands as an example of the grace Mary bears and shares, the grace we celebrate on December 8. We mark December 12 as the day Mary gave Juan Diego the sign requested by the bishop before he would believe that Juan Diego had seen the Virgin. She gave him roses in winter. Many Catholics adorn their crèches with roses on this day in honor of Our Lady of Guadalupe.

Mary has a habit of appearing to the lowliest. She knows what it is to be God's own unlikely choice. Indeed, it would be difficult to find a more unlikely spokesman for the Queen of Heaven than Blessed Juan Diego. Juan Diego was an Aztec Indian and a farmer whose land had been conquered by the Spanish. They were in charge; he, who was among the poorest people in a poor village, had no standing.

Juan Diego's Aztec name, Cuauhtlatoatzin, means "singing eagle." He was an early convert to Christianity, and he walked from his village to Mass every day. One day, in December 1531, he was on his way to church when he saw a vision of a beautiful young woman. She was dressed as an Aztec princess, and she was pregnant. The woman asked Juan Diego to go to the bishop and give him a message from the Virgin Mary: She wanted the bishop to build a church on the spot where she stood. She wanted the church to be a source of help and healing for the people.

Juan Diego had no experience with high officials. When he went to the bishop's residence, he was met with scorn and derision. Juan Diego finally saw the bishop, who said that Juan Diego must be mistaken.

Dejected, Juan Diego went back to the spot where he had seen the beautiful lady. Again Mary was waiting for him. Juan Diego confessed his failure, but Mary assured him of her intentions and his ability to carry them out.

Juan Diego went again to the skeptical bishop, who asked him for some sign as proof of Our Lady's appearance.

Juan Diego went again to the spot, and Mary guided him to a garden filled with roses, blooming in the midst of winter. Juan Diego gathered the roses in his cloak and hurried to the bishop.

When Juan came before the bishop, he unfurled his *tilma*, or cloak, but the roses had disappeared. In their place was an image of the woman who had appeared to the poor man. The bishop wept at the sight and asked forgiveness for doubting. The image on Juan Diego's cloak had not been painted, and, indeed, to this day tests have found no trace of pigment or dye. The cloth of his cloak was so coarse and the weave so large that it would be almost impossible to paint an image on it. Somehow the image was imprinted in the fabric, and the cloak hangs, even now, in the church the bishop built in Mexico City. It is called the image of Our Lady of Guadalupe, and it is honored and revered by believers throughout the Americas and the world.

Juan Diego spent the rest of his life as a caretaker in the chapel of Our Lady of Guadalupe. When he died, he was buried there, a faithful servant to Mary, herself a faithful servant.

The image of Our Lady of Guadalupe is miraculous in many ways. For one thing, since 1531 it has not decayed. Juan's cloak, *tilma* or *ayate*, was made of a cactus fiber cloth that should have disintegrated quickly. Tests have shown that the average life of an *ayate* is twenty years. Yet for 116 years the image of the Virgin of Guadalupe hung exposed to weather, dust, and humidity, as well as the smoke of incense and candles and the oils and dirt from thousands of hands touching it in wonder. Today the image hangs protected behind glass. Four centuries after he unfurled it before the bishop, Juan's humble cloak is in good condition, the image clearly visible.

The Feast of Our Lady of Guadalupe is a gift from Mexico to the rest of the world. Even if you didn't grow up with this feast, you can embrace and celebrate it. You might want to make a Tres Leches (three milks) cake, or some other traditional Mexican dessert, today. If there are children in your life, give them copies of the book *The Lady of Guadalupe* by Tomie dePaola. If you are able, bring roses into your house or office today, or give roses as a gift to another, and rejoice in roses in winter.

## 17

~~~~~~~~~~~~~~~~~~~~~~~~~~~~~~

# THE FEAST OF THE IMMACULATE CONCEPTION OF MARY

Never be afraid of loving the Blessed Virgin too much. You
can never love her more than Jesus did.

-ST. MAXIMILIAN KOLBE

On December 8 we celebrate the Feast of the Immaculate Conception.
The Immaculate Conception of Mary is not the same thing as the virgin
birth. The first refers to the conception of Mary, and the second to the
birth of Christ. Okay, now that we've got that out of the way, let's move
on to just what it means that Mary was "immaculately conceived."

This feast, which has been celebrated since at least the seventh century, and probably before, is really a celebration of the courtesy and con-
sideration, and, yes, the mercy of God. The Church teaches that Mary
was without sin (or immaculate) since the moment of her conception.
She is not sinless because, like Jesus, she is divine. Rather, she is sinless
because God bestowed that grace upon her. God gave Mary the gift she
would need to bear, to give birth to, and to raise the Christ. But Mary,
like all of us who are offered a gift, had to accept it. We are given the gift
of faith at baptism. At some point we have to accept and claim that gift.

When the angel Gabriel calls Mary "full of grace," he is acknowledging the gift God has given her. And he is acknowledging that
Mary is prepared to freely and willingly accept whatever God offers

her. Mary says, "Behold, I am the handmaid of the Lord. May it be done to me according to your word" (Luke 1:38a). Her "yes" prepares her to accept the gift of Christ carried in her womb and raised in her home. Accepting the gift of grace, day by day and hour by hour, has left no room for anything that is not grace, that is not of God. So the phrase "full of grace" is a true description of her life.

We know in our own lives, and we have seen in the lives of others, how people are given the gifts they need, often before they know of their need. They look back and only then understand how God equipped them for a task, a challenge, or a struggle.

So it was with Mary. We do not believe that her immaculate conception meant she never cried or whined as a child. She grew and learned, as all children do. It means that, as she grew, she grew more and more in the direction and likeness of God. Like a flower turning toward the sun, so Mary, in her immaculate nature, turned toward God. She said, yes and again, yes, to God until she was able to say yes to the Incarnation and yes to the passion and death of her only, beloved Son.

It is this grace, or gift of God, that the angel Gabriel understands when he addresses Mary and calls her "full of grace." She is full of God's grace; there is no room for sin.

The Feast of the Immaculate Conception probably began in the Eastern Church as a celebration of St. Anne, who conceived and bore Mary. (Count the months. You'll see that there are nine months between December 8, when we celebrate the Immaculate Conception of Mary, and September 8, when we celebrate the Feast of the Nativity of the Virgin Mary.) The Eastern Church still celebrates the Feast of St. Anne, who waited for many years, longing yet unable to conceive and bear a child. When Mary was given to her and her husband, Joachim, they rejoiced and praised God.

You may be surprised to know how many Marys, both male and female, keep this day, and other Marian feasts, as their name days. Here are some of the many forms of this beloved name: Miriam is the Hebrew form, and it is surely the name by which Jesus's mother was known. Maja is the Croatian form. Moira or Maire is the Irish version, and Marya is the Polish version. In Bavaria, the name is Marla, while in France it is Marie. The Hungarian, Italian, and Spanish form of the name is Maria. Marianna is the Italian name that honors both Mary and her mother. All of these names have nicknames and diminutives, like the Irish Maureen and the Spanish Marita. Sometimes girls are named after Marian appearances, such as girls in Mexico who are named Guadalupe or girls in Puerto Rico who are named Pilar after Nuestra Senora de Pilar, who is said to have appeared at the pillar to St. James the apostle. Many male saints have names, like Alphonsus Mary Liguori, that combine the masculine and the feminine. But other names, now considered masculine, are also derivatives of Mary, like the names Gilmary, Gilmore, Melmore, and Myles, each of which means "servant of Mary."

Like many saints, Francis of Assisi had a deep devotion to Mary. He wrote this hymn to Mary in the thirteenth century. We can pray it with him and believers throughout the ages on this Feast of the Immaculate Conception:

> Hail, O Lady, holy Queen,
> Mary, holy Mother of God.
> You are the Virgin made church,
> and the one chosen by the most holy Father in heaven,
> whom he consecrated with his most holy beloved Son
> and with the Holy Spirit, the Paraclete,
> in whom there was and is
> all the fullness of grace and every good.
> Hail, his Palace!
> Hail, his Tabernacle!
> Hail, his Home!
> Hail, his Robe!
> Hail, his servant!
> Hail, his Mother!
> And hail all you holy virtues
> Which through the grace and light of the Holy Spirit
> Are poured into the hearts of the faithful
> So that from their faithless state
> You may make them faithful to God.
>
> Amen.

~~~~~~~~~~~~~~~~~~~~~~~~

# 18

# MAKING AND PRAYING THE ADVENT WREATH

What is prayer? It is the remembrance of God, the feeling of
His presence; it is joy from that presence. Always,
everywhere, in all things.

–FR. ALEXANDER SCHMEMANN

Advent is the season of spiritual preparation before the celebration of Christmas, which means "the feast of Christ." In the Northern Hemisphere, Advent comes before the winter solstice.

Most people are powerfully affected by the change in seasons. I know that it's easier for me to be anxious and doubtful in the dark nights of winter. When it's freezing outside I often feel housebound and constricted. My hands and feet get cold, my shoulders tense. I miss being outdoors and having the windows open. Nothing is growing in the garden, and the branches of the trees are stark and bare. The only outside work is scraping ice off car windows and shoveling snow.

Year round, of course, there are things to worry about and losses to grieve. Yet it's easier, somehow, to trust in the goodness of God when sunlight is streaming through your windows.

Surprisingly, some of my most powerful experiences of prayer have taken place in the long nights of winter, around the Advent wreath. Perhaps this is because, as St. Oscar Romero once wrote:

No one can celebrate a genuine Christmas without being truly poor. The self-sufficient, the proud, those who, because they have everything, look down on others, those who have no need, even of God—for them there will be no Christmas. Only the poor, the hungry, those who need someone to come on their behalf, will have that someone. That someone is God, Emmanuel, God-with-us. Without poverty of spirit there can be no abundance of God.

In our awareness of our own fragility, dependence, and need, we draw closer to Jesus, the source of life and hope, and the light no darkness can extinguish.

Of course, people cope with real or perceived scarcity in different ways. Some spend all of Advent shopping or eating or drinking, unconsciously storing up against the dark and cold. As Christians, of course, we do these things, too, but we also bring a simple sign of light and hope into our homes in the form of an Advent wreath.

The wreath itself is not new to Christianity. Long before there were any Christians, people brought evergreen branches into their homes in the dead of winter as reminders of the eventual return of spring. Catholics simply adapted this tradition to speak also to the light and hope that come into the world with the birth of Christ.

You can purchase an evergreen wreath or make your own by gathering pine branches and using twine to wrap them around a circular candleholder or form. A wire hanger can also be repurposed into a circle to create a base for your wreath. When people purchase a live Christmas tree, often they will remove the lower branches so that the tree can be placed in a stand. These discarded branches can be used to make an Advent wreath. The circular wreath symbolizes the eternal God in whom there is no beginning and no end.

Because the Advent wreath is a sacramental, it is fitting to say a blessing over it before praying around it.

**Blessing the Advent Wreath**
Lord our God,
We praise you for your Son, Jesus Christ:
he is Emmanuel, the hope of the peoples,
he is the wisdom that teaches and guides us,
he is the savior of every nation.

Lord God,
let your blessing come upon us
as we light the candles of this wreath.
May the wreath and its light
be a sign of Christ's promise to bring us salvation.
May he come quickly and not delay.
We ask this through Christ our Lord.

Amen.

Ever since the time of Pope St. Gregory the Great, Advent has been a four-week period of prayer, fasting, almsgiving, and preparation for Christmas. This is why there are four candles on the Advent wreath. Some Catholics pray Evening Prayer or Vespers around the wreath, in their homes, often immediately following dinner. Before beginning your prayers you might want to turn off all or most of the lights and be silent.

One candle is lit on the wreath the first week, two the second, and so on, until all four are ablaze. Hope and light increase, as we get closer and closer to the birth of Jesus.

Traditionally, three purple candles and one pink candle are used (but any four candles may be used). The purple candles represent the penitential nature of the season. Advent is a time to pray, do good works, and turn away from sin, in order to make room in our hearts for the birth of Jesus. As Pope Benedict XVI writes,

> The first thing we have to accept is . . . this reality of an enduring Advent. If we do that, we shall begin to realize that the borderline "before Christ" and "after Christ" does not run through historical time . . . and cannot be drawn on any map; it runs through our own hearts. Insofar as we are living on a basis of selfishness, of egoism, then even today we are "before Christ." But in this time of Advent, let us ask the Lord to grant that we may live less and less "before Christ," and certainly not "after Christ," but truly *with* Christ and in Christ: with him who is indeed Christ yesterday, today and forever (HEB 13:8).

The pink candle is lit on the third Sunday of Advent, Gaudete Sunday. *Gaudete* is Latin for "rejoice." So Gaudete Sunday is a minicelebration, as it marks the midpoint of Advent and we are aware that Christmas is drawing near. Some Christians put up their Christmas decorations on Gaudete Sunday, or they might do something celebratory, like going sledding.

The daily Mass readings in Advent are among the most beautiful readings of the year. The first two weeks of the Advent lectionary focus on Christ's second coming: "Come, Lord Jesus." The second two weeks focus on His nativity and Incarnation.

Vespers, or the Evening Prayer of the Church, is prayed in the early evening during the winter, shortly after the sun has gone down. The person lighting the candle or candles might say or sing, "Jesus Christ is the Light of the world." All respond, "A light no darkness can extinguish."

Then there is an opening hymn such as, "O Come, O Come, Emmanuel," or "Come Thou Fount of Every Blessing" or "Come Thou Long Expected Jesus" or "Creator of the Stars of Night." If you have an Advent calendar, someone might open the window and read what is inside, then the Mass readings for the day. At the end of the reading the reader says, "The Word of the Lord." All respond, "Thanks be to God."

After that many people pray intercessory prayers (where everyone prays for their needs and the needs of others). For example, "For John who is in the hospital, we pray to the Lord." All respond, "Lord, hear our prayer." After this there is a concluding Lord's Prayer or Glory Be, and then, if you are praying with others, of course, a Sign of Peace is exchanged, and then my children's favorite part, which is blowing out the candles.

If you are praying the Divine Office in the last days of Advent the "O Antiphons" will be added to your evening prayer. They are more than a thousand years old. Originally used in monastic communities, they gradually came to be used by the whole Church.

### December 17
O Wisdom of our God Most High,
guiding creation with power and love:
come to teach us the path of knowledge!

### December 18
O Leader of the House of Israel,
giver of the Law to Moses on Sinai:
come to rescue us with your mighty power!

### December 19
O Root of Jesse's stem,
sign of God's love for all his people:
come to save us without delay!

### December 20
O Key of David,
opening the gates of God's eternal Kingdom:
come and free the prisoners of darkness!

### December 21

O Radiant Dawn,
splendor of eternal light, sun of justice:
come and shine on those who dwell in darkness and in the
shadow of death.

### December 22

O King of all nations and keystone of the Church:
come and save man, whom you formed from the dust!

### December 23

O Emmanuel, our King and Giver of Law:
come to save us, Lord our God!

# 19

# THE CRÈCHE

The Advent mystery in our lives is the beginning of the
end of all, in us, that is not yet Christ.

–THOMAS MERTON

The Christmas tree is part of most American Catholic homes, but it
is not the central visual or devotional element. That honor belongs to
the crèche, or manger scene.

The story of the first crèche comes from the life of St. Francis of Assisi. In December 1223, Francis was visiting Grecio, a town in the mountains of Italy. He realized that the local Franciscan hermitage was too small to hold the people who wanted to celebrate Christmas Eve Mass. So Francis found a rock cavern, before which he placed a stone altar for the priest. Inside the cavern, Francis placed a live ox and donkey amid piles of hay. It is said that the worshippers saw the infant Jesus lying there, though Francis had brought no baby to the scene, and that the infant's holiness shone through him and fell upon those gathered in the darkness.

This is how St. Bonaventure described that night in his book *The Life of St. Francis of Assisi*:

> It happened in the third year before his death, that in order to excite the inhabitants of Grecio to commemorate the nativity of the Infant Jesus with great devotion, [St. Francis] determined to keep it with all possible solemnity; and lest he should be accused of lightness or novelty, he asked and obtained the permission of the sovereign Pontiff. Then he prepared a manger, and brought hay, and an ox and an ass to the place appointed. . . . The man of God [St. Francis] stood before the manger, full of devotion and piety, bathed in tears and radiant with joy; the Holy Gospel was chanted by Francis, the Levite of Christ. Then he preached to the people around the nativity of the poor King; and being unable to utter His name for the tenderness of His love, He called Him the Babe of Bethlehem. A certain valiant and veracious soldier, Master John of Grecio, who, for the love of Christ, had left the warfare of this world, and become a dear friend of this holy man, affirmed that he beheld an Infant marvelously beautiful, sleeping in the manger, Whom the blessed Father Francis embraced with both his arms, as if he would awake Him from sleep.

The crèche spread from Italy to other lands. In some Italian crèches, an entire village springs up around the manger. Mary and

Joseph and the shepherds watch over the Christ Child along with the butcher and the baker, or, in our time, the car dealer and the barista, all of whom gaze from their shops at the one Francis called "the Babe of Bethlehem."

Most American families have simpler crèches: animals and angels and human figures as described in, and inferred from, Scripture. Neither Matthew nor Luke's Gospel says that any animal attended Jesus's birth, but we assume a stable will have animals in it. In the center of the crèche, an empty manger awaits the Child Jesus, who is placed there after Mass on Christmas Eve.

The magi, whose story is told in Matthew's Gospel (2:1-12), start off at a distance from the crèche and are moved a bit closer each day until on the Feast of Epiphany (the Feast of the Three Kings as it is called in places like Cuba and Puerto Rico) they are to be found standing with the others around the manger bed. Children delight in moving the figures of the magi, along with their camels, toward the manger crib. You can start them at some distance from the Holy Family and make the movement of the magi part of your daily Advent prayer. It is a reminder that Christmas is coming, and a reminder, as well, that even those of us who begin the journey from a long way off are welcomed to the Christ Child, there to worship him and be loved by him. Though you may want to keep the reading of the magi's journey for the Feast of Epiphany, consider reading the story of the prodigal son (Luke 15:11-32) as the magi make their way toward the manger. It is a long reading, and it can be broken up over several nights. Talk about the ways in which the son in the story began his journey to his father from an even greater distance than the magi had to travel. Discuss how the father's own son felt himself to be a stranger and an alien in the house where he had grown up. One can be a member of a household and still be a stranger, and yet there is always room in God's house. How do we make room for the strangers? How do we welcome them? Let the magi's journey inform your own.

A crèche—which can be set up on the First Sunday of Advent, and perhaps added to as the days go by—may be made from any worthy material: wood, clay, ceramics, cloth, porcelain, or papier-mâché. The figures may be purchased (many Fair Trade organizations sell crèche sets handcrafted in developing countries) or made at home. You can mix a Peruvian-made Mary with a German-made Joseph, or a kindergartener's clay sculpture of a lamb with a finely detailed porcelain one. Don't be afraid to bring the universality of the Christmas story into your crèche.

If you wish to purchase a crèche, consider buying from a Fair Trade company such as Novica or Ten Thousand Villages, organizations helping to ensure a fair wage for artists and craftspeople in the developing world.

If you make a crèche, use your imagination when it comes to materials. One family with limited space made a felt board to put on an easel. Then they cut out felt figures that could be positioned and repositioned according to the days of Advent. The magi and their animals, for example, started in a far corner of the board and moved closer and closer to the Christ Child.

For families who wish to honor the Holy Father's teachings on the environment by using and reusing objects rather than buying something new, the advantage of a crèche is that you can bring out the same set year after year. Indeed, its familiarity becomes a part of the devotion. Like the story of Jesus's birth, the home crèche is known and loved, though ever fresh in its display and use.

Crèches are also good for households sharing small spaces. The studio apartment that would be overwhelmed by a live fir is well served by miniature animals, kings, angels, and the Holy Family on a shelf or against the wall.

Some households follow the custom of keeping a dish of straw in the house. For each kindness or act of devotion a child or adult performs, that person places a piece of straw in the waiting manger. Children want to prepare a soft bed for the baby, so they are encouraged to see their good deeds turn a hard floor into a generous resting place for Jesus. Adults can keep this custom, too, perhaps adding a straw for each time they practice daily prayer or attend Mass, for each seat offered to someone else on an overcrowded bus. In our sin we each contribute to the cross from which Christ hangs. In our acts of love we each can contribute to the soft bed on which the Infant Christ is laid.

Here is a blessing for the crèche. It comes from *Catholic Household Blessings and Prayers*, published by the United States Conference of Catholic Bishops. All make the sign of the cross as the leader says: Our help is in the name of the Lord. R/. Who made heaven and earth.

One of those present or the leader reads a text of sacred Scripture, for example, **Luke 2:8** (lines 1-8) or **Isaiah 7:10-14** (lines 10-15, the birth of Emmanuel).

**Reader: The Gospel of the Lord.**
R/. Praise to you, Lord Jesus Christ.
*The leader prays with hands joined:*
God of every nation and people,
from the very beginning of creation
you have made manifest your love:
when our need for a Savior was great
you sent your Son to be born of the Virgin Mary.
To our lives he brings joy and peace,
justice, mercy, and love.
Lord,
bless all who look upon this manger;
may it remind us of the humble birth of Jesus,
and raise our thoughts to him,
who is God-with-us and Savior of all,
and who lives and reigns forever and ever.
R/. Amen.

# 20

# DECORATING THE CHRISTMAS TREE

*The tree of life my soul hath seen,*
*laden with fruit and always green.*

-JOSHUA SMITH, *Divine Hymns, or Spiritual Songs*

One of the tasks for Catholic households is to honor the journey that is Advent and to celebrate the destination that is Christmas.

A household keeping Advent is not yet keeping Christmas. The members of the household are moving toward Christmas, but like the three kings on their way to Bethlehem, they have not arrived. The spare scriptural accounts of Jesus's birth, found in the Gospels according to Matthew and Luke, feature journeys. Mary and Joseph journey to Bethlehem and then to Egypt. The shepherds journey from their fields to the manger. In the Church's memory of the nativity of Jesus, journey matters. A journey, leading always toward the child in the manger, shapes the season of Advent.

For Catholics, the journey and the destination cannot be divided, but they can be distinguished. Each has its role and its time, its rhythm and its tone. If we think of Advent and Christmas in terms of journey, it helps us order the life of the household.

The use of the Christmas tree is modern. Its origins are found in the medieval mystery plays that depicted the tree of paradise and the Christmas light or candle that symbolized Christ, the Light of the World. But the Christmas tree as most of us know it is a German tradition that made its way, thanks to Queen Victoria's German-born Prince Consort, Albert, to the British court and from there to the United States. So any customs we have are recent and did not originate in the Church but in the home. Setting up a Christmas tree is truly a domestic custom, and it varies from household to household. Any suggestions you find here are based not on church teaching, but on questions we ask about how the metaphor of journey can help us keep both Advent and Christmas. A good way to approach the question of when to set up and decorate a Christmas tree is to start with a reflection of the Advent journey.

Most of us have the experience of getting a house or a room ready for guests. The preparation happens in stages, from planning to cleaning to stocking extra rolls of toilet paper in the bathroom to putting towels on the nightstand to opening the door in welcome. Think of decorating the tree like putting out flowers for guests. Other things have to happen before the finishing touches of flowers appear.

The Catholic household can make preparing the house for Christmas part of Advent practice by dividing the work to be done by the weeks of the season. In week one we might focus on cleaning out and giving away the excess clothes, books, kitchen equipment, toys, and electronics that clutter our lives. What has become a hindrance for us could be of great use to another. And, whether the guest who is coming is your mother-in-law, your college roommate, or the Holy Family, room must be made.

Week two might be centered on cleaning and rearranging spaces for quiet, for reflection, for prayer, for sleep. We need room in our hearts and minds, as well as in our physical spaces, to welcome others. Think of how difficult it is to listen to someone telling a story all the while watching the television or scrolling through e-mails. Now enlarge that image to include our whole lives: we're always multitasking, listening to bits and pieces of many conversations, virtual and in real life. This week of cleaning is all about focus. Put on music while you clean. Light a candle and fill the air with fragrance. Invite the rest of the household to join in and share a festive meal when

you are done working. Many people have warm memories of string-
ing strands of light on porches and house eaves, work that is argu-
ably harder and colder than cleaning inside. It's the associations that
make the work pleasant. Think of ways to create those happy connections. One way to do this is to make a dish that is forever after
associated with the season and the work.

In my family, wash day lasted all day, with the washing and the
ironing done for the whole family. Supper was always the same: red
beans, mashed potatoes, cornbread, and onions sliced thin and served
soaking in vinegar. These dishes could be prepared, or prepped, early
in the morning before the laundry work began. Though it was simple
food, all of us children, now long grown, and our parents passed,
still remember it with fondness. It was the dish we always requested
on trips home. Think of something like this meal and make it your
Advent after-cleaning staple.

Weeks three and four (since the length of the fourth week of Advent varies with the day of the week on which Christmas Day falls
and doesn't always allow for seven days) seems a good time to begin
preparing the living space for the Christmas season, for guests, for
celebration, for joy of every sort.

We've been talking about making room. It's certainly true that
you have to make room to bring a tree into the house. The question for Catholics is, "When?" When is the right time to set up and
decorate the Christmas tree? Walmart says mid-October; Catholic
custom, based on what parishes do, says Christmas Eve. One of the
considerations is being able to leave the lit and decorated tree up
through the Feast of Epiphany, when the Twelve Days of Christmas
come to an end. The later you bring a fresh tree into the house, of
course, the longer it can stay in a dry, heated indoor space.

Households who keep the tradition of decorating and lighting the
tree on December 24 make it one of the customs of the day, because
that is when the tradition of a tree in the house began. Its origins
come from Christmas Eve as the feast day of our earliest ancestors,
Adam and Eve, who are named as saints in the calendars of the Eastern Churches. Greeks, Syrians, and Copts all honor them. This was
the day when people named after our first parents celebrated their

name days. Though Adam and Eve are not named as saints in the Roman Church, Catholics in Germany in the sixteenth century began putting up a "paradise tree" in their homes to honor Adam and Eve. That is where what we have come to know as the Christmas tree began.

If you choose to follow the custom of decorating on Christmas Eve, consider bringing the bare tree into the house during the last week of Advent. Be sure to keep a fresh tree watered. (You might consider a potted tree that can be planted when the season ends.) This simplifies the work to be done on Christmas Eve, a busy day in most households. The bare tree also reminds us of our expectation, our hope. We look forward. We wait.

For households with children, the need to strike a balance between Catholic tradition and what children see in the stores and in their friends' houses may lead to the compromise my husband and I settled on: set up the tree and decorate it on Gaudete Sunday. (If you don't have ornaments, string cranberries or popcorn.) Or begin decorating it on Gaudete Sunday and add a bit to the tree each day, finishing the work on Christmas Eve. The church names this Third Sunday of Advent "Rejoice" because our journey is nearing its end. We are close to the light of Christmas. Whichever day you choose, think about finding figures of Adam and Eve to place on the tree on Christmas Eve, in honor of their feast day.

Setting up and decorating the tree is a communal event. Mary and Joseph traveled together. The kings traveled together. A host of angels appeared to a group of shepherds and a flock of sheep.

The Catholic living alone may want to invite friends or family to decorate the tree. The Catholic family may want to invite other families or single friends to join them for the decorating. Because the Christmas tree is a sign of the evergreen grace and mercy of God made flesh in Christ, it is fitting to bless the tree. The blessing that follows is from *Winter: Celebrating the Season in a Catholic Home*, published by Liturgy Training Publications:

> God of Adam and Eve,
> God of all our ancestors,
> we praise you for this tree.
> It stirs a memory of paradise,
> and brings a foretaste of heaven.
>
> Send your Child, Jesus,
> the flower of the root of Jesse,
> to restore your good earth
> to the freshness of creation.
>
> Then every tree of the forest
> will clap its hands,
> and all creation will bless you
> from these shining branches.
>
> All glory be yours,
> now and forever.
>
> Amen.

~~~~~~~~~~~~~~~~~~~~~~~~~~~

# 21

# THE FEAST OF ST. NICHOLAS

*And now, O all-blessed Nicholas,*
*Never cease praying to Christ our God*
*For those who honor the festival of your memory*
*With faith and with love.*

–ORTHODOX LITURGY

For Catholic children, Advent is a long season. A lot of their non-Catholic friends may have been celebrating Christmas since Thanksgiving, while the Catholic children wait, impatient for the feast to arrive. Look to the liturgical calendar for help and relief. The days of Advent are filled with feast days: Andrew the Apostle (depending on when Advent begins), Francis Xavier, John of Damascus, Ambrose of Milan, the Immaculate Conception of Mary, John of the Cross, and Mexico's gift to the church, the days of Las Posadas.

A bright day early in the season, December 6, is the feast of St. Nicholas, the fourth-century bishop of Myra and the patron saint of children. The story goes that Nicholas learned of a man who, because he had no money for dowry payments, decided to sell his three young daughters into prostitution. Nicholas went one night and threw a bag of gold into the window where the poor girls lived. He returned the next night and the next: three bags of gold for the three young women, enough to get them out of that cruel house and into a respectable marriage.

In paintings and drawings of the story, the three purses gradually took on the shape of balls. Three balls are a traditional mark of a pawnshop. Nicholas is also the patron of pawnbrokers. And Greece. And sailors. And children. And young women seeking husbands. He may be the saint with the most causes associated with his name.

Born in Asia Minor to devout Christian parents, Nicholas was orphaned young. He gave away his inheritance to the poor and sought religious orders. Some traditions say he was exiled and imprisoned during the persecutions ordered by the Roman emperor Diocletian. Other traditions say he survived those persecutions to attend the Council of Nicaea in AD 325. We do know that he was made a bishop in Myra, a port city located in a region that at the time was Greek but that today is part of Turkey. The devotion to Nicholas began early and continued to grow, even as the saint was transformed in the United States into the figure of Santa Claus. The origins of Santa can be found in his nickname, "Old Saint Nick."

A tenth-century Greek writer recorded:

> The West as well as the East acclaims and glorifies him. Wherever there are people, in the country and the town, in the villages, in the isles, in the furthest parts of the earth, his name is revered and churches are built in his honor. . . . All Christians, young and old, men and women, boys and girls, reverence his memory and call upon his protection. And his favors, which know no limit of time and continue from age to age, are poured out over all the earth; the Scythians know them, as do the Indians and . . . the Africans as well as the Italians.

St. Nicholas Day, December 6, is kept throughout the world, and the outlines of this feast day are ancient. Hopeful children put out their empty shoes on the eve of Nicholas's day. They rise in the morning to find that the saint has left the shoes filled with treats. Some children, like the young women of Myra, find gold in their shoes, chocolate coins wrapped in gold-colored paper. In another widespread tradition, children write letters to the Child Jesus and leave them out alongside their waiting shoes. The saint takes the letters to the Lord.

In places like Croatia, children polish their shoes and put them out on the eve of the feast for the saint to find. They awake on December 6 to find the shoes filled with candy, fruit, and gifts. In Croatia, where the Feast of St. Nicholas, and not Christmas Day, is the occasion for giving and exchanging gifts, it is believed that St. Nicholas travels with a companion named Krampus. Krampus leaves golden twigs for naughty children, a custom that will remind Americans of the coal Santa Claus is sometimes said to leave. In Croatia, every child gets a golden twig and candy. The naughtiest children get the biggest twig and the smallest amount of candy, but no one goes without.

You may want to make this feast day your own. When our children were at home we celebrated on the evening of the feast, with a dinner of favorite foods: no leftovers were served that night, nor any dish whose sole attraction was its "good-for-you-ness." This was a day for butter and cream and chocolate, for roast beef and mashed potatoes, and fluffy yeast rolls. (Nicholas is also the patron saint of bakers.)

Dinner would drag for the younger children who, either through experience or the tales of older siblings, knew what was coming. Near the end of dinner, the doorbell would ring, and the children jumped to answer it.

We opened the door to find just a letter, written by St. Nicholas and addressed to the children of the house. We would settle in to hear the letter read aloud. My husband sometimes wept, as he did the year one of our daughters was graduating from high school and leaving for college. Nicholas sent her off with these words:

> Be assured of this: You will leave the shelter of your parents' house; you can never leave the shelter of their hearts. You are rooted forever there.

And sometimes he would laugh, as when the patient saint asked the two youngest children "to eat cheerfully and gratefully the meal your parents give you," and then added,

> Yes, that means plain milk, and, yes, that means all the food that comes *before* dessert.

And some years the table would grow quiet, as it did on December 6, 2001, when our St. Nicholas addressed our communal grief over September 11 with a reflection on Paul's Letter to the Romans, in which he told his disciples, "You know what time it is, how it is now the moment to wake from sleep." The saint wrote:

> Paul says we are like people in the moments before dawn. If one wakes then with no way of telling the time, one might think it the depth of night. It is so dark before the sun breaks the eastern sky and begins its ascent, flooding the earth with light. But, Paul says, we, the baptized, *do* know what time it is. Though the sky is dark and night seems everywhere, we know that dawn is breaking; a new day is upon us.

Then, finally, at last, their father would turn to the rhymed riddle at the end of the letter, with its clues to the hiding place where a bag of candies and small gifts could be found. One year the bounty was, well, you figure it out:

> *They have these for weddings,*
> *And babies, too,*
> *With gaily wrapped packages*
> *In white, pink, and blue.*
> *What could it be?*
> *I know. Do you?*

Those gifts were found in the bathroom shower stall.

There doesn't have to be a letter. There could be another way for the saint to communicate. And you don't even need to have or live with children to keep the feast. If you do not live in a household with children, consider acting on the good saint's behalf this day. Perhaps you know of a family with a sick child or a parent who is out of work. Imagine their delight and wonderment at finding an envelope with cash (or grocery store coupons or some helpful gift certificates) in their mailbox or slid under their door. A short note signed "St. Nicholas" would surely gladden the heart of the bishop who worked so hard for others. Perhaps a needy family might get a phone call from a landlord or a car repair shop telling them that St. Nicholas has paid their bill. If this is beyond your means alone, enlist friends, relatives, neighbors, or co-workers in the happy plan.

If you think a St. Nicholas letter would be welcome at your house, here are sample rhymes embedded with clues to where children will find small treats and sweets:

> *I run night and day, but I never go away.*
> *I'm very often heard, but I never say a word.*
> *I must have a mouth (tho' I don't know where).*
> *'Cause Mom says I eat socks and underwear! What am I?*
> *(The gifts are hidden in the tub of the washing machine.)*

> *If shoes are houses for feet, and a candy jar houses a sweet,*
> *and hats are houses for heads, and bedrooms are houses for*
>    *beds,*
> *then everything has a house, I think,*
> *from the kitchen table to the kitchen sink.*
> *This house is for us, but it's not where we eat,*
> *or sleep or bathe or bring friends we meet.*
> *This house is close, but still off a ways.*
> *This house is where someone (or thing)—not us!—*
> *spends its days. What am I?*
> *(The gifts are hidden in a garage, dog house, or toolshed.)*

## 22

~~~~~~~~~~~~~~~~~~~~~~~~~~

# ST. LUCY'S DAY

*Hallow the vespers and December of our life, O*
*martyred Lucy:*
*Console our solstice with your friendly day.*

–THOMAS MERTON

Some feasts don't travel well. The feast of St. Lucy is all about light in the darkness, warmth in the cold, and the pleasure of not getting out of bed on a freezing winter morning. These are not necessarily concerns in Tampa or Phoenix or San Diego, or even Sicily, the land where Lucy lived and died. There, December 13 may dawn sunny and fair, with a forecast for an afternoon high in the midseventies.

But for those who live far enough north to know the pain of bare feet on a chilly floor, this is a feast to relish.

Lucy died during the fourth-century Diocletian persecutions (named after the Roman emperor in whose name and by whose decree Christians were killed). She was probably beheaded, and her body was finally brought to rest in what is now Santa Lucia Church in Venice. Her name means "light" in Latin, from the noun *lux*, which in its genitive form is *lucis*, meaning "of light." Because she is St. Light, she is the patron of the eyes. People who suffer blindness and diseases of the eye ask her to intercede for them. When there were lamplighters, she was their patron saint. In many cities where lamplighters went about their work in the early darkness of her feast day, December 13, there were ceremonies in Lucy's honor.

We don't know much about the facts of Lucy's life, but stories have been told about her for centuries. The best known is that Lucy was the daughter of wealthy pagans who had promised her in marriage to another pagan. Lucy knew Christ had called her to consecrated virginity and poverty in his service. She went to St. Agatha's tomb to pray for her mother's healing. She hoped the healing would awaken her mother to the power and truth of Christianity. Lucy's mother was healed and heard her daughter's desire to give her inheritance to the poor and to devote her life to serving Christ. But the spurned suitor turned Lucy in to the authorities. One account says that when the soldiers came for Lucy, she was filled with the power of the Holy Spirit and became so stiff and heavy that even a team of oxen could not move her. Eventually she was taken to trial. She was tortured—some say beheaded, others say burned, others say she was blinded when the emperor's guards dug her eyes out with a fork—and martyred for the faith. By the sixth century, word of Lucy's courage had spread to Rome. Still today, you will hear her name spoken in Eucharistic Prayer I, the Roman canon, at Mass.

In the Middle Ages, before the liturgical calendar was reformed, St. Lucy's day fell on the winter solstice, the shortest day of the year. "Lucy fires" burned outdoors and "Lucy candles" were lit within. The farther north the Church went, the brighter the celebration for this saint. Her day marked the beginning of more sunlight, longer days, and the approach of spring and summer. It was dark, indeed, and cold. It would remain cold for some time, but the night would not grow longer, but shorter, and the darkness would gradually recede.

If you have a fire pit, or outdoor barbecue, consider kindling a "Lucy fire" and inviting friends and neighbors to bask in its light and warmth on this feast day. If you don't have access to an outdoor area, light a Lucy candle (or several) indoors and rejoice in the coming of the Light of the World.

## BREAKFAST IN BED

St. Lucy's Day, in its Scandinavian, and most popular, form, is a simple affair. According to tradition, the eldest daughter rises in the dark, dresses in a white robe, and places an evergreen wreath adorned with lit candles in her hair. She prepares a tray with steaming coffee and warm pastries and carries it from room to room, awakening sleepers with the good news of breakfast in bed, thanks to the stubborn teenage saint whose name means "light."

For twenty-first-century Americans, this generally means that a parent will rise and help the daughter. The white garment can be a bathrobe, and though the light-bearing wreath in the hair is essential, please, no lit candles. We're living in a litigious age. Substitute an artificial evergreen wreath through which tiny, battery-powered lights are woven. Or have an adult carry the lit candle.

If there are children in the house, hot cocoa or cider may replace coffee or be offered alongside.

Some families will sing a song, such as "The King Shall Come When Morning Dawns," to announce the day. Mother (or father) and daughter sing to awaken the other sleepers.

Once everyone else is served, the servers crawl into the largest empty bed and have their own treats.

One of my children always declared it her favorite saint's day. She loved the luxury of staying in bed on a cold morning and eating something rich and flaky instead of the usual Cream of Wheat. She also savored the chance to lounge about while eating, thinking her own thoughts and not having to take part in any conversation about schedules or chores. It felt like a small vacation on what was usually a typical school day.

## BREAKFAST FOR ROOMMATES OR CO-WORKERS

But you don't have to have children, or even other people, in your household. If you do have roommates, consider making breakfast, or buying rolls, and treating everyone to an early-morning December treat. If you live alone, you might celebrate by bringing rolls or doughnuts to neighbors or co-workers and greeting people, whatever their faith traditions, with, "Happy St. Lucy's!" on this friendly day. Or get up before dawn and watch the sun rise. Invite a friend to join you.

One of the customs of the day is to serve Leisst Kattor, or St. Lucy's Cats. For people with the time, talent, and the desire to make these treats, you can find the recipe in Florence Berger's 1949 *Cooking for Christ*. (Don't bother searching for some theological connection between St. Lucy and cats, she warns. Mrs. Berger writes of the Swedish custom that St. Nicholas watches over schoolboys, while St. Lucy watches over schoolgirls. She adds, sensibly, "Most little girls like kittens," and gives us her recipe.)

At our house, we like warm **poppy seed bread**. Here's our recipe for one loaf.

> Preheat oven to 350 degrees.
>
> MIX IN A SMALL BOWL
> 2 cups flour
> ¼ cup poppy seeds
> ½ teaspoon salt
> ¼ teaspoon baking soda
>
> CREAM TOGETHER IN A LARGE BOWL
> 1 stick butter
> ¾ cup sugar
>
> ADD TO THE BUTTER/SUGAR MIXTURE
> 2 eggs, one at a time
>
> BLEND IN
> ¾ cup sour cream
> 1 teaspoon vanilla
>
> Gradually beat in the dry ingredients just until blended. Do not overmix. Bake in a greased bread loaf pan until a knife inserted into the center of the loaf comes out clean. (You can make this bread weeks ahead. Just wrap the loaf well and put it in the freezer. If you want to warm up a single slice, put it in the microwave on full power for 45 seconds.)

~~~~~~~~~~~~~~~~~~~~~~~~

# 23

# KRISTKINDLS

Your kindness should be known to all. The Lord is near.
Have no anxiety at all.

–PHILIPPIANS 4:5-6

When we defend others we defend ourselves, because God knows,
there will come a time when we need defending.

–GRAHAM GREENE

One of the tasks of Advent is to get ready. After all, the word "advent" means "coming," and we know that cleaning is one of the ways we prepare for people who are coming to our houses. Another house we clean in Advent is the house of our heart. We want to get rid of all the anger and resentment and jealousy and despair that litters the place. We want to have plenty of room for the Christ to come in and be at home.

A good way to clean the rooms of our hearts and make room for Christ is to ask each member of the household to pick a Kristkindl for the season. The Kristkindl is someone in the house, someone you promise to treat each day as though that person were Christ.

The word "Kristkindl" is from an Austrian dialect, a form of the German "Christ Kind," or Christ Child. This Kristkindl practice is simple, in that it requires no purchases, no crafts or cooking, but it is not easy, because it requires daily acts of mercy and works of love. In every household there are people who are easy to love and people who are hard to love. That's why Kristkindls must be picked randomly and in secret.

On the First Sunday of Advent, before or after the prayers around the wreath, someone passes out slips of paper; on each slip is written the name of a household member. The paper slips are folded, the names meant to be kept a secret from everyone but the one who opens the slip of paper. So each person reads the name on their slip, but doesn't tell anyone else whose name they have drawn. (This can also be done with roommates or with residents of an apartment building or dormitory. It's possible the practice could turn roommates or neighbors into friends.)

In households with small children, or others who cannot read, one person should be prepared to help. It is often a parent or older sibling who knows the name a little one has drawn and who helps the child do the heart-cleaning acts of kindness. In a household with an older disabled individual, it might be the man or woman most actively involved in daily care and assistance who adds this duty to their list.

A person living alone might choose a particular person or organization as one's Kristkindl. Pray for your Kristkindl. Help however you can with the church or service organization or school you have chosen to serve. You might choose an elderly neighbor or family member as your Kristkindl. You might choose a co-worker, or even a stranger you see each day as you ride the bus or walk to work. You might choose a family member or friend from whom you are estranged. Pray for God's blessings upon them. Pray for their good, and for their health. Listen for the needs God will reveal in prayer.

It is useful for members of a household to have some pre-Advent discussion of the ways in which a Kristkindl might be honored. Being less hard on a child. Countering with an apology instead of an argument, offering to clear the table for another who has extra homework one night, sharing a favorite toy or article of clothing, saying prayers for one's Kristkindl, making oneself available for help with math or reading or music practice, not sharing an embarrassing story about another, listening and not interrupting, showing up to cheer at another's race or meet: These are all ways, visible and invisible, seen and known by the recipient or seen and known to God alone, that we learn what it means to make a place for God to be born and to dwell within us.

There may need to be a discussion on the First Sunday of Advent when the names are drawn. I can remember a child who mimed throwing up when the name slips were opened and read. While it wasn't technically a revelation of the secret, we knew, based on current intrafamily spats, which sibling the offender had drawn. So a "No Obnoxious Pantomime Rule" had to be implemented. I know, it's not very spiritual, or attractive, but we have to work with the material at hand. Just as God does.

Working with the material at hand means there will undoubtedly be a need for reminders along the way. Adults will need to model the art of holy ignoring and holy forgetting. Those who require the most help and make the most demands will have to practice patience. Everyone will have to work on saying "Please" and "Thank you." Perhaps part of our daily prayer will be a reminder that the Christ we worship understands all that it means to be human, in strength and in weakness, in power and in helplessness, as the served and as the servant.

How do we learn to do this? We might begin by asking, What practices foster hospitality to God and to God's bearers and messengers? What practices foster hospitality to the stranger? What if Mary had not welcomed the angel Gabriel? (Luke 1:26-38) What if Joseph hadn't listened to the angel who came to him in a dream, telling him to go ahead with his marriage to Mary and to raise the child as his own? (Matthew 1:18-21) What if someone had not made room in the stable for Mary and Joseph? (Luke 2:6-7) What if the magi had not seen and followed the star? What if they had not listened to the warning they received in a dream—that they should not return to Herod's palace, but go home by a different route? (Matthew 2:1-12) What if Joseph had not heeded the angel's command to take Mary and Jesus and flee to Egypt? (Matthew 2:13-15) We have to live each day in such a way that we are receptive to God's guidance and receptive to the demands of hospitality.

On Christmas Eve, after Mass, or prayers, if you attend Mass on

Christmas morning, you might gather and enjoy guessing and revealing the identities of the Kristkindls and their servants. This is another time when adult guidance is helpful. If a child's deeds were easily ignored or hard to discern, the adults can guide a conversation that honors the one who chose the little way. This might be the moment to reread and retell the nativity legends of the animals, each of which contributed in some small way to preparing Baby Jesus's bed. Think of the birds bringing straw for softness or the sheep offering wool for warmth. Just so, we do our part, however modest, and make a home for God.

In serving one another throughout Advent, in allowing others to serve us, we find the cobwebs cleared, the windows wiped clean, and the light flooding in.

# CHRISTMAS

# 24

# CHRISTMAS LEGENDS

*The Christ-child stood at Mary's knee,*
*His hair was like a crown,*
*And all the flowers looked up at Him,*
*And all the stars looked down.*

—G. K. CHESTERTON, "A CHRISTMAS CAROL"

People have found all sorts of ways to tell and retell the Christmas story. We imagine the journey from Galilee to Bethlehem and from Bethlehem to Egypt. We imagine the birth, the shepherds' wonder, and the shining star. We imagine ourselves into the story, as well as the plants and animals that may have played some part in Jesus's birth. Many of the stories about plants and animals underscore the truth that Christ comes for all of creation, making all things new.

## THE CHRISTMAS TREE

One of the earliest legends of the Christmas tree is told about St. Wilfrid, a bishop born about 634 in Northumberland in what is now England. Most of the people he served were not Christians, but Druids. They worshipped oak trees and held all their sacred ceremonies in oak groves. On stone tablets in the grove, they offered sacrifices, sometimes human sacrifices.

Wilfrid went about preaching Christ crucified, and many Druids came to believe in the risen Lord. But they found it hard to leave the old ways behind. One day, it is said, Wilfrid was with a crowd of newly baptized Christians in an oak forest. He took an ax and chopped down a giant oak tree. This must have been shocking for the people watching. Even if they no longer believed that oak trees were gods, still they were used to seeing them reverenced, not cut down.

The oak fell into four pieces of equal size and length. One piece fell to the north, another to the south, another to the east, and another to the west. From the center of the stump, a new young fir tree began to rise. Wilfrid put down his ax and spoke to the people, saying,

> *This tree shall be our holy tree.*
> *It is the wood of peace,*
> *For our houses are built of fir.*
> *It is the sign of eternal life,*
> *For its leaves are evergreen.*
> *Its branches grow in the shape of the cross.*
> *Its spire points to heaven,*
> *As Jesus points the way to heaven.*
> *We will call it the tree of the Christ Child.*
> *We will not gather about this tree in the wild woods,*
> *But in our homes.*
> *This tree will not shelter spilled blood.*
> *This tree will shelter only our loving gifts*
> *And our acts of kindness.*

## THE PARADISE TREE

Another legend about a tree has a weeping Adam and Eve leaving the Garden of Eden. Like all of us who must leave our homes behind, they wanted something to keep, something to help them remember Eden. So they cut off a branch of the tree of life and carried it with them.

In their new home, Adam and Eve planted the branch and watered it. It took root and began to grow, but it never flowered or set fruit. It never sprouted a single leaf. For hundreds of years the tree stood, tall and bare, reaching up to the sky.

It is said that on the day Christ was born in Bethlehem, in Judea, the tree burst into bloom and bore fruit. It stood, flowering, for many years until one day soldiers came and cut it down. They split the ancient tree into logs and nailed the logs together to form a cross. It was on this tree, sprouted from the tree of life, that Jesus was crucified.

## THE BALSAM PLANT

Many stories are told among the Christian Copts in Egypt about the Holy Family's sojourn there. They say the three arrived in Matariyah, a town that still exists in Egypt. There the Infant Jesus brought forth water from a spring. He drank the water and Mary washed his clothes in it. She poured the wash water on the ground, and where the water flowed the balsam plant sprang up and blossomed. Egyptian balsam is still considered among the finest variety of that oil. Balsam is added to olive oil and used for the holy oil called chrism, which is used for the sacraments of baptism, Confirmation, and holy orders.

## THE ROSEMARY BUSH

There are many stories about the Holy Family as they fled Herod and went into Egypt seeking refuge. One legend has it that they stopped by a stream to rest and wash their dirty clothes. Mary looked around to find a place to hang the laundry. She spied a sweet-smelling bush and hung the wet clothes on its branches. It is said that God the Father rewarded the bush for its service to Mary. God gave the bush blossoms the same blue as Mary's robe. And God gave the bush a name, rosemary, after the name of the Mother of God.

## THE PINE TREE

Another story from the Holy Family's flight into Egypt involves a towering pine tree. The family was on the road when they heard Herod's soldiers approaching. Mary was too tired to run, and Joseph would not leave her side. They looked about and saw an ancient pine with a hollow trunk. It is said that the tree beckoned them inside its trunk and then crossed its boughs over the opening, concealing the three inside. The soldiers searched and searched, but the Holy Family slept, safely hidden in the tree, all through the night.

In the morning the Infant Jesus raised his arms in blessing over the faithful pine. Some say that if you cut a pine cone in half you can still see the imprint of Jesus's hand.

## THE POINSETTIA FLOWER

There are many stories of poor people who want to give a gift to the Christ Child but who have nothing to offer. One of these legends comes from Mexico. Maria was the child of poor farmers. It was the custom in her village for each person to bring a gift to Mass on Christmas Eve and place it before the Christ Child in the manger. Maria had nothing and she was ashamed, for she loved the Child Jesus. As she walked to Mass, she saw some weeds growing along the road. She picked an armful and carried them with her into church. But once she saw all the beautiful gifts before the crèche, she hung back, embarrassed by her lowly offering. Only the prompting of her parish priest caused her to come forward and offer her weeds to Jesus. She closed her eyes and knelt in prayer before the Christ Child.

When Maria opened her eyes, she saw that her bouquet had been transformed. There, before her, were flowers of brilliant red. The petals of what we know as the poinsettia flower formed a star shape, like the star of Bethlehem. From that day to this, these flowers are called Las Flores de Noche Buena, the "Flowers of the Holy Night."

## THE MANGER IS SPARED

Christian pilgrims began going to the place where Jesus was born as early as the second century. The Roman empress Helena, the mother of Constantine, built a church over the site in AD 339, and it was called the Church of the Nativity. When war came to Bethlehem several centuries later, Persian soldiers invaded the church to destroy it. According to Palestinian legend, the soldiers saw a painting on one wall of the church. It showed the magi, the Three Kings, all in Persian dress. The soldiers retreated, and many of the elaborate floor mosaics were spared. They can be seen today in the Church of the Nativity, rebuilt on the same site in AD 565 by the emperor Justinian.

## THE TALKING ANIMALS

Many countries have stories about the gift God gave to animals in honor of their care for the Holy Family on the night Christ was born. The story goes that the animals warmed the newborn with their breath, and so each Christmas Eve, God allows the animals to speak. But no one ever hears what they say, because in almost every country where these stories are told, it is considered bad luck to eavesdrop on the animals. In rural Poland, unleavened bread is broken and shared before the Christmas Eve dinner. Guests share the bread with one another and with the farm animals. Then the people sit down to dinner at a table on which the dishes sit atop wheat and straw, a reminder to all of the animals' hospitality on that holy night.

In France, birds are honored as first among all the animals at Christmas. The French legend says that it was the raven, flying through the night sky, that first heard the angels singing the news of Christ's birth. The raven flew to tell the other birds. The wren (known in France as *la poulette de Dieu*) wove a blanket of feathers and leaves to cover the baby. The nightingale soothed the crying child with its lullaby. The robin spread its wings to shield the baby from the cold wind. The rooster, in France, as in Mexico, is said to have announced the birth to all the animals. "*Christus natus est*," he cried. "Christ is born!"

## 25

~~~~~~~~~~~~~~~~~~~~~~~~~~~~~~~~~~

# ST. STEPHEN AND THE
# COMPANIONS OF CHRIST

A voice was heard in Ramah,
Sobbing and loud lamentation;
Rachel weeping for her children,
and she would not be consoled,
since they were no more.

−MATTHEW 2:18

We sometimes want to turn the nativity story into "White Christmas: The Prequel." You know, how God got a bunch of good-hearted souls together to save an inn in Vermont, and, oh yeah, also the universe?

Christmas is so cozy (babies, candles, gifts, carols) that we want to settle in and stay there forever. That's where the liturgical calendar hits us upside the head with the bracing news that Herod, and his descendants, are on the march and that we are on a path that leads to the cross.

## THE FEAST OF ST. STEPHEN

December 26 marks the first of a series of saints' days we call the Comites Christi, the Friends of Christ. St. Stephen, whose life is chronicled in chapters six and seven of the book of Acts, was the first martyr (a Greek word meaning "witness"), as well as the first deacon (a Greek word meaning "servant" or "helper"). He was one of the first seven men chosen to care for the physical needs of the Jerusalem church.

The author of the book of Acts says that Stephen was "filled with grace and power" (Acts 6:8). He not only cared for the widows and orphans; he went out into the city proclaiming the crucified and risen Christ.

Stephen soon came to the attention of the authorities. When the high priest summoned him, Stephen gave an account of salvation history, from Abraham to Christ. His judges sentenced Stephen to death by stoning. The Scriptures record Stephen's faithfulness unto death:

> As they were stoning Stephen, he called out, "Lord Jesus, receive my spirit." Then he fell to his knees and cried out in a loud voice, "Lord, do not hold this sin against them"; and when he said this, he fell asleep (ACTS 7:59-60).

In what must have grieved St. Paul to his death, he, then an ardent foe of the Christians, agreed to Stephen's execution and took part in the mob violence against Christians that broke out after Stephen's death (Acts 8:1-3).

It has long been a tradition to do some kind of servant or helper work on this day in honor of St. Stephen. Perhaps you could visit an ill or elderly person who is alone on these days of Christmas. Or you could invite someone who might otherwise be ignored to share a meal, or you could shovel the snow from a neighbor's walk.

## THE FEAST OF ST. JOHN THE APOSTLE

The next day, December 27, is the feast of St. John the apostle, who must have wondered why he, alone of all the disciples of Jesus, was spared a martyr's death. His brother, James, was the first of the disciples to die. We can imagine how John grieved his brother. We can imagine his grief as he heard the news of each successive martyrdom.

John was not killed, but neither was he spared suffering. He was imprisoned on Patmos, and we do not know all he endured there. But he survived and went on to become the bishop of Ephesus (in what we now know as Turkey). There, according to the tradition, he lived with the Virgin Mary until her assumption into heaven.

Perhaps John was spared so that he could give his eyewitness account of the life, death, and resurrection of Jesus. Perhaps he was spared that he might follow Jesus's exhortation from the cross to care for Mary as his own mother (John 19:26-27). Perhaps he was spared to give us all a model for a good priest and bishop.

The story that is told of John is one to carry and remember and live. It is said that he was known for preaching the same homily, over and over, day after day, "Little children, let us love one another."

A delegation from the church came to ask him, please, to preach a new lesson. John is said to have replied, "Of course, as soon as we learn this one."

## ST. JOHN'S WINE

One of the customs of this feast day is to make St. John's wine and share it. It's easy to prepare. Just take one bottle of red wine and pour it into a saucepan. Add these spices: 2 whole cloves, 2 (2-inch-long) sticks of cinnamon, 1 cardamom seed, and ½ teaspoon freshly grated nutmeg. Boil the wine and spices for about 5 minutes. Strain the wine and serve it hot. Toast each other with the traditional toast of the day: "I give you the love of St. John."

## THE FEAST OF THE HOLY INNOCENTS

The most difficult of these days of Comites Christi is December 28, the feast of the Holy Innocents. Sts. Stephen and John and Thomas Becket (whose feast is on December 29) chose to follow Christ. But the infant boys of Jerusalem died, never knowing why. Visitors from the east had brought news to Herod of a newborn king, whose birth had been heralded by a star. Unable to find the child of whom the visitors spoke, Herod resolved to kill all the male infants in the region, all the male children two years old and younger.

Perhaps this feast is so troubling because it is repeated in every age: children abandoned, aborted, beaten, abused, and starved. St.

Paul writes of the scandal of the cross, the horror that God should die. But what of the scandal that God should be born, and born in the way all babies are born—helpless, needy, dependent? How could the Creator of the universe come into the world without the strength to hold up his own head?

Sometimes when we gaze at the cross we might think, "At least Jesus died as an adult. He journeyed to Jerusalem knowing he would die there. He journeyed freely, aware, and willing."

But the wonder of this day is that God did not come to earth as an adult. He freely entrusted himself to the unreliable mercies of adults. Jesus is not, like Superman, a baby from the planet Krypton, rocketed to earth and able, if the need arises, to destroy Brainiac, all the while *appearing* as helpless as Clark Kent. Jesus *is* helpless, and it is that soft-skulled, weak-necked truth that causes us to tremble. Luke tells us that, forty days after his birth, Jesus was brought to the Temple in "Jerusalem to present him to the Lord." There, Simeon takes Jesus "into his arms." Jesus does not walk; he is brought (Luke 2:22-38).

Born far from home, a stranger whose parents must beg a place for his birth, Jesus is born into peril. The king, Herod, seeks to kill him. Matthew gives us a sense of the threat when he writes that Joseph, warned of the dangers in a dream, gathered up his little family and ran with them into Egypt, the place where his ancestor, Joseph, had also found refuge (Matthew 2:13-15).

Somehow, by becoming one of the helpless, Jesus casts his lot with, and his mercy upon, the children everywhere whose dependence makes them prey. By having no place to lay his head, Jesus redeems every shanty and shelter. Through his flight into exile, Jesus sanctifies every mother and child crossing the river by night, creeping through the streets at dawn, all those who flee the knife, the gun, the falling bomb, the raised fist. By becoming one who can be passed around, given and taken without his knowledge or consent, Jesus makes holy every defenseless person handed over to those who cannot, or will not, defend her or protect him.

Consider keeping this day by learning more about the needs of children in your own neighborhood, city, country, and around the world. Then decide how you will help: by volunteering at a local shelter for those fleeing domestic violence, donating to Catholic Relief Services and other organizations seeking to help Christians fleeing persecution, or working with your local Catholic Charities as they work to feed families and help them find housing and jobs.

## THE FEAST OF ST. THOMAS BECKET

December 29, the feast of St. Thomas Becket (1118–1170), offers a good opportunity to get together with friends and family to watch a movie. The 1964 movie *Becket* stars Richard Burton and Peter O'Toole, and it stays pretty close to the actual story of the twelfth-century martyr.

O'Toole plays the English king Henry II. When Henry and Thomas were both young men, Henry appointed Thomas as his chancellor. Thomas enjoys the advantages of his closeness to the king, but he also begins to take seriously the demands of his office.

Then, when Henry needs an archbishop of Canterbury, he decides to promote his childhood friend and companion in the high life. Henry believes their easy friendship will continue, as he understands the archbishop's role to be nothing more than another perk-laden appointment. Thomas isn't a priest; he is a deacon. But Henry insists that he be ordained and accept the appointment, as does Pope Alexander III. Thomas as a potential "yes man" who can hear his confession—this is what Henry has in mind.

Thomas, who has indulged his baser instincts right along with Henry, nevertheless understands that the office of archbishop is larger than any of the individuals who occupy it. The office doesn't fit the man; the man must grow to fit the office.

When Thomas begins to grow into his office, Henry, who wants Thomas to be a friend first and a bishop second, is alarmed. Thomas begins to dress simply, pray daily, and turn his attention to the poor. He rejects crony appointments to the Church and looks instead for holy and faithful men.

Thomas and Henry clash politically, and Thomas seeks refuge in France. When he returns to England, still unwilling to bend to Henry's demands, the king calls for Thomas's death. And he gets his wish.

Perhaps nothing demonstrates more the kind of man Thomas

became than the manner of his death. He receives a letter warning him that knights loyal to the king are hunting him. On December 29, 1170, Thomas prepares, as he does daily, to celebrate vespers in Canterbury Cathedral.

When his devoted brother monks tell him that armed men are coming, Thomas neither runs nor hides. He continues to prepare for the sacraments. He does what he has been appointed to do. The loving monks try to hold the doors against Thomas's killers.

The knights shout, "Where is Thomas the traitor?"

Thomas answers, "Here I am, no traitor, but archbishop and priest of God."

The knights rush in, striking Thomas repeatedly with their swords. He sinks to his knees and cries, "For the name of Jesus and in defense of the church, I am willing to die."

He died near the altar, a faithful son of God, just as thousands of Christians around the world continue to die for the name of Jesus and in defense of the Church, faithful sons and daughters of God.

# 26

# CELEBRATING THE NEW YEAR

Fly swifter round, ye wheels of time,
And bring the welcome day.

–ISAAC WATTS

All people mark time. We call special occasions names such as "birthdays" and "anniversaries." We remember the day we were born or the day we entered religious life or were married. We remember the death days of friends and loved ones. My husband and I mark the anniversary of our first date.

We call the first month of the year "January," a word taken from the name of the Roman god Janus, who ruled beginnings and endings. Drawings of Janus show him with two faces, one looking backward and one looking forward. Because he is the god of beginnings and endings, he is also the god of passageways, gates, and doors. The close of one year and the beginning of another is a kind of gate or door. We commonly wish one another health and peace in the New Year. It is a wish, and not a command, because we never know the reality onto which the new door will open, or the places this passageway will lead.

Because people have a sense of moving from the known to the

unknown at the end of the old year and the beginning of the new, many cultures have "lucky foods" that are always served on that day.

In my childhood the lucky food on New Year's Day was black-eyed peas, or cowpeas. The legend of black-eyed peas begins with the Siege of Vicksburg, during the Civil War. The citizens of this Mississippi River town ran out of food. Just in time, they discovered black-eyed peas and found a food to sustain them until the siege ended.

## WHY WE CELEBRATE THE NEW YEAR

People always have a "start-over day" when they celebrate a new year. Hindus in India celebrate a New Year that moves according to their lunar/solar calendar. The date even varies from region to region, but it almost always occurs near the start of spring. This makes sense when one considers the Hindu notion of reincarnation, of creation and destruction, always in cycle, much like the ongoing cycle of creation and destruction that is the world coming out of winter and into spring.

Different people count the years differently. Buddhists count time from the Year 0, which is when the Buddha achieved parinirvana, or, nirvana after death. Nirvana is the highest state of enlightenment, where one's personal desires and sufferings go away. Parinirvana is a kind of doubling of enlightenment, both during life and death.

Muslims count the years from when the prophet Mohammed fled from the city of Mecca to the city of Medina.

The Jewish New Year is said to be the anniversary of creation. This celebration, which is called Rosh Hashanah (from the Hebrew word meaning "head," or "first of the year"), falls close to the autumn equinox, when day and night are of equal length. After all, when God created the world in perfect harmony, day and night must certainly have been equal.

Christians begin their count of years with the days just before the birth of Jesus, on the First Sunday of Advent. The way we count time begins with our looking forward to, and our expectation of, the One who will redeem time and the creation that is marked by time. During the days that we celebrate Jesus's birth, the whole world marks a common ending of the old year and the beginning of a new one.

Food scholars say that the American custom of making and sharing Christmas cookies really began as a New Year's Day custom. Visitors would come calling, and according to an early-nineteenth-century cookbook, the proper dish to serve them was cookies and a cordial called Cherry Bounce. Consider how Cherry Bounce is made: Fill a quart jar with 2 cups of fresh cherries, ⅓ cup of granulated sugar, 1 lemon peel, and 3 cups of bourbon, or more, if needed, to cover the other ingredients, and then leave the jar, sealed, in a dark place for two months before serving. You can see why a cook might move the cookies to Christmas Day. Who is going to want a cookie when he can have a bounce?

Create your own household customs for the start-over day. One family we know keeps a jar filled with scraps of paper. Throughout the year, members of the family jot down a prayer answered, a happy event, a kindness given, beauty seen or heard. It doesn't have to be long or complicated—something like "morning walk through the Garden of the Gods." On New Year's Day, they gather and read aloud the good memories from the past year.

Catholics believe that all our years, when we put them together, are different from what is represented by the two-faced god Janus, who keeps beginning and ending, beginning and ending, but going nowhere. Time really isn't like the moon, growing full and then growing dark, again and again. We believe that time had a single beginning and will have a single ending, a belief reinforced by the prevailing cosmological theory of the Big Bang, developed by the Belgian priest, astronomer, and physics professor, Father Georges Lemaitre. The universe had a beginning and it will have an end. Likewise, we begin in God and we end in God. Each year brings us closer to Christ and to the eternity that we are promised.

~~~~~~~~~~~~~~~~~~~~

# 27

# BLESSING A HOME, MAKING WINDOW STARS, AND KEEPING THE FEAST OF EPIPHANY

*The magi followed the star,*
*and found Christ who is light from light.*
*May you, too, find the Lord*
*when your pilgrimage is ended.*

–SOLEMN BLESSING ROMAN RITE

The Feast of Epiphany, January 6, falls on the last day of the Twelve Days of Christmas, and commemorates the magi who followed a star to find the Christ Child. The word "epiphany" comes from a Greek word meaning "to reveal." The Feast of Epiphany is a celebration of the Incarnation, when God became man. Catholics traditionally bless their homes on Epiphany night. The Epiphany blessing asks that we might find the Lord when the pilgrimage that is our lives is ended. It also reminds us that we should be looking for God, and finding Him, all along the way.

On the Feast of Epiphany, Catholic households begin where the magi ended, not in a palace or a temple, but in the stable, the poor home that Mary and Joseph fashioned for Jesus's birth. They were on the road, those two, and where they settled for the birth, everything, even the building, was borrowed and begged. Yet it was over that place that a star shone, and angels sang, and in that place kings bearing gold bowed down in homage. For within those rough walls God came to earth.

Gather with your household on Epiphany night. If you have a

number of people in your household, each may take a figure from the crèche on the journey through the house. Someone should carry a bowl of holy water for blessing the rooms, someone else might carry a lit candle.

As you proceed from room to room, consider singing "We Three Kings of Orient Are"—just the first verse and the chorus. The song is easy for small children and adults to learn. True, it's a lugubrious tune, but most people know it and are agreed in their desire to be led by God's "perfect light."

Singing, walk from room to room, blessing them one by one. It is understood that the person who lives or works chiefly in a room gets to bless it. In a bedroom a teenager might pray for privacy or the ability to get some sleep. In a home office a single person might sprinkle water on stacks of paper and pray for order or peace.

The person who does most of the cooking should bless the kitchen, praying that many might be fed and welcomed there.

The house blessing ends at the front door, where someone writes in white chalk over the door the annual inscription, the first initials of the names of the wise men along with the numbers of the new year. The names of the magi, according to the tradition, were Caspar, Melchior, and Balthasar, so the inscription will read "C+M+B" and the year "2016," or whatever year has just begun. You might pray that all who enter will be treated with dignity and love, and that those who come into this home might find, as did the magi on their journey, the true and ever-living Christ.

It takes practice to recognize Christ in all the places and faces. It takes work to remember that he is found in the most familiar faces, the ones most likely to be yelling at one another over borrowed clothes, unpaid bills, or misplaced car keys.

We pray to find the Lord when our sojourn is ended, but we know the finding must begin here, in our daily life. Epiphany reminds us that Christ came first to a humble shelter, and to the people dwelling there.

### An Epiphany House Blessing
Lord God of heaven and earth,
 you revealed your only begotten Son to every nation

by the guidance of a star.
Bless this home and all who inhabit it.
Fill us with the light of Christ
that our concern for others may reflect your love.
We ask this through Christ our Lord. Amen.

## EPIPHANY WINDOW STARS

Epiphany reminds us that God makes himself known both in the everyday act of being born, and in signs and wonders. In the Hebrew Scriptures, God often speaks through the natural world. For example, the Angel of the Lord appears to Moses in a burning bush. Likewise, God reveals his presence to the Israelites in a pillar of cloud and a pillar of fire. In the same way, the magi were led to the Christ Child, to the wondrous reality of God made flesh, both by asking directions of the chief priests and the scribes (Matthew 2:1-12) and by following a star in the east. For this reason Epiphany is sometimes referred to as "the Day of Lights."

If you are so inclined, celebrate the Feast of Epiphany by making transparent paper stars and hanging them in a window in your home. This is an easy craft to do on your own or with children, and it's a lovely way to meditate on the Epiphany story. Hanging these kite paper stars in a bedroom or kitchen window gives members of the household an opportunity to stop and reflect on the ways in which God's love is expressed in creation.

## MAKING EIGHT-POINTED WINDOW STARS

You will need eight squares of colored kite paper, tissue paper, or even plain folding paper (though paper that is transparent works so that the light can shine through), and a glue stick or any kind of clear-drying craft glue. The eight sheets of paper need to be perfect squares when you begin.

1. Fold one perfect square of paper in half creating a sharp crease. Then unfold or open it.
2. Fold the paper in half the other way, creating another sharp crease. Then unfold or open it. You should have a square of paper with four boxes or quadrants.
3. Fold each corner down to the center point to make a smaller square.
4. Orient the smaller square toward you in a diamond shape, with a point facing toward you. Take one outer edge and fold it toward the center. Do the same thing on each side, creating a kite shape.
5. Once you have repeated this process with the other seven

squares of paper, so that you have eight kite shapes, arrange them so that their points meet in the center and glue them together along their overlapping edges.

6. Because these stars are so simple, mixing colors looks best. Once they are dry, hang them in a window.

～～～～～～～～～～～～～～～～～

# WINTER ORDINARY TIME

～～～～～～～～～～～～～～～～～

# 28

~~~~~~~~~~~~~~~~~~~~~~~~~

## ORDINARY TIME

This is the day to shape the days upon.

–CORMAC MCCARTHY, *The Road*

Since the reforms of the Second Vatican Council, the term "Ordinary Time" has entered our vocabulary. Someone may announce at Mass, "Today is the Fourth Sunday in Ordinary Time." We might hear the word "ordinary," and think it means "dull," or "run-of-the-mill." And yet, babies will be born and men and women married and the dead buried—all extraordinary events in the life of the Church, all in Ordinary Time. Solemnities, like the Most Holy Trinity, are kept during Ordinary Time. Mass is celebrated daily throughout Ordinary Time, and there is nothing dull, or run-of-the-mill, ever, about receiving the Body and Blood of Christ. What distinguishes Ordinary Time is that it is not a season; it is a period of time between seasons, or, perhaps more accurately, a period of time broken up by seasons.

The Easter season, for example, lasts for fifty days, which is seven weeks of seven days plus one day. Easter comes to a close on Pentecost, and then Summer Ordinary Time begins on the Monday after Pentecost. It lasts until another season, Advent, begins, and then Winter Ordinary Time resumes after Christmas.

"Ordinary" is the English form of the Latin word *ordinalis*, a word that refers to a number in a series. In this sense, the weeks between seasons are ordinary, that is, numbered. We number the weeks from the first Sunday following Epiphany to the First Sunday of Lent. Then we number the weeks from Pentecost to the First Sunday of Advent.

Before the Second Vatican Council, we still counted the weeks, but we called Ordinary Time by two different names: "the Season after Epiphany" (the First Sunday after Epiphany to the First Sunday of Lent) and "the Season after Pentecost" (the First Sunday after Pentecost to the First Sunday of Advent). Time is counted from Sunday to Sunday in the liturgical calendar, but in practice most of us see Ordinary Time in wintertime as ending on Shrove Tuesday, or Fat Tuesday, the day before Ash Wednesday.

Ordinary Time is the longest period of time in the Church year, lasting from 33 to 34 weeks. It is the longest period in the Church year just as our own ordinary time, the time between births and baptisms and graduations, weddings, and burials is the longest period in a human life. Because other liturgical seasons begin or end with moveable feasts, the length of Ordinary Time can vary. The longest period of Ordinary Time each year is that between Pentecost and Advent.

All people live their lives in cycles: school years and graduations, planting time and reaping time, marriages, pregnancies, first steps and last steps, first words and final words. The Church, too, is rooted in cycles and seasons. There are the major feasts and seasons. Easter, as the focal point of our faith, and so also our lives, is both a feast and a season. But what enables us to truly celebrate Easter? It is the daily work of mercy and prayer, of obedience and faithfulness that leads us to the life-giving font, to the baptismal waters of Easter.

The Protestant reformer Martin Luther once asked, "What will you do in the days of mundane faithfulness?" What will we do

with most of the days of our lives, days that are filled with small re-peated acts—of work, of rest, of play, of prayer, of weeding the gar-den? How will these daily steps bring us closer to God? There is a way in which "ordinary" here also means something close to "mundane," which comes from a Latin word referring to the world (*mundus*) in contrast to heaven. That is why some will argue that "ordinary" in this context is closer to *ordo*, a Latin word meaning "order," as in "the regular order of things." We might characterize Ordinary Time as mundane, or, in the regular order of things, in that most days are not Easter, just as 364 days of every 365-day year are not my birth-day. Most days we are not at weddings, anniversaries, or funerals. But what is it that makes it possible for us to marry well, to cele-brate anniversaries of long marriages, to lay our beloved to rest in faith and hope? It is the work that never gets praised or perhaps even mentioned, the ordinary moments that make up most of our days. A bride may tell you that watching her groom's patience with his deaf grandmother back when they were dating, and not the day he was named teacher of the year, is what turned her heart toward him. After my grandfather died, my grandmother recalled how he would come in from the farm calling, "Woman, where's my food?" and how she missed that brusque greeting most of all.

We mark special days in special ways, but we know that the love and faithfulness that make it possible for us to enter into those mo-ments are formed and shaped by the daily work of love and life in community. Think about weddings. Weddings are the result of all the ordinary time a couple has spent—talking together, being with friends and family, finding out what they treasure—that brings them to the wedding feast. Much of the hours spent may not be memorable in the way the wedding day is memorable, yet those quiet days are the foundation on which the wedding and the marriage are built. It is in the "ordinary time" of church life, as in the "ordinary time" of our life at home and at work, that the good seed is sown. Then, when the season of harvest comes round again, there is fruit, ripe and rich and plenty.

# 29

## THE FEAST OF
## THE CHAIR OF ST. PETER

"And so I say to you, you are Peter, and upon this rock
I will build my church, and the gates of the netherworld
shall not prevail against it."

–MATTHEW 16:18

When my father-in-law died, I observed that no one among his six
sons, their wives, and his many grandchildren wanted to sit in his
chair at the table. It wasn't fear or dread, it was something much simpler: the chair, *that* chair, belonged to Leonard. It always had, and, in
some sense, it always would. We had eaten so many meals with him
sitting at the head of the table in his chair. We had played so many
games of cards with him at the head of the table in his chair. I understood as I watched us take our places at meals after his death that the
chair stood for Leonard and his place among us.

February 22 is the Feast of the Chair of Peter, Apostle. Each
bishop has a chair, the bishop's chair, from which he presides. The
Latin word for a bishop's chair is *cathedra*. That is the source for our
word "cathedral," which is the bishop's home church in his diocese.
You may have heard the phrase "ex cathedra," for those times when
a pope speaks definitively, that is, "ex," or "from," the "cathedra," or
"chair," of Peter. When the pope speaks ex cathedra, he speaks about
a matter of divine revelation under the guidance of the Holy Spirit

and in full authority as the successor of St. Peter. These are teachings the Church deems infallible, that is, they are doctrines of the faith that are solemnly proclaimed and that the faithful must believe.

Some people think popes speak ex cathedra all the time, for instance, about personal preferences or political matters. Not so. There are only two times in Church history when popes have spoken ex cathedra: the teaching about Mary's Immaculate Conception was declared by Pope Pius IX in 1854, and the teaching about Mary's Assumption into heaven was declared by Pope Pius XII in 1950. Neither of these were new teachings; both of these tenets had been acknowledged and celebrated throughout the centuries, from the early days of the Church and going forward. These proclamations were statements of what was already known. Think of it like a wedding. It is a public declaration of something that has already been promised, the intention for two people to so join their lives as to live as one. That doesn't just happen at the Church when the processional music begins to play. It happened long before, and now, at the ceremony in the church, the time to announce and witness that declaration has come.

Does that mean the Church has spoken definitively about only two teachings? When the Church teaches, we talk about its magisterium (which is derived from a Latin word meaning "teaching"), that is, its God-given authority to make pronouncements on matters of faith (Matthew 16:18). There are three levels of magisterial teaching: papal, ecumenical councils (when all the bishops around the world are assembled, or convened), and episcopal synods (when bishops from a certain region are assembled, or convened, such as the bishops of the United States of America making pronouncements particular to the diocese of that nation). The three persons, or groups, represented in those levels are the official interpreters of Scripture (derived from the Latin word scribere, meaning "to write") and of the apostolic tradition (that which has been revealed by God to the Church and handed on from the beginning). They are the interpreters of something that belongs to the whole Church, the Body of Christ, throughout time.

Ecumenical councils have also spoken infallibly about matters of faith. (The First Vatican Council, an ecumenical council, declared the doctrine of infallibility only in 1870.) The first example we find is in the New Testament book of Acts, chapter fifteen. A controversy threatened to tear the new Church apart, because some Christians, led by Peter, believed that Gentiles had to follow Jewish dietary law, and, if they were men, be circumcised. In Acts 15:1b, we hear what Peter's group taught, "Unless you are circumcised according to the Mosaic practice, you cannot be saved."

Others, led by Paul, believed that Gentiles did not have to undergo a de facto conversion to Judaism in order to become Christians. The Church leaders met in what has come to be called the Council of Jerusalem in AD 53. Peter, who had received a divine revelation that brought him into agreement with Paul and his followers, stood with James, who gave the final and authoritative teaching: "It is my judgment, therefore, that we ought to stop troubling the Gentiles who turn to God, but tell them by letter to avoid pollution from idols, unlawful marriage, the meat of strangled animals, and blood" (Acts 15:19-20). Gentiles did not have to undergo a two-step process of conversion, becoming Jews first, before becoming Christians. That teaching remains true today.

Less than three hundred years later, at the Council of Nicaea in 325, another ecumenical council, the bishops gathered to consider the relationship of God the Father and God the Son. There was wide agreement that Jesus was the Messiah, the One who had died and was risen, but there were still deep divisions regarding this Father-Son relationship. Did the Father create the Son? That was a big question. And, if the Father created the Son, was there, then, a time when the Son was not? The Council of Nicaea answered those questions in a definitive, authoritative, and, using modern language, infallible way in what we know as the Nicene Creed (from the Latin word *credo*, meaning "I believe"). Listen to the words through which the one substance (*homoousios*) of the Father and the Son is expressed:

> *God from God, Light from Light,*
> *true God from true God,*
> *begotten, not made, consubstantial [one in Being or*
>     *homoousios] with the Father*

It may remind you of arithmetic classes, where you learn that the equation "2+4" and the numeral "6" can be distinguished from one another, but they are equal. In the same way, the Council of Nicaea affirmed that God the Father and God the Son are two persons, but they are equal, that is, of one substance. That teaching is still held, and indeed, the recitation of this creed is part of the liturgy of the Mass. Eastern Rite Catholics, Anglicans, and many Protestant denominations also use the Nicene Creed, making it a powerful source of unity among otherwise divided Christians.

If you go to Rome and visit St. Peter's Basilica, you can see an ancient wooden chair that we believe to have been Peter's, when he was the Bishop of Rome. We preserve the chair, and honor it, because it stands for the long, unbroken history of bishops, from that day to this. The chair is a sign of our unity and of our tradition and history.

You may have a bowl or a plate that belonged to an ancestor or a friend who has died, one you use on special occasions. Perhaps when it comes out at Thanksgiving or Christmas, you tell the story of the person who used it before you. You tell the stories of the meals and gatherings where you remember it being used. Perhaps you have some item of clothing or jewelry that reminds you of a dead loved one. When you think of the Chair of Peter, think of all the ways we remember and give thanks for the chain of mothers and fathers, stretching back to the beginning of time, which links us to them and to one another. And give thanks for the Church, which continues—despite wars and scandals and plagues and attacks—to lead us home to God, and to those who wait for us there.

~~~~~~~~~~~~

# 30

# FEBRUARY HOLY DAYS AND CELEBRATIONS: CANDLEMAS, ST. BLAISE, AND VALENTINE'S DAY

> Love a friend, a wife, whatever you like. Then you
> will know there is a God.
>
> —VINCENT VAN GOGH

You can make the argument that February is the longest month of Ordinary Time, even if it is the month that has the fewest number of days. That's because February is often cold and dark and dreary, with none of the excitement of December and early January to warm us. But February has some wonderful surprises.

## CANDLEMAS—FEBRUARY 2

Though by this time of the year most of us have long ago thrown out their Christmas tree and packed away the crèche, today—the Feast of the Presentation of the Lord, or Candlemas—is actually the official end of the Christmas season. (If your crèche *is* still up, the tradition is to decorate it with flowers to mark the end of the season.)

February 2 marks forty days since the celebration of the Nativity of the Lord. It's the day when we celebrate Jesus's presentation before the Lord in the Temple in Jerusalem. This was, Luke tells us, the custom from the time of Moses (Luke 2:22-38).

Mary and Joseph took the baby Jesus to the Temple, where they found two elderly people, Simeon and Anna, who had been waiting all their lives for the Promised One of Israel. When Anna saw Jesus, the Gospel says, "she gave thanks to God and spoke about the child to all who were awaiting the redemption of Jerusalem" (Luke 2:38).

God had promised Simeon that he would not die until he had seen the Messiah of the Lord. When Simeon saw Jesus, he took the child in his arms and declared the prayer we say each night in Night Prayer, or Compline:

> Now, Master, you may let your servant go in peace,
> according to your word,
> for my eyes have seen your salvation,
> which you have prepared in sight of all the peoples,
> a light for the revelation of the Gentiles,
> and glory for your people Israel (LUKE 2:29-32).

When you pray today, think of some prayer you are waiting to have answered. Think of some deep desire you long to be realized. Then consider Anna and Simeon, who grew old waiting, all the while waiting in faith. Commit to learn Simeon's prayer by heart, as we commit to learning Simeon and Anna's patience by heart.

And, be sure to have candles on your dinner table today. Use a candle at Evening Prayer and Night Prayer. Because today is also Candlemas, when all the candles that will be used in church for the next twelve months are blessed.

## MEMORIAL OF ST. BLAISE, FEBRUARY 3

Feeling achy? Coughing? Know someone who is sick? It's midwinter and we're deep into the cold and flu season. Time to turn to St. Blaise, a fourth-century physician, bishop, and martyr, who is the patron saint of all who suffer diseases of the throat.

According to the tradition, Bishop Blaise saved a young boy who was choking to death on a fish bone. This Armenian bishop is still invoked to intercede and protect those whose throats are unwell.

Go to Mass today and ask your priest for the blessing. This blessing may be offered before or after Mass. The priest or lay minister uses two blessed candles tied together in the shape of a cross and touches the candles to the necks of the faithful while saying this prayer:

> Through the intercession of St. Blaise, bishop and martyr, may God deliver you free from every disease of the throat, and from every other disease. In the name of the Father, and of the Son, and of the Holy Spirit.

## VALENTINE'S DAY, FEBRUARY 14

St. Valentine did not own a greeting card company. He wasn't a candy maker or a florist. He was either a bishop martyr (and just try finding a greeting card to mark that occasion) who died in the middle of the third century, or he was a priest, physician, and martyr (ditto the printed candy heart) who died around the same time as the bishop. They were both named Valentine.

Tradition tends toward the physician priest, because it is said that he wrote notes of love and encouragement to fellow Christians who lived in fear of persecution, arrest, and death. Some say it was his example that started the custom of sending love notes on this day.

Both Valentines would be astonished to find aisles of Walmarts across the country bearing their name. We suggest a return to the original custom by calling it "Say 'I Love You' Day." You don't need to be "in a relationship" to keep the memorial of St. Valentine. Pick up the phone and tell a friend, "I love you."

Drop a card off at a neighbor's house that says, "I love having you as a neighbor." Send a note to your priest, "I love having you as a pastor." Tell the clerk at the grocery store who always has a smile (even for the twenty-item folks in the fifteen-item line), "I love shopping with you." Thank the waitress who always remembers that you like extra ice, and say, "I love having you wait on my table." Put a card in your child's lunch sack that says, "I love having you as my daughter [or son]." Stop by your folks' house just to say, "I love you," and "Thanks."

Give your wife or husband a kiss and say, "I love you." Then tell your spouse at least one thing he or she does to enrich that love. Say it aloud, and mean it.

Think of all the people you can add to this list: a teacher, yours or your child's, a doctor or nurse, the crossing guard, the dry cleaner, the aide at your nursing home, your coach, your conductor, your bus driver, your mechanic. And if you can't say, "I love you," or it wouldn't be appropriate, then think of something kind and encouraging that you can say.

It won't cost a cent to speak or write messages of love, and you might even get an "I love you, too," in return.

## MEMORIAL OF STS. CYRIL AND METHODIUS, FEBRUARY 14

Every American knows that February 14 is Valentine's Day. But, if you are of Slavic origin, or if you speak and write using the Cyrillic alphabet, this memorial trumps candy hearts and greeting cards. It is the day we remember Sts. Cyril and Methodius, who, with St. Benedict, are the patron saints of Europe. And, if you're not a fan of chocolate or red candies, you might want to keep this day with a bowl of red borscht, the beet soup that is a staple in much of Eastern Europe.

These saints were brothers, and brother monks, born in Greece in the ninth century. They were sent as missionaries to the Khazars, a tribe in what is now southern Russia. Before they began spreading the Gospel, they learned the Khazar language.

From Russia, they went to Moravia (which is part of what we

know as the Czech Republic) and there once again they learned the native tongue, Slavonic, before they began preaching and teaching. At the time they learned Slavonic, it had no written alphabet. So the brothers used their native Greek letters to compose a Slavonic alphabet. To this day, it bears a name, Cyrillic, which honors St. Cyril.

The brothers used this new alphabet to translate the Bible and liturgical books. Some church officials denounced the use of a "barbaric" language for Holy Scriptures and holy rites. But the pope stood with the brothers, who are blessed and honored to this day in Central and Eastern Europe for their faithfulness in bringing Christ to these lands. In your prayers today, remember our brothers and sisters in Eastern Europe, especially those threatened by war.

## MEMORIAL OF ST. POLYCARP, FEBRUARY 23

St. Polycarp was a bishop in Smyrna, in what is now Izmir in Turkey. St. John the apostle named him a bishop, and his people, who came to love him for his courage, goodness, and good humor, cherished this link between Jesus, John, and Polycarp. We have the account of his martyrdom in AD 155, written by Marcion, who was an eyewitness to the execution, and who shared his report with the churches in the region. It is a wonderful story and one that should be read and told again and again. You can tell this story to children, beginning when they are about ten years old. It's easy to find "The Martyrdom of Polycarp," usually in an anthology of Early Christian writings. Marcion writes that the Roman governor did not want to kill an old man. He urged the bishop, "Take the oath and I will let you go."

Polycarp answered, "Eighty and six years have I served Him, and He has done me no wrong. How then can I blaspheme my King and my Savior?"

Polycarp was burned alive. Marcion writes,

> The fire took on the shape of a hollow chamber . . . and there
> was he in the center of it, not like a human being in flames

but like a loaf baking in the oven or silver ingot being refined in the furnace.

Bake bread today or buy a loaf of good bread from the bakery and share it with friends or family. Remember the holy man who prayed in thanksgiving for being allowed to share the cup of Christ's suffering and death.

# 31

~~~~~~~~~~~~~~~~~~~~~~~

# HOW TO CARNIVAL

*Wherever the Catholic sun doth shine,*
*There's always laughter and good red wine.*
–HILAIRE BELLOC

Joy is the noblest human act.
–ST. THOMAS AQUINAS

If you ask, "When does carnival begin?" expect a puzzled stare by way of reply.

"Carnival? You mean the school carnival? That was last October." Or "Carnival? Isn't that on Mardi Gras? Down in New Orleans?"

Carnival, the weeks preceding Lent, begins when Christmas ends. If a Russian Orthodox friend is celebrating Christmas Day on January 7, then you, as a Roman Catholic, are entering carnival.

The first hint to the meaning of these days can be found in the name. *Carne vale* is Latin for "farewell to the flesh," or "Good-bye, meat." Another Latin term, *carnelevarium*, means, "removing the meat." The French term *Mardi Gras* means "Fat Tuesday," the day before Ash Wednesday when the last stores of fat (and in a farming culture, that would be animal fat) had to be consumed. The names signal the last days of meat eating before the forty days of Lenten fasting begin.

It's hard for us to understand what it means in a cold climate, in a community that relies on subsistence farming, to anticipate fasting from meat and animal products for forty days. People struggling to consume *enough* fat and calories to survive are grateful, indeed, for a leg of lamb and fearful of passing one by. We, who struggle to consume *fewer* fats and calories in order to survive, often look forward to Lent as a convenient excuse to go on a diet.

Maybe Lent would take on new meaning for us if the fast in the developed Western nations involved abstaining from the use of smart phones and computers. Imagine the confusion, and even despair, many of us would feel about being asked to undertake such a stringent fast.

What would you do to prepare? Probably you would send all the e-mails and texts you could, make all the phone calls you could, and spend (even more) hours than usual visiting your favorite websites and blogs before giving up the use of these technologies. It might not be play and it might not be partying, but you would Internet hard. You might even—is such a thing possible?—discover that you are ready for some quiet, ready to live the non-virtual life for a while.

That's the idea behind Carnival. If you're going to keep a Lent of prayer, fasting, and almsgiving—never easy—then you need to be ready. The Church is like a mother with her kids before a long car ride who says, "Better run around now and get out some of that energy. You're going to be sitting for hours."

And, in a farming community, depleting the available stores of meat before a fast necessarily means enlisting everyone in the eating, which necessarily means parties, and lots of them. So many, in fact, that Lent, with its quiet and restraint, will, when it comes, be welcome.

The origins of carnival are probably pre-Christian. Many people in northern climes observed the days when winter begins to die and spring to be reborn. The day when Carnival begins varies from once place to another. In Bavaria, Carnival, or Fasching, begins on the Feast of Epiphany, January 6. In France, the celebration also begins on January 6, with the climax coming during the ten days up to, and including, Fat Tuesday. In parts of Spain, Carnival continues through

Ash Wednesday. A good general rule is to observe Carnival from the Sunday before Ash Wednesday (this Sunday was once known as Quinquagesima, a word that means "fiftieth," because it falls 49 days, or 50, if you count Easter Sunday, before Easter begins) through Fat Tuesday, or Shrove Tuesday. ("Shrove" is the past tense of the word "shrive." To shrive is to hear a confession, give the penitent a penance, and then absolve the penitent from sin. The word comes from the practice of going to confession on the day before Ash Wednesday. Lent, then, becomes a season for repenting of and repairing the wrongs done by our sins.)

"More parties?" you're wondering. "But didn't we just get through a round of Christmas parties?" Were they really parties, or were they simply social obligations, office cocktail receptions, and school concerts? Were they really parties or command performances? The fact that we often can't tell the difference is yet another argument for indulging in a playful Carnival.

So keep Carnival. Here are some ways to do so, which increase the play without increasing the frenzy of preparation—as happens with the shopping, the wrapping, and the mailing that so often turn Christmas parties into Christmas chores. More fun, less exhaustion; that's our Carnival goal.

Get some friends together and go bowling, or ice-skating, or dancing. Go out in a group and have fun. It doesn't matter if you hug the rail of the rink all night or if you find yourself doing the twist, or some other "no-step," to "Waltz Across Texas." What matters is that you have fun.

If you live where there's snow, get some friends together and go skiing. If there isn't snow, go hiking. Organize a pickup basketball game. Invite the neighbors over for Saturday morning doughnuts—which are a Carnival staple in many European countries—and coffee.

Host a games night. Set up card tables and chairs and have several different games going at once. Ask everyone who comes to bring a snack that can be eaten during the game, that is, nothing too messy. You provide the drinks, and keep them simple and inexpensive. The star of the evening isn't the food, but the games and the gamers.

You'll notice the emphasis here is on community, a community getting their sillies out before the season of cleaning house and heart begins.

In New Orleans, people serve King Cake from Epiphany to Fat Tuesday. This yeasty cake can be filled with cream cheese or with a streusel-like spread made of chopped nuts and brown sugar. (Any good coffee cake recipe that uses yeast can be turned into a King Cake, so feel free to use your own non–New Orleans recipe.) The one constant seems to be the brightly (hand-) colored sugars on the top of the cake and the tiny plastic figure of a baby Jesus tucked somewhere inside. Whoever gets the piece with the figure has to provide the next King Cake.

During Carnival, the doors of houses in New Orleans are decorated with Mardi Gras wreaths, and purple, green, and gold bunting adorns the porch railings. Some people put up Mardi Gras lights in the same three traditional colors. Hardware stores announce the arrival of Mardi Gras ladders, which have small wooden boxes nailed to the top in which children can sit above the crowds, ready to catch the beads thrown by parade marchers and float passengers. Neighborhoods host progressive parties, and people go from one yard to the next, eating and visiting.

In Haiti, Carnival is known as Rara. A central part of Rara involves traveling bands of musicians, and the expression "*to fe rara*" (make rara) can be translated "to make a big racket." The musicians play drums and tin trumpets and bamboo horns. As they play, dancers and singers perform with the band. Vendors follow along, selling *fresko*, the Haitian snow cone.

A German specialty during Carnival is hot pretzels. In Argentina, you'll find street vendors selling tamales. Belgians snack on apple fritters dusted with powdered sugar. In the Tuscan region of Italy, a Carnival staple is pork chops in wine sauce. Just think "fat" and you'll come up with a good Mardi Gras—Shrove Tuesday—Carnival recipe. When our children were small, we made ice cream sundaes or banana splits after supper on Fat Tuesday. We put out a variety of ice cream flavors and toppings and let each person design their own dessert.

# LENT

# 32

~~~~~~~~~~~~~~~~~~~~~~~~~~~~~~

## KEEPING LENT

I am a sinner whom the Lord has looked upon.

-POPE FRANCIS

My junior year of college, at the end of Lent, I made an appointment with a priest someone had told me was a good confessor. It had been a long time, and I had a lot to say. As I began to make my confession my hands shook. The priest listened prayerfully, gently asking if there was more. I shook my head no. Then he pointed to a Bible open to Psalm 51 and asked me to read the page aloud: "Have mercy upon me O God according to thy loving kindness; according to the multitude of thy loving kindness blot out my transgressions." As I read the words, tears of relief streamed down my face. When the priest spoke the words of absolution on behalf of Jesus, "I absolve you in the name of the Father, and of the Son, and of the Holy Spirit," my heart felt light. I walked out into the night, my burden lifted. I felt so happy that I broke into a run in the freezing rain, the words of the psalm echoing in my head, "Create in me a clean heart O God . . . that the bones which thou hast broken may rejoice."

While Lent is indeed a season of penance, it isn't about taking pleasure in pain. On the contrary, we repent during Lent in order to experience God's kindness. To remain in loving relationship with anyone, we must be willing to sometimes say, "I'm sorry." Only when we admit that we are sinners are we able to experience fully the mercy and love of God (Micah 7:14-15, 18-20). Every Lent we read the parable of the prodigal son (Luke 15:11-32), and remember that whatever we have done or left undone, God delights in welcoming us home. We repent in order to be reconciled.

The prodigal son who squanders his father's inheritance on drinking and prostitutes returns to his father and asks forgiveness saying, "Father, I have sinned against heaven and against you" (Luke 15:21). Before he can even get the words out of his mouth his father embraces him and kisses him. God's forgiveness knows no bounds.

We are all sinners in need of God's mercy. One way to think about the season of Lent is as a kind of spiritual spring-cleaning. We ask ourselves, "What sin has accumulated in our lives over the past year that it is time to acknowledge? What is preventing us from being the people God longs for us to be?"

The word "Lent" comes from the Old English word *lencten*, which means "spring." The season of Lent reminds us that we are all in need of renewal. When asked in an interview, "What's wrong with the world today?" the Catholic author G. K. Chesterton is said to have replied, "I am." In Lent, all Christians must admit the same.

We need to make room in our hearts. As the poet Gerard Manley Hopkins put it, so that God might "easter in us, be a dayspring to the dimness of us, be a crimson-cresseted east."

## ASH WEDNESDAY AND THE BEGINNING OF LENT

Lent begins with Ash Wednesday. At this Mass we receive ashes on our foreheads in the shape of a cross. Anyone can receive ashes. The ashes are the burned palm fronds from the previous year's Palm Sunday. They symbolize our

mortality and sinfulness, our need for repentance and repair. The person distributing the ashes will typically say (from Genesis 3:19), "Remember that you are dust, and to dust you shall return." Hearing this signed on your forehead and the foreheads of those you love is a powerful reminder of the truth that we are all going to die. Sometimes the person distributing the ashes will say (from Mark 1:15), "Repent, and believe the Gospel." On Ash Wednesday Catholics fast, abstain from meat, and contemplate their sins.

Wearing ashes on one's forehead until they wear off of their own accord echoes the ancient practice of putting on sackcloth and ashes as a sign of mourning or penance. In the early Church the ashes were actually sprinkled on top of one's head. As it says in the book of Job 42:6, "I abhor myself, and repent in dust and ashes."

People often feel discomfort about walking out of church and going about their day marked with ashes. I used to hate it when my parents would make me go to Mass before high school, as I would spend the day having people tell me that there was dirt on my face. Yet when we think of all the other brands and logos we proudly wear and allow to define us, perhaps the cross of ashes is a mark we need to bear, at least once a year, a reminder of a deeper identity.

In a world that doesn't encourage silence or introspection, Ash Wednesday is also an opportunity to look inward and take stock. It is a reminder that before spring there is winter. God does not need Lent, but we do. A period of self-denial helps us to appreciate better all the good things in life that we so often take for granted. It helps us to rein in our selfishness and practice gratitude and radical dependence on God. In Lent we tame our appetites as a way of disciplining our souls. We start with small things, like abstaining from meat, or television, and work up to harder things, like turning the other cheek. The Lenten fast is also a practice for old age and dying, when the things that define and distract us—career, status, health, or possessions—will be taken away.

## THE FORTY DAYS

Since the fourth century, Lent has been a forty-day period of prayer, fasting, and almsgiving that precedes the celebration of Easter. During the first three centuries, most Christians only fasted during Holy Week. Eventually the fast was extended to forty days (not including Sundays) to imitate Jesus's forty-day fast in the desert. Forty is a symbolic number in Scripture. For instance, the Israelites were in exile for forty years, and the flood lasted for forty days (Genesis 7:12). When we fast we attempt to imitate Jesus, and we stand in solidarity with the poor and those who go hungry.

The three-pronged practices of Lent—prayer, fasting, and almsgiving—begin with getting one's own house in order, and end with giving back to God, and God's people, from the abundance one has received. As Caesarius of Arles wrote in the sixth century, "Let us fast in such a way that we lavish our lunches upon the poor."

## PRAYER

Prayer can be done at all times, when running, commuting to work, or before sleep. Prayer is an opportunity to examine one's life and enter into the mystery of God. In prayer we ask God to show us what delights Him about our lives and also what grieves Him, so that we might make amends and ask for grace. Some people commit to Evening Prayer, or Vespers, after dinner in Lent. They use their candleholder and candles from Advent, but without the greenery, and light one candle each week.

Others pray and meditate on the daily Mass readings during Lent. Doing so helps them enter into the story of salvation history. Get a good book of Bible stories and read them to your children along with the lectionary, matching the stories in the child's book to the ones you are reading. You can also get the readings of the day on your smart phone with the Laudate app (unless, of course, you're fasting from using your phone).

All Catholics are asked to make a confession and pray a sincere act of contrition at some point during Lent.

You might also consider going to a Friday evening Stations of the

Cross service at your church, or going on retreat. Many parishes offer retreats during Lent for busy people.

Some Catholics cut small branches of a forsythia bush or flowering fruit tree, like a cherry tree, bring them into their home, and arrange them in a vase filled with water at the beginning of Lent. By Easter the buds will start to bloom. These branches can be a reminder of the mystery and paradox of the season. When death appears to have the final word, as in the dead of winter, or on the cross, there is yet to come new life, spring, and resurrection.

## FASTING

Fasting is an exercise in self-denial or self-control for a greater purpose. All the world's religions acknowledge the need to deny, occasionally, one's appetites, in order to make progress in the spiritual life. Where there is excess in our lives, a fast brings us back into right order. Fast days are opportunities to reflect on our lives, express sorrow for our sins, and resolve to lead a more Christian life. When we fast we also imitate Jesus, who fasted in the desert for forty days and was tempted by the devil to turn a stone into bread (Luke 4:1-13).

Catholics are required to fast from food on Ash Wednesday and Good Friday, and to abstain from meat on Fridays during Lent. (Young children, the elderly, pregnant women, and people with medical conditions are not required to participate in the fast. If you need to eat for medical reasons, do so.)

Before Vatican II, Catholics abstained from meat every Friday of the year, and the Church still recommends this practice as a way of showing respect for Christ's death on the cross. It is also a good way of honoring creation, as eating less meat is good for the environment. If you are already a vegetarian, then go vegan on Fridays, or for all of Lent.

In the ancient world "meat" referred to four-legged animals. In the Roman world, these were the animals that were sacrificed to the gods, so it was good for Christians to abstain from killing and eating these animals. Fish was permitted, as it was not considered meat. (Also the fish is an ancient symbol for Christ. In Greek, the phrase

"Jesus Christ, Son of God, Savior" is "Iēsous Christos Theou Yios Sōtēr." The first letters of each of these Greek words, when put together, spell *ichthys*, the Greek word for "fish.") Another reason some Christians abstain from meat during Lent is that in the Garden of Eden, before the Fall, the first people were vegetarian.

Some Byzantine and Eastern Rite Catholics don't eat any animal products for the entire forty days of Lent. This is called the Great Fast. (Sundays are a break from the fast, as every Sunday is a little Easter and honors the resurrection.) If you want to go vegetarian or vegan for Lent, we recommend Mark Bittman's cookbook *How to Cook Everything Vegetarian*.

Another idea is to change what you drink. Some people drink only water in Lent as a reminder of their baptism. Others add something, like building homes for Habitat for Humanity, instead of giving something up.

People can decide for themselves what they would like to fast from during Lent. Some people might fast from social media, or drinking, or gossip, or spending money on themselves, or anything that has become for them an addiction, or a distraction, from being the person God longs for them to be. Of course, failure is part of the process. Don't worry when you fail, which you will. Perfection is not the point; growth is.

## ALMSGIVING

A fast for the rich is a feast for the poor. The money saved from abstaining from something, like meat, or shopping, or your daily coffee drink, should be given to the poor. This money can be placed in an alms box or rice bowl and then given to the Church, Catholic Charities, Caritas Internationalis, Catholic Relief Services, or some other charitable organization on Holy Thursday. Catholic parishes often give out Catholic Relief Services rice bowls at the start of Lent. In the past forty years, through the CRS rice bowl program, Catholics in the United States have given $250 million to prevent hunger worldwide.

If you don't have a rice bowl, an envelope will do the trick. Small children enjoy putting money in the alms box. If money is tight, you could also make a commitment to give alms by doing something for a neighbor or family or church member for the entire season of Lent. Time and presence, in a world where everyone is always working, are tremendous gifts.

Almsgiving can also mean giving of yourself. Try to perform one of the seven corporal works of mercy during Lent. These are based on Jesus's sermon on the Judgment of the Nations (Matthew 25:35-36). The corporal works of mercy are feeding the hungry, giving drink to the thirsty, clothing the naked, sheltering the homeless, visiting the sick, visiting the imprisoned, and burying the dead. If you have small children, it shouldn't be tough to clothe the naked or give drink to the thirsty. If you live alone, you might need to be a bit more creative. Consider reading the book *Mercy in the City: How to Feed the Hungry, Give Drink to the Thirsty, Visit the Imprisoned, and Keep Your Day Job* by Kerry Weber.

Practicing hospitality is also an aspect of almsgiving. Consider having people over for a fish supper on a Friday during Lent. You and your family will come to associate fried fish with the season.

# 33

# PALM SUNDAY AND MAKING PALM SUNDAY CROSSES

*All glory, laud, and honor*
*To Thee, Redeemer, king:*
*To whom the lips of children*
*Made sweet hosannas ring.*

—BISHOP THEODULF OF ORLÉANS, NINTH CENTURY

Holy Week, the week leading up to Easter Sunday, begins with Palm Sunday, or Passion Sunday, when the Church throughout the world remembers Jesus's entry into Jerusalem. The entrance is joyful and triumphant, as befits a king. The Mass for this day begins on that high note, but it also, and always, includes the full Gospel reading of the passion and death of Jesus. This ritual is an ancient one, kept by the Church from its earliest days.

We know that in Syria, by the first half of the third century, a Great, or Holy, Week was kept during which the events of Christ's entrance into Jerusalem and his arrest and crucifixion were remembered and celebrated. The Palm Sunday liturgy, marking the beginning of this important time, is also very ancient. We have accounts of the liturgy from a pilgrim, a woman named Egeria, who probably traveled to Jerusalem from either Galicia or Aquitaine in the late fourth century. Read her writing and consider how much of it is familiar.

As the eleventh hour draws near, that particular passage from Scripture is read in which the children bearing palms and branches come forth to meet the Lord, saying: "Blessed is the one who comes in the name of the Lord." The bishop and all the people rise immediately, and then everyone walks down from the top of the Mount of Olives, with the people preceding the bishop and responding continually with "Blessed is the one who comes in the name of the Lord" to the hymns and antiphons. All the children who are present here, including those who are not yet able to walk because they are too young and therefore are carried on their parents' shoulders, all of them bear branches, some carrying palms, others, olive branches. And the bishop is led in the same manner as the Lord was once led. From the top of the mountain as far as the city, and from there through the entire city as far as the Anastasis [the buildings, erected by Constantine after his conversion, centering on the tomb of Christ], everyone accompanies the bishop the whole way on foot, and this includes distinguished ladies and men of consequence, reciting the responses all the while.

We also begin Palm Sunday with a "particular passage from Scripture," a reading from one of the four Gospels describing Jesus's entrance into Jerusalem. We process into the church, singing hymns and bearing palm branches, with our children carried or in tow. We all walk together—the rich and the poor, the mighty and the meek—to hear again the story of Christ's passion. And we all, as Christians have done since the beginning, confront again the mystery and the scandal of the Incarnation. It is a scandal that God would take on human flesh with all its weaknesses and flaws. It is a mystery that God would love us enough to do so. The text for our education in Incarnation is Jesus himself. His life is our book, and the Palm Sunday liturgy asks us to enter into the book by walking the path with Jesus.

How should a king die? Surrounded by faithful servants and

his adoring people? Cared for and soothed, his every need met? Or should he die in pain and abandoned, mocked and despised? Palm Sunday is the introduction to Holy Week, when we see the truth of the Incarnation, that Jesus is both fully human and fully divine. His full divinity is revealed on Easter. But in Holy Week we see his full humanity as he shares the death we must all die, and, further, shares the death the least among us suffer. Every man or woman left to die, unmourned, untended, alone, shares this suffering with Jesus Christ. As the story unfolds, beginning on Palm Sunday and continuing throughout the week, we watch as Jesus bears every weight known to the sick, the wounded, and the dying. He is afraid. He is betrayed. He is abandoned. He is tried. He is ridiculed. He is beaten. He is burdened. He is in pain. He endures, but so does the pain. He dies. As we proclaim in the renewal of our baptismal promises during Easter, "[He] was crucified, died, and was buried."

In Matthew's account of Jesus's passion, we see the Son's humanity as he speaks to God the Father about the suffering to come. He prays, with people throughout time and around the world, "My Father, if it is possible, let this cup pass from me." Then, with the faith to which we are all called, he adds, "yet, not as I will, but as you will" (Matthew 26:39b).

And Jesus prays knowing the answer to his request may be no. Jesus hears, and feels in his flesh, the no that is heard by parents standing helpless in emergency rooms and hostages being tortured and children and victims of violence standing before the knife, the gun, the raised fist.

Jesus does not hide his fear from the Father. He is not ashamed of his pain, nor does he welcome future pain. Jesus is not a superhero; he is a man, with the natural and good desire to avoid suffering, for himself and for others. But he is a man in full communion with the Father, accepting of and ready to follow the Father's will, whatever that may be and wherever it might lead.

When Adam and Eve heard the Father's no, they went searching for a way to become gods themselves. Their break with God broke creation itself and set us on a painful path. Jesus's trust in God, his willingness as a man to follow God, even to the cross, heals what

Adam has destroyed. What is revealed in this story is that the human nature Jesus shares with us is the *fully* human nature intended for and bestowed upon us by God. When God the Father breathes into the man Adam, it is the very breath, or life, of God which we are all given. It is a life in communion with God, the One whose breath and spirit we are to share. Human life, fully human life, is life in intimate relationship with God. Sin, and its killing separation, has neither part nor place in what God has made. What Jesus shares with us, and shows to us, *is* human life. What he invites us to cast aside is the gangrenous appendage—sin—which is attached to our life but filled with death.

In Eucharistic Prayer III the priest prays, "All life, all holiness comes from you." Life and holiness are linked in the prayer because they are linked in the fully human, fully divine person of Jesus. Life and holiness are linked in the prayer because God linked them at creation and relinked them in Christ's death and resurrection.

When Jesus, spent, cries "out in a loud voice, 'Father, into your hands I commend my spirit'" (Luke 23:46), we are hearing the voice of the new Adam. He does not deny the pain he knows, nor does he dismiss it. He never says he is no longer afraid. He just tells the truth: "I am yours, in life, and in death. I am in your hands." Jesus speaks the way a beloved child cries out to a parent in the midst of pain and fear. She is afraid; she is in pain; her mother is her refuge. It is to that face, those hands, so known and dear, that she will turn. This does not guarantee a surcease of suffering; it only guarantees

that both, mother and child, are where they ought to be, in communion, in relationship, embraced and welcomed, at home.

This is a story that has held us fast for two thousand years.

Palm Sunday is a solemn day, but it is not a sad day. We walk with the One who shows us our full humanity and invites us to join in it. So for a very long time Palm Sunday has had a certain festive tone. Perhaps it is all that greenery, though not every place uses palms. In Italy, people wave olive branches. In Ireland they wave yew branches. In England, Poland, and Lithuania they use willow branches. In some of these places, the day is called Willow Sunday or Willow-twig Sunday. If you find a missal from the years before the Second Vatican Council, you can read an antiphon (a verse sung or read before or after a portion of the liturgy) after the blessing of the palms that mentions other flowers. In many parts of Europe, Palm Sunday thus became a day for blessing all the spring flowers. Catholics would decorate the graves of their beloved dead with flowers, a custom you might want to make your own.

In places like the United States where Christians do use palms, some churchgoers weave the sturdy branches into crosses and keep them as sacramentals in the home.

~~~~~~~~~~~~~~~~~~~~~~~~~~~

# 34

# HOLY WEEK: KEEPING TRIDUUM

We venerate your cross, O Lord, we praise and glorify
your holy resurrection: because of the wood of the tree, joy
has come into the whole world.

-FROM *The Glenstal Book of Prayer*

Triduum is the three days that are one, three days that are a single
day. This three-in-one day begins at sundown on Holy Thursday and
concludes with the Easter Vigil on the night of Holy Saturday.

Think of all the moments in your life when time stood still. How long did you hold your newborn when she was first placed in your arms? How long did that moonlit walk last on the night you realized you were in love? How long did you sit in the waiting room, watching the door each time it opened, willing the surgeon to come out with good news?

We all know these glimpses of time out of time, time that does not follow a clock or obey the ordinary rhythms of minutes and hours. When we say, "It seemed to take forever," or "It went by so fast," we're not calculating elapsed time but something that shatters our understanding of time itself.

The ancient Greeks understood this phenomenon, so they had two words for time: *chronos* and *kairos*. Chronos is time as it is measured in hours and days. Kairos is a moment of opportunity, an opening into meaning. Kairos is a moment when meaning overtakes measurement.

Triduum is kairos. Triduum is when time stands still, when, as the *Catechism of the Catholic Church* puts it, "The kingdom of God enters into our time" (CCC, 1168).

The postures of Triduum are startling. We begin with Holy Thursday, when we imitate Jesus, who washed the feet of his disciples before the Passover meal (John 13:1-17) and tells us to do the same. We wash one another's feet and have our own feet washed. Holy Thursday exposes hard, yellow toenails and dry, calloused feet. Freed from shoes and stockings, our feet are caressed and bathed and patted dry. We usually wash our feet at home and wear shoes in the world, but not on this day. On this day, we are unshod, like Moses before the burning bush. Barefoot, we set off into the mystery.

Good Friday is the day when we recall and revere Christ's passion and death on the cross, the day we venerate the cross, that instrument of torture that has become the instrument of our salvation. This day finds the bishops and priests prostrate, lying facedown on the floor of the church they have entered in silence. Their faces pressed to the ground, they cannot see who approaches; they cannot watch the faces of the assembly. They are unguarded. There is dirt on the floor. They lie in it. Adults do not stretch out, prone, in public. We stand, or sit, careful to keep at the same level with those around us. Dead bodies lie while others stand, pitying or horrified, above them. But not on this day. On this day, our shepherds, like David crying out to God, assume the posture of "the slain, who lie among the dead." They are prone before the mystery that God, the Creator of the universe, would die, would allow himself to be handed over and killed.

In the quiet of Holy Saturday, the church remembers Christ's descent among the dead. He goes down among the graves, in the place where every human body molders and decays. The risen Christ goes down into death and brings life. He goes down into darkness and brings light. He goes down into dust and, fulfilling Ezekiel's prophecy, raises the dry bones (Ezekiel 37:1-14). On Holy Saturday we are silent before the mystery that, rejected and murdered, Christ continues to invite us all, even the dead, into new life.

Holy Saturday night, at the Easter Vigil, we begin in darkness and watch light spread from candle to candle throughout the church. We hear the ancient words of the Exsultet sung, the song that tells how, from Adam to Christ, God was at work, reconciling us and preparing to bring us home. We hear our ancient stories told, of how we lost faith in God, but how God is ever faithful. We watch as men and women are bathed in the font. Bathing is private, behind locked doors. To be bathed is to give over autonomy and control. Babies and invalids are bathed. The elect give over autonomy and control to Christ.

We watch as these elect, those who have been praying and preparing for many months to join us in the sacraments, enter the water, wearing the white gowns that look more like bedclothes than church clothes. We watch as water cascades over their heads. Their carefully combed hair is ruined; their makeup streaked and smeared. We watch as the chrism, the blessed oil, drips down their faces. They are bathed, like brides before a wedding, and anointed with oil, like athletes before a race. On this night, like Jesus going down into the Jordan River, we set off wet and dripping into the mystery that Christ who died, rises to new life, and that we are invited to join in that new life.

In the same way that the postures of Triduum are startling, so, too, is the way we keep time during these days. For Triduum is a time to put aside daily work and daily recreations and activities. It is a time to turn off televisions and computers, to silence smart phones and radios. It is a time for quiet and prayer, for singing and keeping vigil, for gathering with brothers and sisters to wait and to listen, to remember and to anticipate.

The contours of Triduum date from the earliest days of the Church. St. Hippolytus, a priest in Rome, wrote this in the third century:

> And let those who are to be baptized be instructed to wash and cleanse themselves on the fifth day of the week [Thursday].
>
> Those who are to receive baptism shall fast on the Preparation [Friday] and on the Sabbath [Saturday]. And on the Sabbath the bishop shall assemble those who are to be baptized in one place, and shall bid them to pray and bow the knee.
>
> And laying his hand on them he shall exorcize every evil spirit to flee away from them and never to return to them. And when he has finished exorcizing, let him breathe on them their faces and seal their foreheads and ears and noses and then let him raise them up.
>
> And they shall spend all night in vigil, reading the scriptures to them and instructing them.

Keeping Triduum requires some planning. If it's possible, take those days off from work. Talk to your boss or supervisor or co-workers as far in advance as possible. See if you could switch shifts with a Jewish or Muslim friend who asks the same of you on their holy days. It might mean using a vacation day or sick day. Find out what possibilities exist at your workplace for time off for religious observances. If you can't manage time off, resolve to keep the days at work, say, by refraining from gossip or angry responses during those hours, and praying to see Christ in the face of all you meet.

You'll have to let your child's school know that he won't be in class on Friday, nor is she available for sports activities or performances or field trips during that time. Talk to the teacher first, and assume goodwill and cooperation. You'll probably get it. By the time our fourth child entered the school across the street, her teacher greeted me. She said, "As soon as I saw I had one of your kids on the roster, I made a note about her not being in school on Good Friday."

You'll find most people are accommodating, and you'll find, as well, that making these plans in advance helps you keep them. Once you've told your boss you'll be in church on Friday afternoon, you don't want to be seen at happy hour at the neighborhood bar or at the late-afternoon matinee. Keep these days distinct and set apart.

Try to observe each liturgy in the same church. The unity of time needs a unity of place. To go from the stripped and bare altar following the Holy Thursday liturgy to the silent space of Good Friday to the flower-bedecked and candlelit and alleluia-filled church of the Easter Vigil and the liturgies of Easter Sunday is to understand— visually, aurally, viscerally—the whole journey.

Keeping Triduum at home also requires planning. Sit down with your spouse, or housemates, or older children and discuss how you plan to mark the days. The hardest thing for most of us is to turn off and shut down all the screens that sell us, inform us, and entertain us endlessly. So you will need to think about how to fill Internet and cable-free hours.

If the weather is warm, gardening is a fine way to have silence and sun and the healing work of preparing the ground and the sleeping plants for their own resurrection.

If trees or bushes are flowering, cut some and bring them in to decorate the Easter table. Lilac branches are often free for the taking, and they bring the fragrance of spring into the house.

If you don't already, you might walk, or bike, to and from church, especially on Good Friday, when the liturgy occurs during daylight hours. If you have the time, take it and rediscover streets through which you generally zoom, late for this appointment or that meeting.

Take a nap. Read a book. Read to a child. Tell a story. Sing a song. Lie on your back and look at the clouds.

Start cooking for the Easter feast and involve the whole house-hold. Get one person chopping herbs while another slices onions and another sifts flour for the cake. Teach someone to make pie dough or ask someone to teach you. On Holy Saturday afternoon, gather a group together to dye Easter eggs and get them ready for tomorrow's hunt.

Triduum is a time to be re-membered to our own baptisms, when we were baptized "priest, prophet, and king," even as we anticipate the baptisms we will witness at Easter. What will wash you clean and restore you to new life? Do those things and rejoice. It's almost time to reclaim and proclaim our alleluias.

# 35

# HOW TO MAKE A CONFESSION

Let the Church always be a place of mercy and hope, where
everyone is welcomed, loved and forgiven.

–POPE FRANCIS

Confession is about how God hears, sees, and forgives. Sin isn't new,
and neither is repentance or the need for confession. Jesus teaches
his disciples how they are to handle sin in the community (Matthew
18:15-17) and then gives them the power to bind and loose, that is, the
authority to name sin and the authority to forgive it (Matthew 18:18).
As early as the First Letter of Clement, which was a letter written by
the church at Rome to the church at Corinth around AD 96, there
is a discussion of sinners who need to repent and be reconciled. The
letter stresses that the sinner is not to be thrown overboard. The community is responsible to offer help and healing through prayer and
intercession and holy friendship. During this time, and at least until
the seventh century, all penance was public and was worked out in
full view of the community. Private penance, where the person meets
one-on-one with a priest, probably comes from the Irish missionary
monks who, under St. Columba, spread their regional customs across
Europe.

We all need to confess. "I just wish I could confide in someone." "I need to talk about this."

People need to share, probably because the bigger the burden, the more it weighs. Telling another person can mean getting help to carry the load.

The problem for most of us is that our (little "c") confessions don't stay where we made them. They wind up on social media or making the office rounds.

The other problem with our usual confessions is that they aren't confessions at all, but elaborate justifications. "You didn't hear how he talked to me"—meaning, "You'd have slapped that kid, too." "She just pushes my buttons"—meaning, "You'd have cursed that woman, too."

We waste a lot of time playing both prosecutor ("I acted badly") and defender ("But I had a good reason"). We get caught up in a never-ending round of the "Wrong, but" game, when what we truly desire is healing and forgiveness.

Some people fear looking a priest in the face while making their confession, but we also have the option to sit or kneel behind a screen during confession.

Some people fear they have done something that cannot be forgiven. Read the story Luke recounts in the fifteenth chapter of his

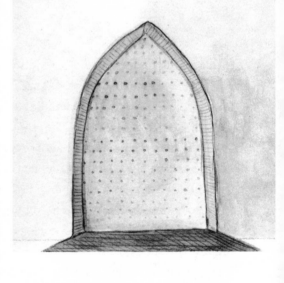

Gospel. It's about a son who is so greedy that he can't wait for his father to die. The son wants his inheritance. When the father gives the son his early inheritance, the son leaves without so much as a thank-you. He goes off and spends the money on drugs and sex, or whatever else Luke means by "a life of dissipation." It's only when the son is living as a farmhand, longing to share the pigs' slop, that he thinks of his father. Even then, his thoughts are not on repentance, but on how much better life is at home. He knows he'll probably have to suffer some punishment, but at least he'll get to eat. While he is "still a long way off" from his home, the son sees his father running to him. The father embraces his son and kisses him and begins making plans for a welcome home party. The son does nothing to impress us with his goodness, or even his good manners or good sense. The goodness belongs to the father. Jesus tells this story to show us who the Father is, and how the Father responds to the hungry children who approach his house. If you are hungry and you want to come home, God is walking the road, watching for you, preparing to run out and meet you, even when you are "still a long way off."

Here's what sacramental confession is, and isn't.

## CONFESSION IS SEALED

The Catechism of the Catholic Church puts it this way.

> Given the delicacy and greatness of this ministry and the respect due to persons, the Church declares that every priest who hears confessions is bound under very severe penalties to keep absolute secrecy regarding the sins that his penitents have confessed to him. He can make no use of knowledge that confession gives him about penitents' lives. This secret, which admits of no exceptions, is called the "sacramental seal," because what the penitent has made known to the priest remains "sealed" by the sacrament (CCC, 1467).

Canon law holds:

> The sacramental seal is inviolable; therefore it is absolutely forbidden for a confessor to betray in any way a penitent in words or in any manner and for any reason (canon 983).

## CONFESSION ISN'T A TRIAL; IT'S A CELEBRATION

The God who spends his last moments on earth asking forgiveness for his murderers is a God who *is* forgiveness. Mercy is his name and his nature. We don't have to beg for it or earn it. We just have to receive it. But you can't accept any present if your hands are already full. Confession is the time to open our hands, let go, and so be made ready and able to receive the gifts God has for us.

The penance the priest gives isn't a sentence; it's a tool. It's meant to help us. Let's say my problem is watching porn online. The penance will probably be something designed to help fill the space I now fill up with my addiction. It's hard to eat three double cheeseburgers if you've just finished a big bowl of salad and downed a quart of water. It's hard to pray the Hail Mary *and* watch women being degraded and misused.

Penance is not about what we deserve. Penance is about what God desires to give us, which is mercy, which is healing, which is friendship. It's about opening our eyes and hearts and hands to receive that truth. This willingness to receive what God offers is so important that Church law requires us to go to confession at least once each year.

## CONFESSION IS NOT EASY, BUT IT IS SIMPLE

Here are the basic elements:

1. A greeting from and a blessing by the priest.
2. The priest will read some Scripture. The reading is meant to act as a light, to help illuminate the dark places we all have. It may also act as a prompt to contrition and as a call to keep our contrition by changing the ways we act and the ways we spend our time, the things we say and do.
3. The confession. Just say it.
4. The penance. The priest gives it and we accept it.
5. The priest's absolution. The priest is proclaiming this truth: God loves you. God is always ready to welcome you home. Are you willing to walk through the door? (See number 4.)
6. A prayer of thanksgiving and praise and a final blessing from the priest.

Yes, there are written prayers, like the act of contrition,

> My God, I am sorry for my sins with all my heart.
> In choosing to do wrong and failing to do good,
> I have sinned against you whom I should love above all things.
> I firmly intend, with your help, to do penance, to sin no more,
> and to avoid whatever leads me to sin.
> Our Savior Jesus Christ suffered and died for us.
> In His name, my God, have mercy.
>
> Amen.

These prayers are useful and, often, beautiful. Don't worry if you don't have them memorized; copies of the prayers will be provided. All that you need to bring is an open and willing heart. God does the work.

## PREPARATION HELPS

Take some time and think about all that separates you from God, from the people you love, and from your true self. Think about all the ways you want and need to change. It can be helpful to read Scripture, perhaps Psalm 51 or the Ten Commandments (Exodus 20:1-17), before you do this personal inventory. Read and ponder the Beatitudes (Matthew 5:3-12) or review the corporal works of mercy rooted in Matthew 25:34-36. Reflect on what you have done that is wrong and on the good you have failed to do. It may help to write a list you can use when you meet with a priest.

## CONFESSION IS READILY AVAILABLE

Every Catholic Church offers regular times for confessions. Not comfortable going into a church? Many Franciscan priests have established chapels in shopping malls. Check online for locations.

## 36

~~~~~~~~~~~~~~~~~~~~~~~~~~~~~

# STATIONS OF THE CROSS

"At the very least, they can be persuaded that the bodily
position makes no difference to their prayers; for they
constantly forget, what you must always remember, that they
are animals and that whatever their bodies do
affects their souls."

-ADVICE FROM A MASTER DEMON TO HIS APPRENTICE,
C. S. LEWIS, *The Screwtape Letters*

Were you there when they crucified my Lord?

-AMERICAN SPIRITUAL

Movement is important in Catholic prayer. If we associate prayer only
with silent meditation or prayers read or spoken as we sit quietly, it's
possible to begin to think of prayer as a purely mental exercise. The
wisdom of the Church lies in its understanding of Christianity as
enfleshed. What we think matters, but not nearly so much as what
we do. It may not be a good thing to think angry thoughts as we walk
toward the baby's room at three in the morning, wondering why "she
won't just shut up and let me sleep," but what really counts is getting
up and taking care of her needs. Body, not mind, is the issue here,
because the Church knows that what we do with our bodies shapes
our souls.

The Church has many walking prayers, and probably the best
known is the Stations of the Cross. We know from the diary of Egeria, a fourth-century pilgrim to Jerusalem, that a long procession fol-

lowing Jesus's Way to the Cross was part of Holy Week observances in the early church. She writes that early on Good Friday morning the pilgrims would go "at the first cockcrow . . . to the place where the Lord prayed, as it is written in the Gospel." From there, she writes, "all, even to the smallest child, go down with the bishop, on foot, with hymns to Gethsemane." There they would pray, sing a hymn, and listen to a reading from Matthew's Gospel recounting Jesus's arrest.

Then, singing, the pilgrims would go to Jerusalem "on foot, reaching the gate about the time when one man begins to be able to recognize another," just as dawn began to break. They walked through the whole city, before arriving at the place where Jesus was crucified. This is the same way pilgrims walk today, and it is known as the Via Dolorosa, which is Latin for "Sorrowful Way." Egeria writes that, by the time they had made this walk, "The daylight is already growing bright." Then the pilgrims heard the Gospel account of Jesus taken before Pilate. From the sixth to the ninth hour (from noon to three) they went to venerate the cross.

Even today, the Stations of the Cross begin with Jesus before Pilate. Even today, the particular hours for prayer and veneration of the cross on Good Friday are from noon to three.

In the seventh century, Muslim forces conquered Jerusalem, and for the next almost three hundred years Christians were unable to go there on pilgrimage. In 1342, Franciscan friars took custody of the Christian holy sites in the Holy Land. Since that time the Stations of the Cross (a term first used by an English pilgrim, William Wey, in the fifteenth century) has been closely associated with the Franciscan order. It was the Franciscans who brought this walking prayer from Jerusalem to the rest of the world when they first began, in the seventeenth century, to install stations in churches associated with the Franciscan order. By early in the eighteenth century all Catholic churches, regardless of any Franciscan connection, were permitted to install stations. It was at this time, in 1731, that the number of stations was fixed at fourteen. In the twentieth century, Pope John Paul II encouraged Catholics to add a fifteenth station, the resurrection.

Because the Stations of the Cross is a popular devotion, it has been prayed by many people, each adding a particular focus to the prayer. There are Stations of the Cross for persecuted Christians, for victims of abortion, and for victims of gun violence. There are Stations of the Cross for vocations, for global justice and reconciliation, and for the holy souls in purgatory. There are Stations of the Cross for those in recovery from drug or alcoholic addiction, and for the sick and the dying. Stations have been adapted for use with preschoolers, children and teens, and for expectant mothers. A common prayer is the scriptural Stations of the Cross, in which a Scripture passage is read at each of the fourteen, or fifteen, stops.

Pope St. John Paul II led a scriptural Stations of the Cross on Good Friday in 1991. This is interesting, because he took out a non-scriptural element, Veronica wiping the face of Christ (traditionally the sixth station) and replaced it with "Jesus is scourged and crowned with thorns." The pope's change made the stations more amenable to participation by and with Protestant Christians. Since the bishops of the United States have said that a priest, deacon, or layperson may lead the Stations of the Cross, praying the Stations of the Cross is a good opportunity for interfaith worship, as any Christian, of any Christian tradition, can join in this ancient devotion.

Just as movement plays an important role in Catholic prayer, so too does memory. Knowing a prayer by heart (and that doesn't mean "letter perfect," but, rather, deep familiarity with the words and the movements and the order) frees us to stop worrying about what comes next and to enter more fully into the way the prayer is leading. Begin walking the Stations and soon you will learn what each one is and what part of the story it tells. In this way you will learn the story of the passion by heart, from Jesus appearing before Pilate to Jesus taking up his cross to Jesus being laid in the tomb, with all the encounters in between.

## THE ORDER OF THE STATIONS OF THE CROSS

The people gather and the leader opens with a prayer. They may sing a song. For example, "At the Cross Her Station Keeping," or "Stabat Mater," which is a thirteenth-century hymn that is often sung during Lent and particularly when believers walk the stations.

During the song, a procession will begin to the first station, "Jesus is condemned to death." Everyone is invited, and encouraged, to join the procession. This is a good prayer for children, as it allows them to move. (If you are more comfortable remaining in the pew, do so. You'll have plenty of company.) At each station, there will usually be some kind of painting, carving, mosaic, or other image depicting the scene. These artistic depictions vary from parish to parish.

The procession halts and the leader says,

**"We adore you, O Christ, and we bless you."**

Everyone kneels and responds,

**"Because by your holy cross you have redeemed the world."**

There will be a reflection or reading from Scripture relating to this event along the "Sorrowful Way." Sometimes the people will respond to the reflection or reading with a prayer or reflection that they read aloud together. People may kneel or stand during these reflections. Since the order varies according to parish custom or need, just watch and do whatever the leader and other members of the procession do.

If you are singing a hymn such as "At the Cross Her Station Keeping," you'll begin singing the second stanza of the song as you walk or process to the second station, and so on, through all fourteen or fifteen stations. No doubt one of the reasons for this song's enduring popularity is that there are enough verses to go around. The Stations of the Cross is a penitential prayer. It asks us to look at every step Jesus takes to the cross. It invites us to consider his innocence, an innocence that was no protection against a murderous crowd. We are moved to think of all the innocents who suffer, of all who are walking under crushing burdens. The truth brings us to our knees and lifts us up, as in Jesus we are able to pray, "By your holy cross you have redeemed the world."

~~~~~~~~~~~~~~~~~~~~~~~~~~~~~~~~~~

# EASTER

~~~~~~~~~~~~~~~~~~~~~~~~~~~~~~~~~~

# 37

# CELEBRATING EASTER

"Do you know why our master went to the pond every day at
dawn and stayed there for a little while before coming home
again? . . . He was learning the song with which the frogs
praise God. It takes a very long time to learn that song.'"

—MARTIN BUBER, *Tales of the Hasidim*

Easter lasts for fifty days. Fifty days of feasting and singing alleluias
and rejoicing. This is less a promise than a threat for most Western
Catholics. We work. And pay bills. And clean. And strive. And stress.
A fifty-day celebration sounds like too much work. To be honest, the
way most of us plan and host parties, fifty days of parties would be
too much. But what the Church means by fifty days of celebrating
doesn't require either money or shopping. It requires awareness and
attention.

If the number fifty seems intimidating, start with the number
"eight," or the octave of Easter. The Octave of Easter is the eight days,
from Easter Sunday through the Second Sunday of Easter, that the

Church reckons as a single day. Just as the Triduum, or the Three Days (Holy Thursday, Good Friday, Holy Saturday) is reckoned as a single day, so is the Octave of Easter. Seek to do something celebratory and life-giving on each of those days. Set aside time for prayer or sacred readings, for conversation or walks or naps or works of mercy. Let the eight days lead you into the fifty.

Look to the lectionary and the practices of the Church for guidance on how to keep the Easter season. A lectionary is a book of scriptural readings for each Mass of the year, Sundays, weekdays, and special occasions, such as weddings or funerals. At each Mass there will be a reading from the Old Testament (though this changes during Easter), followed by a psalm. Then there will be a reading from the New Testament, usually from one of the epistles, or letters, of St. Paul or others. Then there is a reading from one of the four Gospels. The lectionary runs in three-year cycles, called Year A, B, and C. In Year A we hear mostly Matthew's Gospel; in Year B we read Mark's Gospel as well as John 6; and in Year C we have Luke's Gospel. Readings from John's Gospel are interspersed; the passion narrative at the Good Friday liturgy, for example, is always taken from John's Gospel. These four elements will be printed out in the lectionary for each Mass of the year.

What you'll notice during Easter is that the usual reading from the Old Testament is replaced by a reading from the book of Acts, describing the life of the early Church in Jerusalem. It doesn't matter if we are in Year A, B, or C, on the Second Sunday of Easter, for example, we will always hear this reading from the book of Acts as the first reading,

> The community of believers was of one heart and mind, and no one claimed that any of his possessions was his own, but they had everything in common. . . . There was no needy person among them, for those who owned property or houses would sell them, bring the proceeds of the sale, and put them at the feet of the apostles, and they were distributed to each according to need (ACTS 4:32, 34-35).

The question that gripped these early Christians is the one we continue to ask: "How then shall we live?" Because to witness a man die and rise again is a life-altering reality. We can't leave the empty tomb and go back to the way we lived when we thought death had won. We know something we did not know before. We have news, Good News that not everyone has heard. "How then shall we live?"

That question forms the basis for what the Church practices during the fifty days of Easter: Mystagogia. Mystagogia is a Greek word that denotes the time when the newly baptized are immersed ever more deeply into the mysteries of faith. Those already baptized are called to this reflection, study, and prayer with the newly baptized. Another way to put it might be to ask, "I am baptized. What does that mean for how I live my life?" It requires what St. Cyprian, a bishop in third-century Carthage, pronounced long before Alcoholics Anonymous and its twelve-step program coined the phrase "Fake it till you make it." Cyprian taught, "We who have been sanctified by baptism pray that we may persevere in what we have begun to be . . . regenerated . . . reborn in spirit. Let us *imitate*, therefore, what we will *be*." In other words, mystagogia is a time to learn to act like the person you are called to be until, in truth, you become that person.

In the lectionary during these days, we hear the stories of the first Christians who had to answer the same question asked of Christians in every age. Did they answer the question "How then shall we live" perfectly? No, they did not. But they continued to seek and find the risen Christ. They continued to do the works of mercy. They continued to pray and gather for worship. And they continued to be transformed into faithful followers of the risen Christ. They continued to do what we are called to do, and to act as we are called to be.

One way to think about the days of Easter can be found in *Easter: A Sourcebook* by Liturgy Training Publications. The editors have taken the lectionary as their inspiration, dividing the season into weeks and assigning as a theme for each week one of the mysteries and delights God has given us. There are Scripture readings, as well as poetry and songs and prayers from both the Eastern Church and the Roman Catholic Church. There are reflections from theologians and Church Fathers. It is an invitation into mystagogia and into what the Church means by giving us fifty days of rejoicing and celebrating.

Creation, Table, Ark, Pasture, Garden, Palace, and Temple are the weekly themes. Within each week, there are seven days related to the theme. The days of the first week are Sunday, Light; Monday, Waters; Tuesday, Earth and Plants; Wednesday, Sun and Moon; Thursday, Fish and Birds; Friday, Animals and Humankind, and Saturday, Rest.

The editors have provided readings for each day, with a Scripture reading setting the tone and leading us into all that follows.

Consider bringing one celebratory element into each day. That doesn't mean hosting a party. It can be much simpler. Consider the first week of Easter. Go out and look at the stars on Easter Sunday night. Wade in water on Monday or go swimming or soak in a bubble bath. Plant something on Tuesday or visit a garden or take a walk in the park. Sit in the sun on Wednesday and feel the warmth on your skin. Take a moonlight stroll. Grab your children or godchildren or the children of a friend and visit the local zoo on Thursday. Buy snow cones and slurp up the last of the juice in the paper cone. On Friday, talk to someone. In person. Take a nap on Saturday. Sit in a comfortable chair and read a book. Leave your e-mail. Put off shopping and running errands for another day.

Reading through the topics lets you know that by "celebration" the Church doesn't necessarily mean hilarity or fun. "Celebration" here is closer to the solemn sense of play we see when a toddler blows bubbles for the first time and watches them float into the sky and pop. And Easter celebrations may mean just that: watching, really seeing, some feature of our lives. To stand still and feel the wind, to kneel in silence before an altar, to savor a piece of fresh fruit, smelling its perfume and biting into the flesh and tasting the juice, the pulp, and the skin. These are ways of keeping the Great Fifty Days.

~~~~~~~~~~~~~~~~~~~~~~~~~~~~~~

# 38

# EASTER EGGS, CRAFTS, AND LEGENDS

My Jesus came and rescued me.

–THAD COCKRELL

## EASTER LEGENDS

Easter is a season of paschal joy, which lasts for fifty days. It is both the Christian Passover and the celebration of the Resurrection of Jesus. Many children wake up on Easter morning to find Easter baskets full of sweets, books, or small toys. Children in the United States usually grow up hearing that the Easter bunny brought the baskets, though the legend of the Easter bunny is German and pre-Christian in origin. Unlike Santa Claus, who can be traced to St. Nicholas, the Easter bunny, which, in the original telling, judges whether children are well-behaved or disobedient and brings them gifts accordingly, does not have Christian roots.

In France and Belgium, instead of bunnies, church bells are said to bring the Easter baskets. Legend has it that the bells fly to Rome on Holy Thursday to see the pope. One bell from each church speaks to the Bishop of Rome in secret, telling him the good deeds of all the children. Then the bells return home for the Easter Vigil, to ring happily, bringing treats with them.

## EASTER EGGS

While many Christians omit
the stories of the bunnies
or the bells, Easter sim-
ply wouldn't be Easter
without the eggs.

The early Chris-
tians adopted eggs,
like butterflies, as
symbols of resurrec-
tion and new life. In the
case of a butterfly, a cater-
pillar entombs itself in a co-
coon, only to emerge transfigured.
So, too, the egg was used as a symbol of Jesus's triumph over death,
because, out of something seemingly dead—a stone-like shell—
hatches new life. Jews and other pre-Christian religions also used
eggs as symbols of new life.

In 2006, a two-thousand-year-old Christian burial ground, or ne-
cropolis, was discovered at the Vatican under the via Triumphalis.
Among those found buried in the tombs was a baby less than a year
old. She was found to be holding an egg, a sign of her parent's hope
in the resurrection. Archeologists estimate that the child was buried
between the years AD 50–150.

Similarly, eggs have always had a place at the Easter table. Orthodox Christians abstain from eggs and all animal products during
Lent, in what is called the Great Fast, or Byzantine Fast. One of the
only ways to preserve fresh eggs during the Lenten fast was to boil
them, so boiled eggs have traditionally been part of the Easter feast.
Some Christians even brought blessed eggs to the cemetery on Easter
Sunday or Monday to tell their loved ones asleep in Christ, "Christ
is risen."

Orthodox Christians, then and now, dyed their boiled eggs red,
the color of blood, to symbolize the new life, which comes from
Jesus's death and resurrection. One Easter legend has it that Mary
Magdalene, the first witness to the resurrection, went to Rome to tell

the emperor Tiberius about Jesus's rising from the dead. She went holding an egg as a symbol of the Good News. Tiberius scoffed at her, telling her that a man could no more rise from the dead than the egg in her hand could turn crimson. At this remark, the egg turned a deep shade of red. Because of this tale, St. Mary Magdalene, apostle to the apostles, is sometimes depicted in icons holding a scarlet egg.

## DECORATING EGGS

Most Americans use dye kits, which can be found in any supermarket, to color boiled eggs for Easter egg hunts. Before coloring your eggs try using white crayons to decorate them with Easter symbols or words. Another idea is to color the eggs first, and then use toothpicks dipped in a bleach and water solution to add ornamentation.

### Natural Dyes

Some people prefer to use all-natural dyes such as beets, turmeric, blueberries, carrots, or coffee, but the easiest and prettiest way to dye eggs is to use onion skins. Wrap the damp skins of yellow or red onions around raw eggs, then bundle them tightly in a piece of hosiery. The more onion skins you use, the richer the color. Tie the ends of the bundle with rubber bands or string and then bring your eggs to a slow boil while wrapped. Rub a drop of vegetable oil onto your finished eggs for shine.

Another option is to make red eggs in the Orthodox style.

### Making Red Eggs

1. You can find Pasch (red) egg dye at a Greek grocer.
2. Bring your eggs to a rapid boil in a pot of water with a pinch of salt. Remove the pan from the heat and let the eggs sit for 15 minutes.
3. Place the cooked eggs in cold water.
4. Then dye the eggs according to the instructions and let them dry. The hardboiled eggs are served on Easter with

horseradish or beets. Or, in the American tradition, turned into deviled eggs.

## CENTERPIECES

Another tradition is to use boiled, ceramic, felted, or wooden eggs as centerpieces. Felted Easter eggs are fun to make and give as Easter gifts. Needle felting makes prettier eggs but requires a barbed needle. So for little ones it's best to start with wet felting, which doesn't require a needle, offers them the fun of playing in soapy water, and can even be done outside.

### Wet Felting Easter Eggs

First, fill a large bucket with dish soap and water, making bubbles. You could also just do this in the sink.

Take a plastic Easter egg and wrap it in plain white wool roving or batting until it is covered. Then wrap dyed wool roving over that. You can mix colors and patterns or simply make solid colored eggs. Alternate directions each time you wrap your raw wool around the egg, pulling it tight. Continue until the egg is about 3 times its original size (as the wool will shrink when it gets wet).

Dip your wool-covered eggs in the soapy water and gently work the wool with your hands, squeezing and squishing it to help the fibers knit together. Rub and squeeze it firmly. Let it sit for a bit. Then rinse it with hot water and cold water, alternating a few times, and put it in the sun or on a windowsill until it is completely dry. You can even throw the felted eggs in the dryer on low.

If you want more, you can make baby chicks out of yellow roving (using the same wet felting method). Then simply cut one of your eggs halfway, slip out the plastic egg and place your baby bird inside. (If you like, you can needle felt the face on the baby chick.)

### Needle Felting Easter Eggs

Another option is to needle felt your Easter eggs. Use a sharp felting needle and a pile of roving. Stick the needle into the roving, again and again in a vertical, straight up-and-down motion. All this jabbing can be weirdly therapeutic, plus it takes time, so you can chat with your kids or listen to a book on tape or music while you do it.

You are knitting the fibers together into an egg shape with each stick of the needle. (Don't jab your wool at an angle though, as it will break your needle.) This is better for older kids or adults, as the needles are sharp. Also, you'll need some Styrofoam or something squishy to felt on top of, so you don't mark up your table. Once you have a very firmly felted egg you can add detail and decoration to the outside. Felted Easter eggs can be brought out as table decorations, hidden around the house for Easter egg hunts, or given to friends as gifts.

### REAL EASTER GRASS

Another DIY project, to do on your own or with kids, is to grow your own Easter grass for Easter baskets or as a table decoration.

1. You can grow your grass in a metal or clay pot (with a dish underneath) or right in an Easter basket lined with plastic. If you're using an Easter basket that's deep, you may want to crumple some newspapers and put them in the bottom so your grass will grow closer to the top.
2. Next, add potting soil to your container.
3. On top of the potting soil add a layer of wheat berries (wheatgrass seeds), which you can find in bulk at any health food store. These are edible as is the wheatgrass.
4. Add another inch of soil and keep the seeds damp and on a windowsill until the seeds sprout.
5. It should take 10–12 days for your Easter grass to grow. Some people cover their containers with plastic wrap at the beginning to create a greenhouse effect, which helps the seeds to germinate.
6. As your grass grows you can trim it with a pair of scissors to your desired height.

~~~~~~~~~~~~~~~~

# 39

# EASTER SUNDAY

*O Splendor of the Father's light*
*That makes our daylight lucid, bright;*
*O Light of light and sun of day,*
*Now shine on us your brightest ray.*

–ST. AMBROSE, FOURTH CENTURY

Easter is a day, Easter Sunday, and a season. And though it often doesn't seem so (no decorated houses, no Easter lights or Easter trees or mountains of gifts), Easter Sunday is both the holiest and the most festive day of the Christian year. It is our rebirth day, our triumph-over-death day, and it should smell, taste, and feel both holy and festive.

Two elements should mark the day: the altar table at church and the welcome table at home.

## MASS

Whether you go to the Easter Vigil or go to one of the morning liturgies, go to

Mass. It marks the first time you will hear the Alleluia sung since Lent began. The church will be filled with flowers. The Gloria will resound. Men and women and children will often be dressed in fresh spring clothes and shiny new shoes. The lectionary will have, instead of a reading from the Old Testament, a reading from the book of Acts, telling, again, the story of the earliest days of the Church.

The catechumens who have been hungering for the eucharistic feast will join you there. It is a glorious moment, for them and for all of us who have had our own holy hungers reawakened by their witness.

## MEAL AT HOME

The feast at Mass flows into the feast at home. This is a day to fill your table with guests, and then to set up card tables and fill them, too. This is a day for rich foods, for wine and sweets. But the only way such a feast can be savored is if it is preceded by a fast. So make sure you come to the table hungry.

This is a day to get out and use your best dinnerware, your best glassware, and your favorite family recipes. This is a day for table-cloths and cloth napkins and flowers on the table.

Some foods, like eggs and lamb, evoke Easter for many of us. *The Rural Life Prayerbook* contains this Easter blessing for eggs, and another one for lamb,

> We beg of you, Lord, to let the grace of Your blessing come upon these eggs, which You have made. May they be health-ful food for your people, who eat them in thanksgiving for the resurrection of our Lord Jesus Christ, who lives and is King with You forever and ever. Amen.
>
> O God, when you freed your people from Egypt You or-dered, through Your servant Moses, that a lamb be killed and that both the doorposts of the houses be sprinkled with its blood. Be so kind as to bless and sanctify this flesh which You have made, and of which we, Your servants, wish to partake in Your honor, through the resurrection of Jesus Christ our Lord, who lives and is King with You for ever and ever. Amen.

Our family likes to make deviled eggs (a good way to use dyed, hardboiled eggs). And we use Ina Garten's recipe for roast lamb from *Barefoot Contessa Family Style*. It combines ease of preparation with an elegant appearance and a delicious taste.

## EASTER BASKETS

If there are children in your household, there will be Easter baskets with sweets. Consider putting a book in each basket. (Good luck finding a book specifically about Easter that is worthy of the season. So concentrate on finding beautiful, well-written books. Beauty points the way toward its source.) Here are some suggestions for children, based on age and reading ability. For young children, consider: *Prayer for a Child* by Rachel Field; *Where the Wild Things Are* by Maurice Sendak; *The Easter Story* by Brian Wildsmith; *The Story of Easter* by Aileen Fisher; *The Colt and the King* by Marni McGee; *My First Easter* by Tomi dePaola; *Noah's Ark* by Peter Speiser; *Saint George and the Dragon* retold by Margaret Hodges; *Miss Rumphius* by Barbara Cooney; *The Clown of God* by Tomie de Paola; *Owl Moon* by Jane Yolen; or anything by Virginia Lee Burton.

For older children, consider: *The Golden Fleece and The Heroes Who Lived Before Achilles* by Padraic Colum; *On the Banks of Plum Creek* by Laura Ingalls Wilder; *Little Women* by Louisa May Alcott; *Charlotte's Web* by E. B. White; *The Door in the Wall* by Marguerite de Angeli; *Old Yeller* by Fred Gipson; *A Wrinkle in Time* by Madeleine L'Engle; *My Side of the Mountain* by Jean Craighead George; *The High King* by Lloyd Alexander; *When Shlemiel Went to Warsaw and Other Stories* by Isaac Bashevis Singer; *Sounder* by William H. Armstrong; and *The Grey King* by Susan Cooper.

For teens, consider: *The Diary of Anne Frank* by Anne Frank; *To Kill a Mockingbird* by Harper Lee; *A Separate Peace* by John Knowles; *The Giver* by Lois Lowry; *The Space Trilogy: Out of the Silent Planet, Perelandra*, and *That Hideous Strength* by C. S. Lewis; or *The Chosen* by Chaim Potok.

Seed packets are a good gift for an Easter basket. Make plans to plant the seeds with a child and to watch them grow. If it's still too cold to plant outside where you live, start the seeds indoors and then transplant them.

## EASTER EGG HUNTS

Easter baskets mean Easter egg hunts. If there are children of varying ages, make sure some of the eggs are well hidden and others are hidden in plain sight. Stagger the start times so that toddlers get to go out first, with the oldest children going last. If you have plastic eggs that can be filled, consider these alternatives to candy: stickers, friendship bracelets, hair ribbons or elastics, fancy shoelaces, and finger puppets. If you will have a large group, consider taking apart a puzzle and putting a piece or two in each egg. Then have the hunters (and their helpers) reassemble the puzzle.

When the sun goes down on Easter Sunday, you'll be tired. So when you think of keeping the Easter season, indulge in some small gifts of beauty to keep the season's spirit. Keep flowers in the house. Flowering tree and bush branches look pretty cut and placed in a tall vase. If you don't have flowers in your yard, plant some during Easter and look forward to picking your own bouquets next year.

## NATURE

Since water reminds us of our baptisms, spend time near or in the water. Go fishing or swimming or wading in a river or a creek. Take children to a water park or local pool to play.

Eat outside. Make a picnic and take it to the park or to your backyard. Sit in the sun and revel in its warmth.

Plant a vegetable garden. Plant a tree. Make a potted patio garden, or, if you have no outdoor space, make an herb garden for a kitchen windowsill. Plant tomato seeds in large tin cans and place them in a sunny spot and watch them grow.

Sing an alleluia. Listen to an alleluia. Rejoice. Christ is risen. He is risen indeed.

# 40

# DIVINE MERCY SUNDAY

The Lord is gracious and merciful.

—PSALM 145:8

How can I fear a God who is nothing but mercy and love?

—ST. THÉRÈSE OF LISIEUX

Jesus is a God of mercy: a God who eats with sinners and befriends tax collectors and prostitutes; a God who, even as He was dying on the cross, was asking forgiveness for those who had put him there. "For my thoughts are not your thoughts, nor are your ways my ways" (Isaiah 55:8).

In the same way that human mercy can be transformative, an encounter with divine mercy changes lives. Jesus's mercy is what causes great sinners, as it did St. Matthew, the tax collector and thug, to give up everything and follow him. Without mercy there would be no saints, as James Martin writes in *Jesus: A Pilgrimage*: "Imagine all the good that would never have gotten done if Dorothy Day had said: 'What could God do with me? I had an abortion.' Feelings of inadequacy are human, as Peter shows us, but we are invited to see them in the light of God's love."

And yet, the world is full of people who do not

believe in the mercy of God. The problem is twofold. On the one hand, many people do not believe in the concept of sin. These people desire to live without "guilt," which they think comes from subscribing to an external moral code that calls them to conversion. On the other hand, the world is full of people who believe in sin but do not believe in forgiveness. We live in a culture that wants neither to acknowledge sin nor to offer pardon. We prefer to push sin out of our minds. We prefer to ignore our own sins, instead of asking for forgiveness, and we prefer to punish the sins of others, often for life.

As Pope Francis emphasized in his first homily at a parish after being elected pope, "This is the Lord's most powerful message: mercy." Indeed Francis has been called the "Pope of Mercy." He even went so far as to declare the third year of his papacy "An Extraordinary Holy Year of Mercy" in March 2015, a jubilee year, for Christians to spread the word of God's forgiveness. He also started the practice of 24 hours for the Lord, in which churches around the world are open 24 hours a day for the Sacrament of Reconciliation during the season of Lent.

Pope Francis is a man acutely aware of his own sinfulness. He speaks openly about his shortcomings, for example, as archbishop of Buenos Aires. But he is also a joyful and unburdened person who knows the transformative power of mercy. Before he was pope, he said: "The privileged locus of the encounter with the Lord is the caress of the mercy of Jesus Christ on my sin." Francis is describing a God who looks at us with all our failures and offers us mercy, like Jesus with the woman at the well.


## DIVINE MERCY SUNDAY

We need to fall more deeply into the merciful arms of God. Divine Mercy Sunday was established in 2000 by Pope John Paul II, to help us do just that. It falls on the first Sunday after Easter, the final day of the Easter octave. This universal celebration of God's mercy developed from the mystical visions of a peasant nun, Faustina Kowalska, who lived in Poland until her death in 1938.

Born Helena Kowalska, Faustina grew up as one of ten children and had only a few years of formal education. At sixteen she left home to help support her family as a housekeeper. At nineteen, after experiencing a vision of a suffering Jesus, she decided to pursue a religious vocation. Because she was penniless and uneducated, she joined the only convent that would take her, the Congregation of the Sisters of Our Lady of Mercy, where she worked as gardener, cook, and housekeeper. In the convent, Faustina continued to experience Jesus calling to her in prayer to spread the message of mercy. Eventually, she found a confessor who believed that what she was experiencing in prayer was real, and he encouraged her to keep a diary.

In prayer, Faustina saw an image of Jesus, "the King of Divine Mercy," with red and white light emanating from his heart (red representing blood, both Christ's sacrifice on the cross and his presence in the Eucharist; and white representing water, baptism, and the gift of the Holy Spirit). With the help of her confessor, Faustina commissioned an artist to paint the image she had seen, with the words "Jesus, I trust in you" inscribed at its base. The Divine Mercy painting and devotion became extremely popular.

Faustina also came to believe that God was calling her to help establish a feast devoted to His mercy, which John Paul II, the first Polish pope, did in 2000, the same year Faustina was canonized.

On Divine Mercy Sunday Catholics around the world are invited to meditate on a God who *is* mercy and forgiveness. We need to recognize the need for mercy in our individual lives and in society. For example, Pope Francis has called for an end to the death penalty as well as life imprisonment, saying, "Life imprisonment is a hidden death penalty." He has said that elderly people should often be paroled, "On the basis of their very errors [they] can offer lessons to the rest of society. We don't learn only from the virtues of saints but also from the failings and errors of sinners." He has warned that we need to move beyond the endless cycle of violence and revenge, and he has argued that we cannot solve social problems by punishment. For example, the United States has the highest incarceration rate in the world, and many felons, once paroled, are unable to find work or successfully re-enter society.

There are many ways to mark Divine Mercy Sunday. If you have hurt some of the people you love the most, your children, for example, and have been too proud to apologize, take a moment from your day to tell them you're sorry. It can be as easy as saying, "I'm sorry I yelled at you." Too often we remain cut off from the people we love the most because we're too proud to admit what everyone already knows, that we're human and we sin.

Or if you have rosary beads, learn how to pray the Divine Mercy Chaplet, a popular devotion, developed by St. Faustina. Following are some guidelines for reciting the Chaplet.

## THE CHAPLET OF THE DIVINE MERCY

The Chaplet of Mercy is recited using five decades of rosary beads. The Chaplet begins with two prayers from *Diary of Saint Maria Faustina Kowalska: Divine Mercy in My Soul* and is followed by a closing prayer.

1. **Make the sign of the cross (at the crucifix):**

    In the name of the Father, and of the Son, and of the Holy Spirit. Amen.

2. **Optional Opening Prayers (on the first bead):**

    You expired, Jesus, but the source of life gushed forth for souls, and the ocean of mercy opened up for the whole world. O Fount of Life, unfathomable Divine Mercy, envelop the whole world and empty Yourself out upon us.

    (Repeat **the following verse** three times:)

    O Blood and Water, which gushed forth from the Heart of Jesus as a fountain of Mercy for us, I trust in You!

3. **Say one Our Father:**

    Our Father, Who art in heaven, hallowed be Thy name;

Thy kingdom come; Thy will be done on earth as it is in heaven. Give us this day our daily bread; and forgive us our trespasses as we forgive those who trespass against us; and lead us not into temptation, but deliver us from evil. Amen.

4. **Say one Hail Mary:**

Hail Mary, full of grace. The Lord is with thee. Blessed art thou amongst women, and blessed is the fruit of thy womb, Jesus. Holy Mary, Mother of God, pray for us sinners, now and at the hour of our death. Amen.

5. **The Apostles' Creed:**

I believe in God, the Father almighty, Creator of heaven and earth, and in Jesus Christ, His only Son, our Lord, who was conceived by the Holy Spirit, born of the Virgin Mary, suffered under Pontius Pilate, was crucified, died and was buried; He descended into hell; on the third day He rose again from the dead; He ascended into heaven, and is seated at the right hand of God the Father almighty; from there He will come to judge the living and the dead. I believe in the Holy Spirit, the holy Catholic Church, the communion of saints, the forgiveness of sins, the resurrection of the body, and life everlasting. Amen.

6. **The Eternal Father:**

Eternal Father, I offer you the Body and Blood, Soul and Divinity of Your Dearly Beloved Son, Our Lord, Jesus Christ, in atonement for our sins and those of the whole world.

7. **On the Ten Small Beads of Each Decade:**

For the sake of His sorrowful Passion, have mercy on us and on the whole world.

8. **Repeat for the remaining decades:**

Saying the "Eternal Father" on the "Our Father" bead and then saying "For the sake of His sorrowful Passion" on each of the ten "Hail Mary" beads.

9. **Conclude with Holy God (repeat three times):**

Holy God, Holy Mighty One, Holy Immortal One, have mercy on us and on the whole world. Amen.

# 41

~~~~~~~~~~~~~~~~~~~~~~~~

## WALPURGIS NIGHT

*Lord, give me light, that I may see your way.*
*Lord, give me strength, that I may follow your way.*
*Lord, give me love, that I may do your will.*
–CONCLUSION OF THE NOVENA TO ST. WALBURGA

Long before there was a *Farmers' Almanac* or a Weather Channel or daily forecasts, people divided the year simply into the warm season and the cold season. May 1 was the start of the warm season, and November 1, All Saints' Day, was the start of the cold season. These days were understood to be liminal, or threshold, moments when, at midnight, the seasons mingled and met. In that in-between place, anything could happen. Some of that memory still infuses All Hallows Eve, or Halloween, a day that is widely kept in the United States.

Less familiar to most Americans is the European counterpart of All Hallows Eve, Walpurgis Night, on April 30, a celebration of St. Walpurga, or Walburga. Like her uncle, St. Boniface, Walburga was born in England, but she devoted her life to the church in Germany, where she died in the year 777. St. Walburga was the daughter of a saint, King Richard of the West Saxons, and the sister of two saints, Willibald and Winibald. You could say she went into the family business when her father took her, at the age of eleven, to be taught by the Benedictine nuns at Wimborne Abbey in Dorsetshire. She lived there from 721 to 748, the year her uncle called her to help with the work of bringing the Gospel to Germany.

Sister Walburga set out with other women from her abbey. The weather was fair when they set sail, but soon fierce storms arose and threatened to swamp their boat. Walburga knelt on the deck and prayed that, as Jesus calmed the winds and the waves for the disciples on the Sea of Galilee, he would calm the weather for her and her companions. The sea quieted and the sailors, who witnessed the miracle, told everyone in the German port where they docked how God had answered Walburga's prayers.

Walburga went on to become an abbess at the Abbey of Heidenheim. She studied medicine, in addition to devoting her life to prayer and administration, and she became known for her ability to heal the sick. After the death of her brother, Winibald, who was the abbot at Heidenheim, she was placed in authority over both the men's and the women's abbeys. Antoine-Frédéric Ozanam, the founder of the lay Society of St. Vincent de Paul, wrote of Walburga and her sisters, "Silence and humility have veiled the labors of the nuns from the eyes of the world, but history has assigned them their place at the very beginning of German civilization."

After Walburga's death, pilgrims came to her tomb seeking cures. When her tomb was opened in 893 to take out a portion of relics for the Benedictine Abbey of Monheim, the nuns found her body covered in oil, and the oil continues to flow from her body today. It flows from her bones into the rocks around her tomb every year from about October 12 to February 25. As the oil seeps through the rocks, the nuns of the Abbey of St. Walburga, in Eichstatt, Bavaria, collect and distribute it. Miraculous cures have been attributed to Walburga's intercession and to the anointing of the healing oil.

There are a number of feast days for this remarkable woman, one of which is May 1, when she is celebrated in Bavaria and Belgium. The May 1 feast day meant Walburga became connected to April 30, when Europeans, especially those in the northern countries, prepared to welcome warm weather.

The customs of Walpurgis Night are many: lighting bonfires to welcome the sun, or dancing through the night in orchards and meadows. All-night dances are still common in Germany, where they are known as Tanz in den Mai (Dance into May) parties. This custom would be easy to make your own.

Take a picnic to the patio, the backyard, or to a nearby park and enjoy your own summer pastures. Welcome the warm season. If you are not close to any green space, open the windows and welcome the warm breeze.

The farther north you go, the more likely you are to find Walpurgis Night customs. Finland and Estonia host carnivals. Bonfires dot the hills of Sweden and the Czech Republic. In some rural areas, cattle raisers adapt the bonfire custom by building two fires and driving their cattle between them before leading the animals to the summer pastures.

Host a block party or parish party. If you can't light a bonfire, fire up the barbecue or fire pit and host a meal around the flames. In Finland, it is traditional to make and eat doughnuts on Walpurgis Night. If you have a recipe for doughnuts, be sure to follow the Finnish tradition and add a little cardamom to the batter.

Another northern European custom is to decorate the house with flowering branches, especially oak branches. Maybe the lilacs or hydrangea in your area are beginning to bloom. Cut some branches, or ask a neighbor for permission to cut some branches, and place them in jars or vases where you can watch the flowers blossom.

Consider making a Walpurgis Night pilgrimage to St. Walburga's Abbey, a daughter-house of the ancient German abbey, here in the United States. The abbey is located in northern Colorado, near the Wyoming border, in the country outside the little town of Virginia Dale. Its location means that April 30–May 1 could be snowy and cold, but even in the snow, signs of spring can be seen. The cloistered nuns pray and work raising crops and farm animals. They lead some retreats, though time and space for retreatants is limited. So contact them before you set out.

Wherever you are and however you keep Walpurgis Night, ask St. Walburga to pray for us in the summer to come, for the healing of the earth, and for an end to the extreme weather that threatens so much of the world.

~~~~~~~~~~~~~~~~~~~~~~~~~~~~~~~~~~~~~

# 42

# PRAYING WITH MARY AND INTERCESSORY PRAYER

Learn how to pray in the streets or in the country. Know
how to meditate not only when you have a book in your hand
but when you are waiting for a bus or a train.

–THOMAS MERTON

## INTERCESSORY PRAYER

Catholics do not worship Mary, but we do honor and venerate her,
just as we honor and venerate all the saints. Devotion to the saints
and intercessory prayer date back to the earliest days of the Church.
Early Christian artwork and devotional items attest to the special
place of honor given to the beloved dead by the early followers of
Jesus, who believed, as do we, that the holy ones who had died were
nevertheless alive in Christ. Just as we might ask a friend who is living to pray for us, so, too, do we ask our fellow believers who have
died, and are with God, to pray for us on earth.

We do not worship or make sacrifice to the saints, but we do keep
them alive in our hearts, like great-grandparents in faith. Sometimes
we ask them to intercede for us to God the Father. My dear friend
Cassie had a grandmother, Nana, who passed away a few years ago.
In life Nana was particularly holy and devout, so whenever Cassie is
facing an obstacle, her mother will say, "I'll ask Nana to pray for you."

Probably the best-known example of this kind of intercessory prayer is the Hail Mary, in which we say to the Blessed Virgin Mary, "Pray *for* us sinners, now and at the hour of our death."

Who better to ask for prayers than the woman who stood in prayer at the foot of the cross, faithful and unafraid until the bitter end, even as the other disciples were in hiding (John 19:25-27)? Mary is our Advocate.

Blessed Teresa of Calcutta once said, "If you ever feel distressed during your day—call upon our Lady—just say this simple prayer: 'Mary, Mother of Jesus, please be a mother to me now.'"

## THE THEOLOGY OF MARIAN DEVOTION

Of all the saints, Mary is uniquely honored. There are thirty-two Marian feasts in the Church calendar (though many of these celebrations are unique to particular regions and are not celebrated universally). Catholic and Orthodox Christians recognize that Mary was and is the Mother of God, closer to Jesus in life than anyone. It was Mary's heartbeat that the unborn Jesus first heard.

St. Cyril of Alexandria named the Blessed Virgin Mary "Theotokos," which is Greek for "the bearer of God." Mary carried Jesus in her womb, nursed him at her breast, and raised him at her side. She made him laugh, taught him language, and comforted him when he was in distress.

The earliest known prayer to the Theotokos is on a fragment of papyrus dating to AD 250. The prayer appears to be from a Coptic liturgy or Vespers and is written in Greek. Coptic, Roman Catholic, and Oriental Churches still use this prayer in worship services. It reads:

> Beneath thy compassion, we take refuge, O Mother of God:
> do not despise our petitions in time of trouble, but rescue us
> from dangers, only pure one, only blessed one.

Catholics believe that Mary was given special grace from the moment of her conception, that she might have the courage to say yes at the annunciation, and that through Mary's yes to the Incarnation, the whole world might be redeemed (Luke 1:26-38). Of course, Mary was free to say no, but she was given the grace to say yes, a grace for which we should all pray.

Catholics consider Mary the first and greatest disciple, and the preeminent member of the communion of saints. She is Our Lady, the Queen of Heaven, and the Cause of Our Joy.

My priest at St. Joseph's parish in South Bend once told me that the bank of votive candles before Mary's icon always received more donations than the bank of votive candles before the icon of Jesus. Perhaps this is because we look to Mary as an example for how to love Jesus. As Jesus said on the cross, Mary is our mother (John 19:26-27). Since Jesus is our brother, his father is our Father, and his mother is our Mother.

As we would expect of any good mother, we expect Mary to be merciful and understanding, and because Mary knew suffering, we hope that she will understand our trials.

Mary always stands with the poor and oppressed. She was poor, she was falsely accused, and she gave birth while homeless and fleeing. Mary was a refugee. Mary was the mother of an unjustly executed son. We draw on her example, thank God for her, and ask her to speak to Him on our behalf. We also look to Mary to teach us how to walk with God, as we see her doing when she advises the servers at the Wedding at Cana, "Do whatever he tells you" (John 2:5).

## PRAYING WITH MARY

Consider learning a Marian prayer such as the Hail Mary by heart during Mary's month, the month of May, or learn the Marian devotion of the Rosary during October, the month of the Rosary.

### The Memorare

Remember, O most gracious Virgin Mary, that never was it known that anyone who fled to your protection, implored your help, or sought your intercession was left unaided. Inspired by this confidence, I fly unto you, O Virgin of virgins, my mother; to you do I come, before you I stand, sinful and sorrowful. O Mother of the Word Incarnate, despise not my petitions, but in your mercy hear and answer me. Amen.

### Salve Regina (Hail, Holy Queen)

Hail, holy Queen, Mother of mercy, our life, our sweetness and our hope. To you do we cry, poor banished children of Eve. To you do we send up our sighs, mourning and weeping in this valley of tears. Turn, then, most gracious advocate, your eyes of mercy toward us; and after this our exile, show unto us the blessed fruit of your womb, Jesus. O clement, O loving, O sweet Virgin Mary.

### The Magnificat (The Song of Mary)

My soul proclaims the greatness of the Lord, I delight in God my savior, who regarded my humble state. Truly from this day forward all generations will call me blessed: for God, wonderful in power, has used that strength for me. Holy the name of the Lord, whose mercy embraces the faithful one generation to the next. The mighty arm of God scatters the proud in their conceit, pulls tyrants from their thrones and has lifted up the lowly. The Lord fills the starving and lets the rich go hungry. God rescues lowly Israel, recalling the promises of mercy, the promises made to our ancestors to Abraham's heirs forever. Glory to the Father, and the Son, and the Holy Spirit: As it was in the beginning, is now and will be forever. Amen.

## The Angelus

V. The Angel of the Lord declared unto Mary.

R. And she conceived of the Holy Spirit.

*Hail Mary, full of grace,*

*the Lord is with thee;*

*blessed art thou among women*

*and blessed is the fruit of thy womb, Jesus.*

*Holy Mary, Mother of God,*

*pray for us sinners,*

*now and at the hour of our death. Amen.*

V. Behold the handmaid of the Lord.

R. Be it done unto me according to thy word.

*Hail Mary, etc.*

V. And the Word was made Flesh.

R. And dwelt among us.

*Hail Mary, etc.*

V. Pray for us, O holy Mother of God.

R. That we may be made worthy of the promises of Christ.

Let us pray.

Pour forth, we beseech Thee, O Lord, Thy grace into our hearts; that we, to whom the incarnation of Christ Thy Son was made known by the message of an angel, may by His Passion and Cross be brought to the glory of His Resurrection. Through the same Christ Our Lord, Amen.

## Litany of Loreto approved in 1587 by Pope Sixtus V

Lord, have mercy.

Christ, have mercy.

Lord, have mercy.

God our Father in Heaven, *have mercy on us.*

God the Son, Reedemer of the world, *have mercy on us.*

God the Holy Spirit, *have mercy on us.*

Holy Trinity, One God, *have mercy on us.*

Holy Mary, *pray for us.*

Holy Mother of God, *pray for us.*

Holy Virgin of virgins, *[etc.]*

Mother of Christ,

Mother of the Church,

Mother of divine grace,

Mother most pure,

Mother most chaste,

Mother inviolate,

Mother undefiled,

Mother most amiable,

Mother most admirable,

Mother of good counsel,

Mother of our Creator,

Mother of our Saviour,

Mother of mercy,

Virgin most prudent,

Virgin most venerable,

Virgin most renowned,

Virgin most powerful,

Virgin most merciful,

Virgin most faithful,

Mirror of justice,

Seat of wisdom,

Cause of our joy,

Spiritual vessel,

Vessel of honor,

Singular vessel of devotion,

Mystical Rose,

Tower of David,

Tower of ivory,

House of gold,

Ark of the covenant,

Gate of heaven,

Morning star,

Health of the sick,

Refuge of sinners,

Comfort of the afflicted,

Help of Christians,

Queen of angels,

Queen of patriarchs,

Queen of prophets,

Queen of apostles,

Queen of martyrs,

Queen of confessors,

Queen of virgins,

Queen of all saints,

Queen conceived without original sin,

Queen assumed into heaven,

Queen of the most holy Rosary,

Queen of families,

Queen of peace.

Lamb of God, you take away the sins of the world, *spare us, O Lord.*
Lamb of God, you take away the sins of the world, *graciously hear us, O Lord.*
Lamb of God, you take away the sins of the world, *have mercy on us.*

Pray for us, O Holy Mother of God. *That we may be made worthy of the promises of Christ.*

Let us pray. Eternal God, let your people enjoy health in mind and body. Through the intercession of the Virgin Mary free us from the sorrows of this life and lead us to happiness in the life to come. Grant this through Christ our Lord. Amen.

After praying the whole litany you might choose one or two lines that resonate with you and repeat them throughout your day. Such as "Queen of families, Queen of peace."

# 43

# THE FEAST OF ST. JOSEPH AND ST. JOSEPH THE WORKER

If you and I are to live religious lives, it mustn't be
that we talk a lot about religion, but that our
manner of life is different.

−WITTGENSTEIN

Even those with only a passing understanding of Catholicism know that Catholics love Mary. This is because of her unique relationship with Jesus. Mary was the woman God created to be his mother, the person closest to him in life. We look to her as a model for how to love him. But what role does the third member of the Holy Family, St. Joseph, play, and how do we honor him?

It is often the case that Joseph, the man who raised God incarnate, gets overlooked. Perhaps this is because, unlike Mary, Joseph is silent in the New Testament. Many scholars believe that he died before Jesus's public ministry began. After he brings the Holy Family to Nazareth, Joseph disappears from Matthew's account (although in Luke's Gospel, Joseph is present for the circumcision and again, twelve years later, when he and Mary take Jesus to Jerusalem for the Passover).

It may also be the case that in choosing to emphasize Jesus's divine paternity, the Church focuses more on Mary, his virgin mother, rather than on Joseph, the man who raised him.

Whatever the case may be, St. Joseph plays a supporting role. And yet, Joseph's willingness to play his essential part, humbly and quietly, has inspired a devotion to him that has grown with time. Joseph is a model of faithful fatherhood. Unlike Mary at the annunciation, Joseph was not consulted about God's plan, yet once he became aware of God's will, he was obedient to God and faithful to Mary and Jesus.

Joseph's actions were heroic. He protected Jesus and Mary from great danger, helping them to escape the wrath of Herod (Matthew 2:13-15). For this reason, Joseph is often pictured cradling the Child Jesus in his arms. Joseph made it possible for Jesus to have a safe and secure childhood. He kept Jesus out of harm's way until it was time for his public ministry to begin. Joseph was also one of Jesus's first and best teachers, as he passed on to his son his craft, training him as a carpenter (Mark 6:3), and taught Jesus to read the Hebrew Scriptures.

In addition to his courage and heroism, Joseph is a saint of great mercy and love. When he discovered that his betrothed, Mary, was pregnant with a child he had not fathered, his first instinct was to divorce her quietly, even though he was meant to adhere to the letter of the law, which at the time required that a woman guilty of adultery be stoned to death. When Joseph was told in a dream to take Mary as his wife (Matthew 1:20-25), he obeyed, sheltering her and raising the Child Jesus with love.

## THE FEAST OF ST. JOSEPH

Around the year 700, March 20 was set aside as a day to honor Joseph. About a century later the date was moved to March 19, where it remains. In the 1300s, the Feast of St. Joseph was declared a solemnity, and in 1870 Pope Pius XI declared St. Joseph the Patron and Protector of the Universal Church.

In Spain people celebrate March 19 by burning bonfires in St. Joseph's honor. Carpenters and woodworkers clean out their shops and burn all the wood scraps on the evening of the patron's feast. Children and men often use the scrap wood to create scenes, many of them symbolic of some event in the past year. The best-made creations receive a prize and are kept in a place of honor. The rest are burned in celebratory bonfires. These outdoor celebrations often include music, dancing, and fireworks.

Adopt this tradition as your own and make something out of wood on this day—a trellis, a shed, a birdhouse—and, if you have kids or grandkids, involve them in the project. In his day, St. Joseph built houses and furniture, as well as plows and yokes. We honor the life of Joseph when we work with our hands.

In Italy people light candles in honor of St. Joseph or put statues of him in their gardens and fields to celebrate the beginning of spring. They might even have their fields blessed by a priest. On St. Joseph's day it is the custom to wear red, just as Americans wear green on the feast of St. Patrick. The feast of St. Joseph falls during Lent, so Italians make a meatless or vegan dish, like minestrone soup, and sprinkle fresh breadcrumbs or croutons on top just before serving. St. Joseph was a woodworker, and breadcrumbs or croutons remind us of the wood shavings and dust that must have been on the ground where he worked.

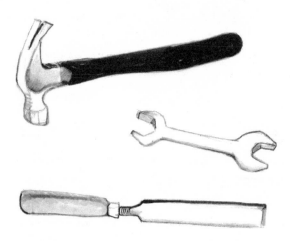

## ST. JOSEPH THE WORKER

In the late nineteenth century, May Day, May 1, was chosen by the Communists as a day for recognizing the workers of the world. In response to the Communist celebration, in 1955 Pope Pius XII established the Feast of St. Joseph the Worker on May 1 as a way of indicating that the Church cares about the rights and dignity of workers as well.

St. Joseph worked with his hands, as a craftsman (Matthew 13:55) to keep his family fed and sheltered. He is often seen in paintings, as in the fifteenth-century Flemish painting by Robert Campin, surrounded by saws, squares, and chisels, the tools of his trade, known as the Mérode Altarpiece. St. Joseph was a peasant and a man from Nazareth, a town that was so tiny and remote that it served as the butt of jokes. Speaking of Jesus people joked, "Can anything good come out of Nazareth" (John 1:44-46)? Joseph knew hard labor and the struggle of daily life in the ancient world. His wife gave birth in a stable, and when Joseph and Mary presented the Child Jesus in the Temple, they could only afford to sacrifice pigeons. (At the time, a yearly lamb was required for a burnt offering, but the poor were permitted to substitute doves or pigeons for the lamb.) He also knew injustice. Much of what Joseph and the other farmers and artisans in Nazareth earned went to support the ruling class in the Roman Empire via an unfair system of taxation. Jesus's family was at the bottom of the economic ladder. This is why Joseph is the patron of tradesmen and workers, travelers and refugees, of the persecuted, of Christian families and homes, of purity and interior life, of engaged couples, of people in earthly distress, of the poor, the elderly, and the dying.

While May is the month of Mary, set aside May 1 to honor St. Joseph the Worker. Adopt a May Day tradition and leave a May basket, a small basket of sweets or flowers, anonymously on the doorstep of a neighbor in need, or pray the Litany of St. Joseph. After you've prayed the litany, meditate or repeat a favorite line or two throughout your day.

### Litany of St. Joseph
Lord, have mercy.
*R./ Lord, have mercy.*
Christ, have mercy.
*R./ Christ, have mercy.*
Lord, have mercy.
*R./ Lord, have mercy.*

God our Father in Heaven,
*R./ have mercy on us.*
God the Son, Redeemer of the world,
*R./ have mercy on us.*
God, the Holy Spirit,
*R./ have mercy on us.*
Holy Trinity, one God,
*R./ have mercy on us.*

After each line respond "Pray for us."

Holy Mary,
Saint Joseph,
Noble son of the House of David,
Light of patriarchs,
Husband of the Mother of God,
Guardian of the Virgin,
Foster-father of the Son of God,
Faithful guardian of Christ,
Head of the Holy Family,
Joseph most just,
Joseph, prudent and brave,
Joseph, obedient and loyal,
Pattern of patience,
Lover of poverty,
Model of artisans,
Example to parents,
Guardian of virgins,
Pillar of family life,
Comfort of the troubled,
Hope of the sick,
Patron of the dying,
Terror of evil spirits,
Protector of the Church,
Lamb of God, you take away the sins of the world, have
    mercy on us.

Lamb of God, you take away the sins of the world, have
mercy on us.
Lamb of God, you takes away the sins of the world, have
mercy on us.

V. God made him master of his household.
R. *And put him in charge of all he owned.*

Let us pray. Almighty God, in your infinite wisdom and love
you chose Joseph to be the husband of Mary, the mother of
your Son. As we enjoy his protection on earth may we have
the help of his prayers in heaven. We ask this through Christ
our Lord. Amen.

~~~~~~~~~~~~~~~~~~~~~~~~~~~~~~~~~~~~

# 44

# PENTECOST

The fruit of the Spirit is love, joy, peace, patience, kindness,
generosity, faithfulness, gentleness, self-control.

—GALATIANS 5:22-23A

One of the holy names of Jesus is Emmanuel, a name that means
"God with us." God is with us always. Since the day that Jesus Christ
ascended into heaven, the way that God is with us is by and through
the presence and power of the Holy Spirit. Pentecost is the feast of
God, the Holy Spirit, and it is rightly linked to the resurrection of
God the Son.

This is how Pope Benedict XVI described it in his homily on the
feast of Pentecost in 2012:

> On that morning, fifty days after Easter, a powerful wind
> blew over Jerusalem and the flame of the Holy Spirit de-
> scended on the gathered disciples. It came to rest upon the
> head of each of them and ignited in them a divine fire, a
> fire of love, capable of transforming things. Their fear dis-
> appeared, their hearts were filled with new strength, their
> tongues were loosened and they began to speak freely, in

such a way that everyone could understand the news that Jesus Christ had died and was risen.

So we might say that the season of Easter begins and ends in life. Jesus Christ defeats death at Easter, and at Pentecost the Holy Spirit empowers the disciples to share that new and risen life with the whole world, Jews and Gentiles, people of every nation and tongue. Pentecost is the birthday of the Church.

Just fifty days before the events in Jerusalem, on the evening of the day of the resurrection, the same disciples were locked in a room, hiding, sure that their Messiah had been killed and worrying that they would be next. There were no men at the empty tomb on Easter Sunday morning; they were crouching in the rubble of their dashed dreams, fearful of getting anywhere near the fallen Messiah, or his grave. Jesus came into their locked room and made it a womb by breathing on them, and into them, the breath of life. He said, "Receive the Holy Spirit," and thereby conceived them as new beings (John 20:22). Jesus made them alive in a way that had not been before, in a way that sent them out of that room and into the community, teaching and preaching the Good News of Jesus's resurrection from the dead. Their community is Jerusalem and the Jews of Jerusalem. The book of Acts records of that first community:

> All these [the disciples] devoted themselves with one accord
> to prayer, together with some women, and Mary the mother
> of Jesus, and his brothers [or, relatives] (ACTS 1:14).

Think of the fifty days between Jesus's appearance in the locked room and Pentecost as a kind of gestation, during which the apostles grew stronger in the womb of the Jerusalem Church. Then the day came when God allowed them to be birthed into the world, the world where they would travel far and wide preaching Christ crucified, the world in which every one of them, save John, would die as martyrs for Christ. And the sign of this universal birth, or sending, was that the disciples were able to speak in foreign tongues, unknown to them but intelligible to people in the crowds gathered for the festival of Shavuot, or the Feast of Weeks. Think of a newborn's first cry into the world; this is the disciples':

> And they were all filled with the holy Spirit and began to speak in different tongues, as the Spirit enabled them to proclaim.

> Now there were devout Jews from every nation under heaven staying in Jerusalem. At this sound, they gathered in a large crowd, but they were confused because each one heard them speaking in his own language (ACTS 2:4-6).

Even non-believers accept this historical fact: a small group of frightened, discouraged men were empowered to boldly proclaim the Gospel of Christ at the cost of their freedom and their lives. They went, using current place names, to Egypt (Mark); to India (Thomas); to Rome (Peter); to Greece (Andrew); to Turkey (Philip); to Turkey, Armenia, Iran (Bartholomew); and to Iraq (Simon and Jude). Some traditional accounts include even wider travel to Spain, England, and Russia. Wherever they went, the disciples left behind a world filled with Christian churches, a world for which they were willing to die. The only disciple to live to old age was John, who after imprisonment on the island of Patmos became a bishop. No one knows why he alone was spared (his brother, James, was the first of the disciples to be martyred), but perhaps it was so that he could record these events.

## THE JEWISH ROOTS OF PENTECOST

Some seasons are ours alone: such as Advent (from the Latin word meaning "the coming, the approach, the arrival") and Christmas, the "Christ Mass." But Pentecost (from the Greek word meaning "the fiftieth") is, in its origin, a Jewish feast, and, like Easter, which is our Pasch or Passover, it has ancient roots. We read about this festival in the Old Testament:

You shall count off seven weeks; begin to count the seven weeks from the day when the sickle is first put to the standing grain. You shall then keep the feast of Weeks for the Lord, your God, and the measure of your own voluntary offering which you will give shall be in proportion to the blessing the Lord, your God, has given you (DEUTERONOMY 16:9-10).

Take one week and multiply it by seven; you get forty-nine days. The next, or fiftieth, day is Pentecost. Jews call Pentecost Shavuot, or the Feast of Weeks. They count it starting from the second day of Passover to the day before Shavuot (Weeks). For Christians, Pentecost is counted starting from Easter Sunday to Pentecost Sunday. Just as it is for Jews, the Christian Pentecost is the fiftieth day. Think about the name. "The fiftieth day" is different from "fifty days." It puts an emphasis on the final, or fiftieth day, making it stand out on its own. We look to Jewish tradition for a clue as to why Pentecost, the fiftieth day, has such a particular character within the Easter season.

Shavuot (Weeks) is one of two anchors of the time between Passover and the giving of the Torah (the first five books of the Old Testament) at Mount Sinai. Jews understand it as beginning and ending in freedom: Passover marked the beginning of physical freedom, and the giving of the Torah marked the beginning of spiritual freedom.

In a similar way, Christians understand the Easter season as being anchored by two commemorations: the resurrection of Christ and the birth of the Church. The Holy Spirit came upon the disciples, all of whom had gathered in Jerusalem for Shavuot (Weeks).

Because Pentecost is a birthday, and, in many places, the beginning of the summer season, get outside today. Fly a kite, hike a wilderness trail, ride a bike, wade in a stream or in the ocean.

Because this is a birthday, make plans in the coming week to collect money or baby clothes or equipment for a local crisis pregnancy center. Perhaps they need volunteers to answer phones or make deliveries. Think of what you can do to support pregnant women or babies and their mothers and fathers in your community.

Jews eat at least one dairy meal on their Shavuot (Weeks). So plan a meal that features cheese or yogurt or sour cream. Or plan a milk-shake party with friends.

The liturgical color for Pentecost is red. So make spinach straw-berry salad or some other berry dish. You might conclude your meal with this prayer from Anglican priest Eric Milner-White:

Enter my heart, O Holy Spirit,
come in blessed mercy and set me free.
Throw open, O Lord,
the locked doors of my mind.
O Holy Spirit, very God,
Whose presence is liberty,
grant me the perfect freedom
to be your servant
today, tomorrow, evermore.

Amen.

# SUMMER ORDINARY TIME

# 45

# HOW TO PLANT A MARY GARDEN

*A garden enclosed, my sister, my bride,*
*a garden enclosed, a fountain sealed!*
*Your branches are a grove of pomegranates,*
*with fruits of choicest yield.*

–SONG OF SONGS 4:12-13A

In the Church, no human being receives more reverence than the Virgin Mary. The term for this is "hyperdulia." It means the veneration (*dulia*), over (*hyper*) that granted to any saint or angel.

We do not worship Mary, but we do honor her in a particular way as the Theotokos, or God-bearer, the one, alone, of all women, asked to carry Christ in her womb and deliver him to a waiting world.

An entire month, the month of May, is devoted to Mary. (The name, "May," is a variant of the name Mary.) It's also the month when we want to go outside and enjoy the warmth of spring.

A good way to honor Mary is to plant a Mary garden, a garden in which every plant has some connection to the Blessed Virgin. Just as God sowed the seeds of eternal life in Mary's womb, so we can sow the seeds of new life in our gardens. There are hundreds of plants associated with Mary, and the tradition of planting gardens in her honor dates from at least the seventh century. Here are some of the hardier and more common Marian plants.

**Lady's Mantle** is a perennial ground cover. The plant grows eight

to fourteen inches high, with lobed silvery green leaves. The scalloped edges of the leaves are said to be like those of a woman's cloak, so the Germans call it *frauenmantle*. But the Italians call it *Madonna Mantello*, or the Madonna's cloak. After a rain, drops of water catch in the lobes of the leaves and glisten like sequins. It is beautiful to see the water cupped and held in the leaves. Some people believe the water caught in Lady's Mantle has healing properties. Lady's Mantle does better where the summer is cool and fairly moist. It will need some protection from hot sun and dry conditions.

**Columbine**, or Lady's Slipper, grows wild in the Rocky Mountains. According to legend, these flowers sprang up under Mary's feet as she hurried to her cousin Elizabeth's house.

Columbine, as befits a wild mountain flower, isn't particular about soil conditions, as long as the soil is well drained. If you live at a high altitude or far north, plant this perennial in full sun. If you live farther south, plant them where they will receive shade in the hottest part of the day.

**Lavender** is said to be the plant on which Mary hung the baby Jesus's diapers during the flight into Egypt. It is hard to imagine a sweeter smelling wash than one hung to dry on lavender. This plant is native to the Mediterranean, so it likes bright sun and fairly dry soil. But there are many varieties of lavender, and you can find one for your area. England is planted thick with lavender, and neither dry soil nor bright sun characterize the climate there. You can use lavender for cooking as well as crafts. For instance, you can make lavender sachets to place under your pillow to aid sleep. Lavender is also useful for repelling fleas and moths.

**Marigolds**, or Mary's Gold, are as easy to grow as weeds, and they come in several varieties and shades of yellow or gold. The story is that thieves accosted the Holy Family on the way into Egypt. Mary gave them her purse. When the thieves opened it, marigolds, rather than money, poured out. In the Middle Ages it was customary to decorate shrines of Mary with this small, sturdy flower. If you plant marigolds, consider using them as a border around tomato plants or other vegetables and fruits. French marigolds repel whiteflies and kill bad nematodes. Mexican marigolds repel harmful insects and wild rabbits. Make sure that any marigolds you plant have the distinctive astringent odor of marigold flowers.

**Violets**, like marigolds, are modest flowers, easily grown, and they spread easily. Beautiful and small, the violet is called Our Lady's Modesty and is said to have blossomed first when Mary spoke to the angel Gabriel saying, "Behold, the handmaid of the Lord."

**Irises and Lilies** are flowers associated with the annunciation. Legend has it that the angel Gabriel was holding a lily when he approached Mary with the news that she was to bear the Savior. Both flowers are hardy perennials, but each has a graceful arrangement of petals that open like a cup. It is easy to see how Mary's grace in accepting God's will is mirrored by the petals of the iris and the lily.

**Snowdrop**, one of the first blooms to appear in late winter or early spring, is called the Flower of Purification, because in some areas it blooms on February 2, the Feast of the Purification of Mary, which is better known in the West as the Feast of the Presentation of the Lord. In Italy, where snowdrops are known to bloom this early in the year, it is the custom to remove small statues of Mary from their places in church and cover the spot with white snowdrops.

**Junipers** are hardy bushes. According to legend, the Holy Family was fleeing into Egypt when Herod's soldiers drew near. A juniper by the road opened its branches and beckoned the Holy Family to hide inside. Herod's soldiers passed by, never guessing how near they were to the Christ Child they sought to kill. Junipers are divided into male and female plants. If you have a female juniper it will bear the small blue berries that are the color of Mary's robe. Juniper berries are the secret ingredient in gin, and they can be used in cooking red meats like venison and pork. Just be sure that the berries on your plants are edible and have not been sprayed with toxic chemicals.

**Larkspur** is called Mary's Tears. It is said that when Mary wept at the foot of the cross, her teardrops fell to the ground and sprang up as larkspur.

**English daisy**, perhaps because of its traditional association with innocence, is known as Mary's Love.

If you have limited outdoor space, you can plant a Mary herb and fruit garden in pots on a porch or in a windowsill. Here are some herbs associated with Mary: **rosemary** (Mary's Bouquet), **thyme** (Mary's Modesty), **parsley** (Mary's Vine), **marjoram** (Mary's Bedding), **spearmint** (Our Lady's Mint), and **sage** (Mary's Cape). **Strawberries** (Mary's Fertility) can also be grown in patio planters.

Often Mary gardens are planted around or near a statue of Our Lady. My husband and I placed a statue of Mary in our yard years ago. Then we decided to build or buy a shelter with a spot to plant flowers or a lit votive candle. We couldn't find what we were looking for. One summer we hired a company to lay a new sidewalk. The laborers were mostly Spanish speakers, born and raised in Mexico. In halting Spanish, my husband began to describe what we had in mind. I drew my medal of Our Lady of Guadalupe from my shirt and held it out. Several of the men pulled out their own identical medals. They smiled and assured us they knew just what we wanted, because they had grown up with similar statues and similar shelters. They spoke of a *cueva*, or cave, and with sketches and gestures they showed us what they meant. It was perfect. They built a platform of concrete bricks about seventeen inches high. The niche for Mary (the statue is about twenty-seven inches high) was crafted of curved rebar over which the workers laid a layer of what looks like chicken wire, but is, in fact, metal lath. The niche measures about thirty-four inches high. The workmen covered the lath with cement, and on top of the cement they laid smooth stones and pebbles, accented with a blue-and-white Mexican tile cross. On the last day of work the men brought cameras and asked us to take their pictures in front of the *cueva*. They wanted to send the pictures home, to their mothers mostly. Later we placed a bench in front of our statue of Mary, making a quiet place for prayer and reflection. Around the statue we planted **holly**, which is traditionally associated with the nativity.

# 46

~~~~~~~~~~~~~~~~~~~~~~

## ST. JOHN'S DAY FIRES

A man named John was sent from God. . . . He was not the
light, but came to testify to the light.

–JOHN 1:6,8

June 24 is the Feast of John the Baptist. Like the birthdays of Mary
and Jesus, we keep John's birthday, which falls around the time of
the summer solstice. (Out of all the followers of Jesus, only John and
Mary are honored with a feast celebrating their birthdays.) The summer solstice marks the sun's highest rise north of the equator. It is the
longest day of the year in the Northern Hemisphere, and it falls on
either June 20 or 21, depending upon the time zone.

Of course, no one knows exactly when John was born. No one
knows exactly when Jesus was born. It is the deep wisdom of the
Church to link their births with the annual movements of the sun. We
keep John's day just as the sun reaches its zenith and begins to sink,
with the days growing shorter and darker until the winter solstice on
December 21. The winter solstice is the longest night of the year.

We keep the Feast of the Nativity, Jesus's birthday, on December
25. By this time, the sun has reached its farthest point south of the
equator and has begun its northward rise. The days grow longer, and
the night shorter, as light reclaims the hemisphere.

Christmas comes just when nights have grown long and it seems that darkness has taken over the world. But, slowly, so slowly we may not be able at first to tell, the sun's light grows brighter and, day by day, overcomes the night.

John's birthday marks the beginning of a decrease in the light. After the summer solstice, slowly, so slowly we may not at first be able to tell, the sun's light grows less, day by day, until the hours of darkness in the day outnumber the hours of light. This reveals a theological truth about the relationship between John, the Prophet, and Jesus the Lord. Jesus's birthday marks an increase. It is just as John himself said of Jesus, "He must increase; I must decrease" (John 3:30).

There is no resentment in John's words, no sense that he feels he has been usurped or ignored. Indeed, he says that all this had to happen, and, "so this joy of mine has been made complete" (John 3:29b). The Gospel of John includes a section of John's own testimony. In it, John the Baptist says,

> I baptize with water; but there is one among you whom you
> do not recognize, the one who is coming after me, whose
> sandal strap I am not worthy to untie (JOHN 1:26-27).

John's decrease before Jesus is as natural and as graceful as the decrease of the winter darkness before the increase of the spring sun.

There is a long European tradition of St. John's fires. On the night

of the 23rd, the vigil of St. John's Day, the 24th, people gather to light fires, especially along riverbanks and lakeshores and ocean shores. Some groups will place lit candles on rafts and set them out on the water. Some place lit candles inside biodegradable paper lanterns and release them over the ocean. These customs remind us of the John the Baptizer, who preached and baptized along and in the River Jordan. John's Gospel says,

> A man named John was sent from God. He came for testimony, to testify to the light, so that all might believe through him. He was not the light, but came to testify to the light. The true light, which enlightens everyone, was coming into the world (JOHN 1:6-7).

The light recalls the One whom John, and the whole world, awaited. When we kindle St. John's fires on the night-shadowed shore or send lit candles onto the ocean waves, the dark water is illuminated.

Because we celebrate John's birth in the Northern Hemisphere summer, flowers and herbs abound. Another custom is to go out and gather wild herbs and flowers. Use the herbs and flowers to make a wreath. You can wear the wreath or give it to a friend to wear. After the wreath dries, place it in your home to keep until the next St. John's Day, when it can be placed on one of the candle-bearing rafts and cast upon the water.

Have a St. John's Day party. Maybe the body of water you illuminate will be the community swimming pool, or a local creek. (Check for fire warnings and restrictions in your area. If you live in a drought area, consider using a fire pit.)

If you live near the ocean or a lake, go and bring a picnic.

Just before you light the fire or share your picnic, retell the story of John's miraculous birth, which you can find in Luke 1:5-25. Luke tells us that Elizabeth and Zechariah were old. They had no children, and their childbearing years had passed. As Zechariah was serving as a priest in the sanctuary of the Lord in the Jerusalem Temple, an angel appeared to him. The angel announced that Elizabeth would bear a son, and that the son was to be named "John." The angel promises that John "will be great in the sight of the Lord" (Luke 1:15). There are echoes of Old Testament stories here: Abraham and Sarah's miraculous conception of Isaac, and the stories of both Samuel and Samson, who, long before John's birth and consecration, were consecrated by a Nazirite vow. (A Nazirite, a title coming from the Hebrew verb, *nazir*, which means "to consecrate," takes a formal oath to God, promising to abstain from drinking wine and eating anything that comes from the vine, like grapes; to refrain from cutting his hair for the duration of the vow; and to retain ritual cleanliness, by never, for example, coming into contact with a corpse. You can read more about the Nazirite vow in Num. 6:1-21.)

Zechariah is understandably surprised when the angel Gabriel appears to him with the news that Elizabeth will conceive and bear a son. He is struck dumb (perhaps out of wonderment, though Luke writes that it is because he did not believe Gabriel's words).

The child arrives. Luke recounts that "[Elizabeth's] neighbors and relatives heard that the Lord had shown his great mercy towards her, and they rejoiced with her" (Luke 1:58). Elizabeth will show great mercy toward her cousin, Mary, rejoicing with her at the news of Mary's pregnancy.

Zechariah gives the baby the name "John," writing the word on a tablet. He chooses this name even though no one in the family carries it. Once Zechariah has declared, "John is his name," his tongue is freed and he begins blessing God (Luke 1:63-64).

As you sit around the fire, tell other stories of births. Recall all the ways God uses other people to bring light into our lives. Parents and grandparents can recall their joy at the births of their children, and children can ask questions of their parents and grandparents. Aunts and uncles and family friends have stories to tell. In families with several children, the older ones can tell the younger ones what they remember of their births. The youngest of our five has always enjoyed hearing how his brother, our eldest, took the occasion of his baby brother's birth to skip school. He figured no one would be paying particular attention to him on that day, and he was right. He declared his own holiday and still remembers it with pleasure.

~~~~~~~~~~~~~~~~~~~~~~~~~~~~~~~~~~~

# 47

# THE FEAST OF CORPUS CHRISTI

I don't partake because I'm a good Catholic, holy and pious
and sleek. I partake because I'm a bad Catholic, riddled by
doubt and anxiety and anger: fainting from severe
hypoglycemia of the soul.

—NANCY MAIR, *Ordinary Time*

The first American-born saint, Elizabeth Ann Bayley Seton, was a
married Protestant and the mother of five children when her husband, William, became ill. His doctor suggested he go to Italy to heal
in the warm climate. In Italy, Elizabeth saw a Corpus Christi procession in the streets, the monstrance (the vessel used to hold and
expose the consecrated Host) held high, and she was driven to her
knees by an invisible force. She felt in her heart that she had seen
God. This event was a turning point in her life. Her husband died
while the family was in Italy, and Elizabeth and her children found
refuge in the home of an Italian family. She observed their life of
charity and hospitality and decided that she wanted to emulate them
in every way, which included converting to Catholicism.

On Ash Wednesday in 1805, she walked into St. Peter's Basilica
in Rome, sank to her knees, and prayed, "My God, here let me rest."

Elizabeth's heavy heart may have rested, but her hands did not.
She returned home to the United States and became a teacher in New
York. Word of her gifts as a teacher spread to the bishop of Maryland,

who asked her to come there and start a school for poor girls. She packed up her children and moved to a ramshackle home in Emmitsburg, Maryland. Though snow fell through the roof and onto their beds as they slept, Elizabeth Ann and her children were happy there.

Near Baltimore, she helped found the first Catholic school in the country. Later she and eighteen other women founded the Sisters of Charity, the first native-born Catholic women's religious order.

Who knows what path St. Elizabeth Ann Seton's life might have taken had she not been in Italy on the Feast of Corpus Christi and witnessed a eucharistic procession?

## THE BODY AND BLOOD OF CHRIST

The Feast of Corpus Christi is a celebration of the Real Presence, the belief that Christ is present in the consecrated bread and wine of the Eucharist. Catholics believe that Jesus, at the last Passover supper before his crucifixion, instituted the Eucharist and keeps it until the end of time.

Catholics take Jesus at his word:

> I am the bread of life. Your ancestors ate the manna in the desert, but they died; this is the bread that comes down from heaven so that one may eat it and not die. I am the living bread that came down from heaven; whoever eats this bread will live forever; and the bread that I will give is my flesh for the life of the world (JOHN 6:48-51).

And again,

> Amen, amen, I say to you, unless you eat the flesh of the Son of Man and drink his blood, you do not have life within you. Whoever eats my flesh and drinks my blood has eternal life, and I will raise him on the last day. For my flesh is true food and my blood is true drink. Whoever eats my flesh and drinks my blood remains in me and I in him (JOHN 6:53-56).

A Protestant friend once asked me why I go to church, and I told him that I go for the Eucharist. He told me he expected to hear something vague about community. I told him that I agree with Flannery O'Connor when she said, "The only thing that makes the Church endurable is that it is somehow the body of Christ and that on this we are fed."

Catholics adore and receive Jesus in the Eucharist at Mass. It is a mystery we will never fully comprehend, yet we take it on faith that by God's action at the consecration, the bread and wine become the Body and Blood of Jesus. The accidents of bread and wine remain ("accidents" refers to what our physical senses perceive when we receive Communion), but the substance of the bread and wine has become Jesus, in his full humanity and his full divinity. This daily miracle is known as transubstantiation.

## THE FEAST OF CORPUS CHRISTI

The Feast of Corpus Christi dates back to the thirteenth century and an Augustinian nun named Juliana of Liège. Juliana had a vision of a dark spot in an otherwise full moon. She understood the moon to be the Church and the darkness to be the result of there not being a feast in honor of the Blessed Sacrament. Her bishop heard and believed her, and he instituted the first celebration of this feast, known then as the *Festum Eucharistiae*, at the church of Saint-Martin in 1247. Pope Urban IV extended the feast to the universal Church, and at his invitation St. Thomas Aquinas composed the poems and sequence for the liturgy. He wrote the well-known hymns *Pange Lingua Gloriosi, Panis Angelicus, Tantum Ergo,* and *O Salutarius Hostia* for the Feast of Corpus Christi.

On the Thursday after Trinity Sunday, or, in the United States, the Sunday after Trinity Sunday, the universal Church celebrates the Solemnity of the Body and Blood of Christ, a holy day of obligation, also known by its Latin name, as the Feast of Corpus Christi.

It is customary for parishes to have a solemn eucharistic procession on the Feast of Corpus Christi. A procession is a way of bearing witness. It is a way of praying with our bodies fully engaged. It is a way of turning a crowd into a community.

The Corpus Christi procession occurs after Mass. The priest carries the Body of Christ, reserved in the monstrance, high above his head. The faithful follow behind. Usually the altar servers carry incense and all sing a litany or hymn. After the procession, the Eucharist is brought to a place of veneration and repose.

Eucharistic processions, like all things Catholic, vary considerably from place to place. In Jinja, Uganda, dancing and drumming might accompany the Eucharist. In Genzano di Roma, Italy, people cover the streets with flower petals in Jesus's honor. In Tarentum, Pennsylvania, parishioners make art from colored sawdust on the pavement where the procession will pass. Traditionally the faithful would kneel in the streets and venerate the Eucharist when they saw it pass.

If your community doesn't have a Corpus Christi celebration, speak with your pastor and see if you can get one started. As uneasy as we may be about getting up from our pews and following the Eucharist out into the streets, eucharistic processions bring God to people who might not otherwise encounter him while going about their day, people like St. Elizabeth Ann Seton. The Corpus Christi procession brings the Eucharist before people who need, without even knowing the need, to see God.

# 48

THE FEAST OF THE
ASSUMPTION OF MARY

*For me a dogma is only a gateway to contemplation and is
an instrument of freedom and not of restriction. It preserves
mystery for the human mind.*

−FLANNERY O'CONNOR

The oldest and the most important of the Marian feasts is the Feast of the Assumption on August 15. It is a feast that grows out of the particular love and devotion Jesus showed his mother even as he suffered and died on the cross. It is a celebration of the courtesy of Christ to the one who bore him and nurtured him in her womb. And it is an acknowledgment of the holiness of the vessel that bore the Holy One.

Sometimes this feast is called the Dormition, or "falling asleep," of Mary. The word "assumption" refers to the ancient belief that Mary, like Elijah the Prophet (2 Kings 2:11-12), was taken up into heaven without suffering the pain or decay of death. We know this belief has been held since apostolic times. We also know that even in the Middle Ages, when the trade in holy relics was at its height, no one ever claimed to have a relic of Mary. There is a tomb near the site where she is believed to have been assumed into heaven, but it has always been empty. Today, the Benedictine Abbey of the Dormition of Mary stands on the site of the tomb.

As God, Jesus loves the whole world, but as a man, as a son, he also knows the particular bond between a mother and her child. John's Gospel says, "He loved his own in the world and he loved them to the end" (John 13:1). That speaks to Jesus's full humanity, for that is the way we learn to love, one person at a time, mother to child and child to mother. Those who are taught well learn to give love more and more, until it spreads like a balm, an ointment, on all they meet.

As Jesus hung on the cross, he took care of his own, his mother, Mary.

> When Jesus saw his mother and the disciple there whom he loved, he said to his mother, "Woman, behold, your son." Then he said to the disciple, "Behold your mother." And from that hour the disciple took her into his home (JOHN 19: 26-27).

John didn't check in on Mary or give her a call each week. He took her into his home. I hear that story and recall the first time our oldest grandchild, Lucas, spent the night with us. After prayers and many cups of water and kisses and a story and some songs, I went in to turn out the light. I heard Luc make this declaration, against the dark, against the fear: "Ma-Maw," he said, "if I call you in the night, you will come."

Jesus gives John and Mary to each other. They stand together, against the dark, against the fear. If Mary calls John in the night, he will come. The tradition holds that Mary lived with John until her death, and we can imagine the care she needed and the care he gave to her in those last days.

The tradition tells us that, as Mary's death grew closer, all the disciples gathered at her bedside. The living and the dead, from foreign lands and foreign graves—they came to be with her as she went to her Son and Savior. There's nothing in Scripture to suggest a close relationship between Mary and Peter or any of the others, yet they come as sons called to their mother's bedside. I like to think the relationships flowered and grew in John's house, as the disciples came to visit, perhaps, or to rest or to seek counsel. Maybe they came to learn more about Jesus from the woman who had raised him.

As Mary lay dying, the apostles, both the living and the dead, gathered at her bedside. The apostles, the living and dead, kept vigil and watched as Mary was taken into heaven, the flesh that had cradled the Christ never falling into corruption and decay.

It is as if God understood Mary's grief at the cross and sought to spare her further sorrow. She would die, but she would not be alone, and she would never know the darkness of the grave into which her beloved child was laid.

Because Pope Pius XII declared the assumption of Mary to be a dogma of the Church in 1950, some people think that this is a recent teaching. (The word "dogma" is from the Greek word meaning "what seems right." It is a definitive or infallible teaching of the Church, one that cannot be denied or changed. It must be found in sacred Scripture or in the postbiblical tradition of the Church and so is a teaching divinely revealed.)

The belief in Mary's assumption into heaven is ancient. When the bishops of the Church gathered in Constantinople for the Council of Chalcedon (in AD 451), the Roman emperor Marcian asked the Patriarch of Jerusalem to bring the relics of Mary to be enshrined there. The patriarch replied that "Mary died in the presence of the apostles; but her tomb, when opened later was found empty and so the apostles concluded that the body was taken up into heaven."

From this testimony it seems that the apostles did not understand God's plans for Mary any more than they understood God's plans for Christ. Both Mary and Christ were laid in tombs but did not remain there. Christ was resurrected and, forty days later, ascended into heaven; Mary fell asleep and was assumed into heaven.

The Feast of the Assumption is one of the holy days of obligation in the Roman Catholic Church. Every Sunday is a day of obligation, that is, a day when Catholics are obliged to attend Mass. In the United States, these are the holy days of obligation that may, or may not, fall on a Sunday:

*Solemnity of Mary, Mother of God* (January 1)

*The Ascension* (except in the several ecclesiastical provinces that, since 1999, have transferred this celebration to the following Sunday) (40 days after Easter Sunday)

*The Assumption of the Blessed Virgin Mary* (August 15)
*All Saints' Day* (November 1)
*The Feast of the Immaculate Conception* (December 8)
*The Nativity of Our Lord Jesus Christ* (December 25)

One way to think of this August feast is that it is Mary's harvesting home. Like a bountiful crop, she is being gathered in. When you gather to eat after Mass today, try to fill the table with the fruits of the late summer harvest. Watermelons and sweet corn and tomatoes and peaches and fresh green beans snapped off the vine weighted down with its bounty—all these foods speak of the fullness of life and fertility that is Our Lady. Mary gave life. She brought forth the Savior of the world, the fruit of her womb. As much as possible, fill your home or the home of a family in need with produce: flowers and fruits and vegetables. St. Catherine of Siena wrote of Mary that "you have given us of your flour. . . . The Godhead is joined and kneaded so thoroughly into our humanity that this union can never be broken, neither by death nor by our ingratitude." Give thanks for the one who shared her flour with us, and ask her to help us on our way.

# 49

~~~~~~~~~~~~~~~~~~~~~~~~~~~~~~~~~~~~~~~~~

## THE FEAST OF STS. PETER AND PAUL

Nothing is more practical than finding God, that is, than
falling in love in a quite absolute, final way. . . . Fall in love,
stay in love and it will decide everything.

–PEDRO ARRUPE, SJ

[Jesus said to his disciples,] If the world hates you,
realize that it hated me first.

–JOHN 15:18

The Feast of Sts. Peter and Paul is observed all over the world, but
especially in Rome, where both men died during the persecutions
ordered by the Roman emperor Nero. (Peter died around AD 64, and
Paul about three years later.) Though the New Testament does not
mention Peter going to Rome, except perhaps in code when he writes
that he sends greetings from "Babylon," that is, Rome, where he is
with Mark (1 Peter 5:13), many letters from the earliest years of the
Church speak of his presence there. When St. Ignatius wrote his Letter to the Romans around AD 107, he was in chains, on his way to his
martyr's death. Ignatius's letter, addressed to the Church of Rome,
speaks of the authority there of Peter and Paul, contrasting it with
his own comparative lack of authority: "They were Apostles, and I
am a condemned criminal" (4.3). Ignatius speaks of the two apostles
as the Church has consistently spoken of them: as co-founders of the
Church at Rome, with Peter its first bishop. Recent archaeological

finds confirm Church teachings about Peter as the first Bishop of Rome, and so our first pope.

Upon an order from Pope Pius XII, archaeological excavations under St. Peter's Basilica, inside the Vatican in Rome, took place from 1940 to 1949, under the leadership of the archaeologist Margharita Guarducci. There, under the main altar, her team found a plain wooden box in which there were bone fragments, some dirt, and scraps of cloth. Years later, when the contents of the boxes were analyzed, they were found to be the bones of a sturdily built man somewhere between the ages of sixty and seventy. What surprised the searchers was the cloth: it was very fine, a purple cloth interwoven with threads of gold. Scholars now believe that the emperor Constantine—who converted to Christianity and who, in the fourth century, built the first basilica on the site of the present St. Peter's Basilica—moved Peter's bones from their original burial spot. Wrapping the bones in royal cloth, Constantine had them placed in the catacombs beneath the church. The bones remained there, untouched, until 1941, when Guarducci found a fragment of the original red wall by the niche where the bones were kept. On it were scratched the Greek words "Peter is here." Other Greek scholars have translated the words as "Peter in peace." (You can read her book about the excavation and its findings; it is called *The Tomb of St. Peter*.)

We know from Scripture and other early documents that Paul was also in Rome. The last two chapters of Acts tell of Paul being taken in chains to Rome. The story of his martyrdom is found in books like *Church History* by Eusebius of Caesaria (AD 265–340). Eusebius quotes earlier writers, such as Tertullian, and records:

> Thus publicly announcing himself (Nero) as the first among God's chief enemies, he was led on to the slaughter of the apostles. It is, therefore, recorded that Paul was beheaded in Rome itself, and that Peter likewise was crucified under Nero. This account of Peter and Paul is substantiated by the fact that their names are preserved in the cemeteries of that place even to the present day (2.25).

There is no doubt Peter and Paul planted the church in Rome, and from there it spread throughout the earth. (Open your Bible and read the book of Acts to learn the stories of the missionaries and early leaders of the Church.)

So celebrate Peter and Paul's feast today. Consider making a flambé dessert in honor of Peter, on whom the flames of the Holy Spirit came down at Pentecost. In her book, *My Nameday: Come for Dessert*, Helen McLoughlin recommends a simple and easy-to-make-ahead treat for this day. She calls it "Snowballs-On-Fire."

Scoop ice cream into snowball-sized balls. Roll the ice cream balls in flaked coconut and place them in the freezer. When you're ready to eat dessert, cover the snowballs with your favorite ice cream sauce and insert food safe sparklers, or birthday candles, in each one. Turn out the lights in the dining room and bring in the "flaming" desserts.

The book of Acts tells us that Paul, before his conversion, was "still breathing threats and murder against the disciples of the Lord" (Acts 9:1). He was on his way to Damascus to search for and arrest Christians there when "a light from the sky suddenly flashed around him" (Acts 9:3). Paul fell to the ground and heard the voice of Jesus speaking to him.

Paul was blind for three days. During that time he neither ate nor drank. That is the beginning of Paul's ministry. In Damascus, rather than rounding up Christians and turning them over to the authorities, he began preaching to non-believers and bringing them into the church.

So a flambé dessert—the flash of light!—would work well for Paul as well as for Peter. Cherries Jubilee sounds too fancy, too much like a restaurant for most home cooks. But Mark Bittman, in his essential *How to Cook Everything*, says Cherries Jubilee is basically a simple cherry stew with a dramatic finish. Here's his recipe:

2 pounds pitted sour cherries
½ cup sugar
¼ cup brandy

Put the cherries in a medium saucepan with 1 cup of water. Stir in ½ cup sugar, or more, to taste. Turn the heat to medium-high. Cook, stirring occasionally, until the cherries are very tender (about 20 minutes). *Carefully pour the warm cherries into a chafing dish that you can safely put on the dining table, and make sure you have another adult to help at this point.* (Have scoops of vanilla ice cream ready in serving bowls.) With everyone assembled, pour ¼ cup of brandy into the cherries and carefully touch with a match. Spoon the flaming cherries over the ice cream and serve.

You could even pour the flaming cherries over the coconut balls and skip the sparklers. Fiery sweets may make the Feast of Sts. Peter and Paul the favorite of your household.

~~~~~~~~~~~~~~~~~~~~~~~~~~~~~~~~~~~~~~~~~~

# 50

# PRAYING WITH
# ST. IGNATIUS LOYOLA

Prayer is a long, loving look at the real.

—WALTER BURGHARDT, SJ

If you ever doubt the power of books to change a life, consider the story of St. Ignatius of Loyola, the founder of the Jesuit order. Ignatius, born in 1491, the youngest of thirteen children, knew his path as a child. He would be a military officer, just like his father. As a young man, he was not interested in anything but the army.

Ignatius became a soldier in service to the Spanish king, and by all accounts a good one, but he was severely injured while defending the fortress of Pamplona against a French siege. (We know Pamplona best today for its annual running of the bulls, but it was first known as a famous military stronghold in the province of Navarre.) Ignatius's legs were badly broken, and then badly set, and he faced months of recuperation in bed. He asked for novels about knights and soldiers to help him pass the time, but the only available books were stories about Christ and the saints. Anxious for any distraction, Ignatius began to read and, in his reading, he was converted. He realized that he wanted to become a soldier for Christ.

When Ignatius could get out of bed, he went to the Shrine of Our

Lady of Montserrat. He placed his sword before a statue of Mary, gave his military uniform to a beggar, and made a lifelong vow, not to the king of Spain, but to the King of the universe, Christ the Lord. For a time he lived like one of the desert fathers in a cave, where he prayed and fasted and grew in faith.

Then the man who did not like to read as a child went back to school. He started at a local grammar school, a grown man among children. He went on to the University of Alcala and then to the University of Paris, where he met six friends—among them St. Francis Xavier—who came to share his vision of a life, living for God alone. St. Ignatius became very learned and, like him, most Jesuits today receive PhDs, or doctorates, before their ordination to the priesthood.

During his lifetime, more and more people were attracted to the life Ignatius and his friends were living. They came together, the first of those who would be called the Society of Jesus, or the Jesuits. By the time Ignatius died in 1556, some one thousand men had joined the society. The earlier Jesuits called themselves "friends in the Lord." In 2013, for the first time, one of their numbers became the Bishop of Rome, Pope Francis. The Jesuit motto, attributed to St. Ignatius, is *ad majorem Dei gloriam*, or the abbreviation AMDG, which is translated into English as "for the greater glory of God." A key tenet of Jesuit spirituality is the idea of "finding God in all things." In addition to Pope Francis, there are many famous Jesuits, men like St. Francis Xavier, St. Edmund Campion, St. Aloysius Gonzaga, St. Peter Canisius, St. Robert Bellarmine, and St. Isaac Jogues.

### PRAYING WITH ST. IGNATIUS LOYOLA

To help his Jesuit brothers in their life together, Ignatius wrote the *Spiritual Exercises*, one of the great works of Christian instruction in prayer and holiness. The Ignatian *Spiritual Exercises* focus on many things, including using one's imagination, in prayer and meditation, to place one's self in the biblical story being contemplated.

You can incorporate this style of praying when you meditate on the readings of the day. The readings of the day can be found online, for example, from the Laudate app or from the USCCB website, or in your missal. Catholics believe that the Holy Spirit inspired the authors of the Bible, and many of the authors of the New Testament also knew Jesus during his ministry. So reading Scripture is one way of allowing God to speak to our hearts. Read the readings of the day slowly, and as many times as needed. Then use your imagination to place yourself in the story being contemplated. For example, if the Gospel is the story of the Wedding Feast at Cana (John 2:1-11), use your imagination to place yourself in the scene. What does the food smell like? When you hear the people grumbling, "There's no more wine," how do you feel? And so on. This technique helps you to draw on your own life experiences to enter more deeply into the Scriptures and the life of Christ.

## DAILY EXAMINATION OF CONSCIENCE OR "THE EXAMEN"

This is a simplified version of the five-step daily Examen that St. Ignatius practiced and required Jesuits to practice twice daily at noon and at the end of the day. Try doing the examination of conscience before falling asleep.

1. Become aware of God's presence. Be still and know that God is present. Ask for God's grace to help you in reviewing your day, to direct your attention where it will be most useful.

2. Express gratitude. Give thanks to God for all the gifts received. Know that God is at work in your life. Savor all the moments of goodness in your day.

3. Review your day. Watch it like a movie in your head. Ask for God's grace to know your sins. Where could you have been more loving? Pay attention to your emotions. When we reflect on the times we did or did not act with God's grace, we can be more sensitive to developing better habits. We can become aware of our need for God.

4. Repent, express sorrow, or ask forgiveness for the times you failed to follow God's will, and ask Him to be with you the next time you encounter a similar situation. Give thanks to

God for the grace that enabled you to follow His will freely. Choose one feature of the day and pray from it.

5. Resolve to cooperate with God's grace and guidance. Look toward tomorrow. Ask God to help you to put your hope and trust in him.

You might conclude with a prayer such as the Our Father or with a prayer by St. Ignatius Loyola called Suscipe or Receive.

Take, Lord, and receive all my liberty, my memory, my understanding and my entire will. All I have and call my own, You have given to me; to you, Lord, I return it. Everything is yours; do with it what you will. Give me only your love and your grace. That is enough for me.

The Examen can also be adapted for use with young children. Focus on gratitude and forgiveness. For young children this might mean asking, "What made your heart happy today?" "What made your heart sad?" As the children grow, the questions grow in complexity or depth: "What helped you grow closer to God today?" "What drew you further away?" The focus is never on shame or blame, but on those practices or acts a child will want to embrace or avoid.

## 51

THE MEMORIAL OF
ST. ELIZABETH OF PORTUGAL AND
THE FOURTH OF JULY

Saint Elizabeth was a peacemaker from birth, a quality that
was totally out of character with her family tradition.

−MARY REED NEWLAND, *The Saint Book*

For most of us who live in the United States, the Fourth of July is a
national holiday, one we mark with picnics and fireworks. For the
universal Church, the Fourth of July is the Memorial of St. Elizabeth
of Portugal. For Third Order Franciscans, whose patron she is, it's a
day to remember the saint who has a special care for their work and
prayer.

A source of confusion for American Catholics arises when the Fourth of July falls on a Sunday and we are tempted to treat this national holiday as a feast day of the Church. Which means that not all the Fourth of July fireworks go off outdoors, at night. Some of them explode in churches on Sunday morning, as the customs of a national holiday celebration collide with the practices of the Universal Church.

We are reminded at Mass, again and again, that we worship with brothers and sisters throughout the world. We are limited by time and space. We are limited to a place, to a people. The God we worship, the Lord and Creator, transcends time and space to gather us all into one as we sing and pray, take bread and bless, take wine and give thanks. We bow and bend as one. We receive from God's gracious hand.

This is not simply an ecclesiastical conceit. We are joined at Mass with Christians in Iraq and North Korea, in Haiti, Cuba, and Venezuela. We are joined at Mass with Christians from countries that are at war with us. Our bond in the Body and Blood of Christ transcends border and race, government and tribe. We are the "one flock," with "one shepherd," that Jesus describes in John 10:16b.

The order of the Prayer of the Faithful reminds us of this every Sunday. We pray first for the world, then for the church throughout the world, and only last for the needs of our local parish.

Still, we love the places where we live. I know the pleasure of driving into the high north plains of the Texas Panhandle, that cloud-dappled and sun-shot sky, stretching out before me as far, and farther, than I can see. And I know the pleasures of returning north and west, back to the mountains I now call home.

I have lived in Colorado Springs for more than thirty years. There is a strong military presence here. It is a place where thousands of men, women, and children know, in their flesh, the costs of war. I unfold the paper many mornings to the news of more soldiers from our local army post killed or injured in foreign wars.

One of the flashpoints at church is the music we sing when the Fourth of July falls on a Sunday. Music directors and choir leaders all across the land know they will get letters and phone calls and e-mails no matter what they choose or omit to sing on the day. There is the "America the Beautiful" crowd—particularly strong here, in the birthplace of the song Katharine Lee Bates composed atop Pikes Peak—and there is the "My Country, 'Tis of Thee" crowd. There are even a few who think "The Star-Spangled Banner"—no matter that no one can hit those "rockets' red glare" notes—is the only appropriate closing hymn for the day. "We should sing these songs," they will tell you; "they're in the hymnal." Which, in most American hymnals, they are.

"America! America! God shed His grace on thee," covers a lot of ground, all of which stops at the border. "The bombs bursting in air" cross the border, but not in the ways in which we are called to cross borders as the Mystical Body of Christ.

A few years ago our music director introduced a new selection to the parish on a Sunday Fourth of July holiday. "This Is My Song," sung to the tune "Finlandia," by Jean Sibelius. Lloyd Stone and Georgia Harkness wrote the lyrics. All three of them had witnessed the destruction of world wars fought in their lifetimes.

> *This is my song, O God of all the nations, / A song of peace*
> *for lands afar and mine. / This is my home, the country where*
> *my heart is;/ Here are my hopes, my dreams, my holy shrine;/*
> *But other hearts in other lands are beating,/ With hopes and*
> *dreams as true and high as mine.*
> *My country's skies are bluer than the ocean,/ And sunlight*
> *beams on cloverleaf and pine./ But other lands have sunlight,*
> *too, and clover,/ And skies are everywhere as blue as mine./So*
> *hear my song, O God of all the nations,/ A song of peace for*
> *their land and for mine.*

I have heard the song called "patronizing" for what many see as a grudging admission of the obvious, that people in other lands have "hopes and dreams as true and high as mine." But there are guarded borders everywhere, even within churches. And this song has helped bring about a truce in my parish, and a crossing over. For that I am grateful.

Even when the Fourth of July does not fall on a Sunday, it is important for Catholics to remember and celebrate the saint whose memorial it is, a saint whose holiness crossed borders, a saint whose life's work was to bring peace among warring nations. So have a picnic and light sparklers in the night sky. Or gather and watch the community fireworks go off. But remember that the Catholic Church is not a national one. It does not belong to any particular people or land or tribe or language. As you have a beer today, drink one in honor of St. Elizabeth, and make her story part of the celebration.

## ST. ELIZABETH OF PORTUGAL

Elizabeth was a twelve-year-old Spanish princess when she married Denis, the king of Portugal. She never gave herself over to the luxuries of the court. Elizabeth's heart was with the poor of her country. Her concern was for the peace of her family and her home. Elizabeth bore and raised two children. She cared for lepers and established hospitals for the care of the sick. She built the first school to teach farming methods. She built orphanages and hostels for pilgrims and strangers. She donated money so that poor girls, who had no dowries, would be able to marry.

Elizabeth and Denis's son, Afonso, grew so angry at the favor he believed his father showed to his illegitimate sons that he rebelled. In 1323 the father and son declared war on each other. Elizabeth rode on horseback onto the field of battle. She put herself between the two armies and reconciled her husband and her son. She is known as the peacemaker.

King Denis lived a dissolute life while his wife lived a prayerful one. It seems that he found her piety tiresome. Then he fell ill, and Elizabeth never left his side. Blessed by Elizabeth's goodness, Denis repented. She cared for him faithfully until his death.

The widowed Elizabeth left the palace and moved to a convent of Poor Clares. In order to do the work to which she was called, Elizabeth put off taking vows until shortly before her death. She left the convent once during these years, when her son, Afonso IV, marched against his son-in-law, the king of Castile.

When Elizabeth heard the news, she hurried once again to the field of battle. The sixty-five-year-old woman was not well when she set out, and the journey hastened her death. But she never wavered in her plans, telling her sisters that she could think of no better way to spend her life and health than by stopping a war. Yes, she might die, but how many would die if war broke out? She went to Estremoz, where the two kings faced each other, ready to fight. Elizabeth stopped the war and arranged a reconciliation.

On her deathbed, it is said that Elizabeth begged her son to put down his weapons and to seek peace. May her plea take root and grow in all our lives.

The most famous miracle attributed to Elizabeth is the miracle of the roses. One day in winter she was leaving the castle, her long skirts gathered to her and filled with loaves of bread. Her husband had heard rumors that Elizabeth was taking food from their larders and distributing it to those in need. He confronted her and demanded to see what she was carrying. Elizabeth answered, "Roses, my lord."

Since it was winter, King Denis refused to believe her and ordered her to open her skirts. When she did so, roses poured out upon the ground.

When, and if, you are buying groceries for a cookout or picnic on the Fourth of July, remember to buy food to be donated to your local soup kitchen or food pantry in Elizabeth's honor and name, and tell your children the story of St. Elizabeth, the peacemaker.

# AUTUMN ORDINARY TIME

~~~~~~~~~~~

# 52

# THE FEAST OF THE ARCHANGELS

*For he commands his angels with regard to you,*
*to guard you wherever you go.*

*–PSALM 91:11*

"Angel" is a word that means "messenger of God." They are, as Augustine explains, spirits who have a special function. Out of all the angels mentioned in Scripture, only three are called by name: Michael, Gabriel, and Raphael. Before the reform of the calendar, each of these archangels had a separate feast. Now we celebrate them all on this one day, Michael's day (September 29) or, as it is called in some places, Michaelmas.

Angels are difficult for us to contemplate. Often they are reduced to greeting card illustrations or viewed as vague deities. It's easy to believe that either Hallmark Company or a daytime talk show guru invented them, but angels as incorporeal messengers of God are found in Scripture and are referenced in each of the Abrahamic religions: Christianity, Judaism, and Islam.

The name "Michael" means "Who is like God?" And in Revelation 12, Michael is shown casting out of heaven those angels who think the answer to that question is "I am."

Perhaps because presuming to be like God is the primary sin,

Michael is known as the protector of Israel and the protector of the Church. In the Eastern Rite Catholic Church, he is known as "the Prince of the Seraphim." He stands guard against those who take to themselves what belongs to God alone.

Gabriel—"God is my strength"—is the bringer of good news. Gabriel interprets Daniel's visions (Daniel 8:16-26; 9:20-27). Gabriel brings the news that John the Baptist will be born to Elizabeth and Zechariah (Luke 1:19-20). Gabriel appears to Mary and tells her she is to be the Mother of God (Luke 1:26-38). Tradition holds that Gabriel will sound the trumpet to awaken the dead on the Judgment Day.

Raphael's name means "God has healed." The story of Raphael and the healing of Tobit's elderly blind father is told in Tobit 11:1-15. This book is filled with stories of the archangel. In Tobit 12, the angel declares, "I am Raphael, one of the seven angels who stand and serve before the Glory of the Lord" (Tobit 12:11-150). In his Gospel, John tells the story of a sick man lying by the pool of Bethesda (John 5:2-9). He wants to go into the waters, which, according to tradition, were stirred up by Raphael. Jesus tells the man, "Rise, take up your mat, and walk." The man is healed (John 5:8).

The Church teaches that each of us has a guardian angel. The image, then, is of a multitude of heavenly helpers surrounding us, leading us, protecting us. (And, by protection, the Church does not necessarily mean safety. It means keeping our hearts and souls in God and with God, whatever may come.) It may seem a bit over-whelming to think of this multitude of beings until you consider how God has established the order of creation. The Godhead is itself a community: Father, Son, and Holy Spirit. We are made in the image and likeness of God, made to live, like God, in community. How fitting, then, that there is an angelic community keeping faith with the earthly community of which we are a part.

There are nine ranks, or choirs, of angels. When we understand the nature of each rank, we understand what St. Augustine meant when he said, "The name angel belongs to its office, not to his nature. You ask what is the name of his nature. He is a spirit. You ask what is the name of his office. He is an angel."

## SERAPHIM

The seraphim are stationed at the throne of God. It is from their lips that we have the song we sing at Mass, "Holy, Holy, Holy, Lord God of Hosts." When the prophet Isaiah had a vision of God "seated upon a high and lofty throne," he saw the seraphim in attendance (Isaiah 6:1-9).

## CHERUBIM

Like the seraphim, the cherubim continuously praise the beauty and might of God. They are described in the book of Revelation as double-winged beings "covered with eyes inside and out." Their eyes gaze always on God's glory (Revelation 4:1-11).

## THRONES

These are angels of humility, of peace, and of submission. They stand as guards of a sort between the higher and lower spheres. You must pass through this rank to reach the heavenly kingdom. What do you need to make the journey? You need humility, peace, and submission.

## DOMINIONS

Dominions are messengers. They relay messages from God to the angels who interact with human beings and the material world.

## VIRTUES

They are called "the shining ones." Their role is to encourage human beings in lives of grace, valor, and courage.

## POWERS

These are warrior angels whose only role is to defend us against evil and to strengthen our own stand against evil.

## ARCHANGELS

The archangels are the most frequently mentioned in Scripture, as they are the angels God uses most often in face-to-face encounters with human beings.

## PRINCIPALITIES

In St. Paul's letter to the Colossians, he writes of thrones, dominions, principalities or powers (Colossians 1:16). Have you ever wondered what he was talking about? He's talking about angels. He even names principalities, which is the general term for heavenly beings that are now in rebellion against God and hostile to the human beings God has made. You may wonder why principalities would be included in the ranks of angels. It is, as Paul makes clear in several New Testament letters, because Christ is sovereign over all that is, even over those in rebellion, even over those who set their faces against him.

## ANGELS

Angels are the closest to us humans and to our world. They bear messages from the heavens to earth, and our guardians are found among their ranks.

## NAME DAY

If this is the name day for any of the Michaels, Michaelas, Gabriels, Gabriellas, Raphaels, or Raphaellas in your life consider serving a dessert like tapioca pudding or something ethereal in appearance and taste.

## PRAYING WITH ANGELS

There are two verses from the Outer Hebrides, dedications that you can use to invoke the angels as you begin the day. The first is for the kindling of the fire. For us, that might mean plugging in the coffee pot or turning on the heat:

I will kindle my fire this morning
In the presence of the holy angels of heaven.

And this is for making your bed:

I make this bed
In the name of the Father, the Son and the Holy Spirit,
In the name of the night we were conceived,
In the name of the night that we were born,
In the name of the day we were baptized,
In the name of each night, each day,
Each angel that is in the heavens.

As you begin this day, ask God to help you be a protector, a bringer
of good news and a healer, this day and every day.

Angel of God,
my guardian dear,
to whom God's love
commits me here,
ever this day,
be at my side,
to light and guard,
to rule and guide.

Amen.


INVOKING THE ANGELS

For an angel of peace, faithful guardian and guide of our
souls and our bodies, we beseech thee, O Lord. Amen.
—FROM THE ORTHODOX TRADITION

# 53

# THE FEAST OF ALL SAINTS

*Come to our aid, O saints of God. Come to*
*meet us on our journey.*

—ANTIPHON FROM VESPERS ON THE FEAST OF ALL SAINTS

We tend to think of Halloween as a singular celebration, a day for dressing in costumes and getting candy. But Halloween is a door to the more important feast, Hallowmas, or, as it is better known, the Feast of All Saints. We learn that from its name: "All Hallows Eve," or Halloween, is not a stand-alone day. It is the vigil of the Feast of All Saints. The word "hallow" means "holy," so Halloween is the vigil of the Feast of the Holy Ones.

One of the things we know about evil is that it hates holiness and tries, always and everywhere, to destroy it. We also know that God, who is Goodness, will triumph over evil. So it makes sense to have a vigil celebration where we make fun of monsters and ghosts and all the manifestations of death in our midst. We are the people who know how the story ends, and so we can rejoice.

If Halloween is about rehearsal and remembrance, All Saints' Day, which dates from the seventh century AD, is a banquet table set with the fruit of rehearsal and remembrance. We begin with the banquet table that is the altar of the church, for the Feast of All Saints is a holy day of obligation. Make sure that going to Mass is at the center of your observance, because this is a day for children to glimpse the grown-up life for which they are rehearsing, a day for adults to remember the grown-up life to which they are called.

The celebration of the Feast of All Saints continues at the day's main meal. Consider inviting some of the trick-or-treaters who came to your door in the darkness of Halloween to come to your table for an All Saints' dinner. If Halloween is a snack-sized candy bar and bubble gum, All Saints' is homemade bread and roast chicken with potatoes, a feast that will, as my mother, and probably yours, said, "stick to your ribs."

You can find paper autumn leaves at craft and discount stores during this season, or cut your own. Write one guest's name on each leaf. Then write something about the saint for which each guest is named. For an Eva, you might write, "The mother of all the living." For a Stephen, you might write, "The first deacon and the first martyr." If the guest has a name that is not a saint's name, look for one that is close, like "James" for a "Jaden." (Also inquire about middle names, or for older children, Confirmation names. Sometimes the saint's name is tucked in there.) For flower names, look to Scripture: "The Lily of the Valley," or "The Rose of Sharon."

Put a leaf on the plate of each guest, child and adult. Read the names aloud. Have stories ready to tell about each saint or attribute of God. Encourage questions. Recall the saints known to the whole church, and remember the holy men and women known to our parishes and our families and neighborhoods. Talk about favorite saints and odd saints and funny saints and challenging saints.

You could sing "For All the Saints" as a table prayer or have someone read Revelation 7:14b-17 aloud. Pray in thanksgiving for the men and women, so various, from every place and time, every race and tribe, who have witnessed to the love of God and neighbor with their lives and in their deaths. Asking the saints to pray for us reveals how saints can, and do, become companions on the way, sturdy friends and faithful helpers.

The Feast of All Saints invites us to sit at a table with those whose days of practice and rehearsal, of striving and seeking, are done. They are whole and healed, forever in the presence of the One who made and pursues us all.

Don't make the mistake of separating Halloween and All Saints' Day. Keep the link, and enjoy the day. Consider making a lemon and herb roasted chicken with vegetables for your main dish.

Conclude your meal with this prayer from *A Christian's Prayer Book*, published by Franciscan Herald Press. (You may need to shorten the prayer, depending on the ages of your guests. The first two lines of the prayer might be just right for very small children at the table.)

> Father, you are the source of all holiness. Through the
> prayers and examples of your saints, lead us to holy lives.
>
> As you have called us to be perfect in love,
> so make us perfect in your service.
>
> Lord Jesus Christ, you came to serve, not to be served.
> Make us truly humble in your service and in service to our
> brothers and sisters.
>
> The saints bore your cross willingly throughout their lives;
> enable us to bear any suffering in this life for your sake.
> We thank you, Lord, for those who have chosen poverty or solitude
> for your sake, for men and women of prayer, for saints in every
> walk of life, and for all who in purity of life have endured pain with
> patience in the strength of Christ Jesus our Lord.
>
> Amen.

## 54

~~~~~~~~~~~~~~~~~~~~~~~~~~~~~~

# THE FEAST OF
# ST. THÉRÈSE OF LISIEUX

In the heart of the Church I will be love.

–ST. THÉRÈSE OF LISIEUX

On October 1 the Church celebrates the Feast of St. Thérèse of Lisieux. Thérèse lived a short and seemingly unremarkable life, in a quiet corner of northern France. She was a cloistered Carmelite nun, totally unknown outside the walls of her convent. In fact, her life was so ordinary that her Carmelite sisters were unsure what to write in her obituary when she died at the age of twenty-four from tuberculosis, having seemingly achieved so little.

Thérèse was the daughter of devout parents Zélie and Louis Martin, themselves now canonized saints, and the youngest of nine children (five of whom entered religious life). Her parents attended daily Mass and raised their children to see all people as brothers. They regularly invited the poor to dine in their home and visited the sick and homebound.

Thérèse was the baby of her family and by all accounts a spoiled child. She refused to do housework and indulged herself in fits of tears whenever she was disappointed. She was highly emotional and very stubborn, but as the baby of the family, she was also adored. Her mother died when she was only four, and she grieved her terribly, but she was devoted to her sisters and her father. Eventually, she had a conversion experience and found that she was able to put childish ways aside and think of others. After begging everyone (from her father, to her local bishop, to Pope Leo XIII himself), she received a special dispensation to join two of her older sisters in the Carmelite monastery at Lisieux at the age of fifteen. For the next nine years, until her painful death from tuberculosis at twenty-four, she lived what looked like an unexceptional life inside the convent. She prayed, did housework, and read. But quietly and without fanfare, she battled temptations of temper and taste, preference and mood. In her pursuit of holiness, she made a point of performing the most unpleasant tasks and eating the most unpleasant foods without complaint.

Thérèse recognized that—by the world's standards—she was never going to lead an especially noteworthy life. Indeed, like her, most of us will lead ordinary lives. We will never be rich or famous, run countries or corporations, or appear on TV. And yet, Thérèse came to believe that all of us are called to perform hidden acts of love and sacrifice, small acts done with great love. As the Catechism of the Catholic Church puts it, "Love is the fundamental and innate vocation of every human being" (CCC, 2392). Or, to paraphrase 1 Corinthians 13: 1-4, if we do not have love we are nothing.

Servant of God Dorothy Day once described Thérèse of Lisieux as "the saint we need" because Thérèse knew that it was the small acts done hour by hour and day by day that constitute a character and build a life.

Thérèse wrote in her autobiography, *The Story of a Soul*, that she longed to be of great importance, to be a missionary to foreign lands or a knight like Joan of Arc, but she understood that it was the "little way," a lifetime of mundane tasks done with great love, that surely leads all souls to heaven.

After her death *The Story of a Soul* was published and went on to become an international bestseller. In it Thérèse describes what she terms "a little way of spiritual childhood." She advocated small deeds done without complaint, offered up to God. The "little way" might look like the alcoholic who faithfully attends AA meetings, or a family member being yelled at, who stubbornly refuses to yell back.

Thérèse understood that most of these small acts would not be recognized by anyone but God, yet she taught that Christians are called to turn the other cheek, and keep on turning it, until it becomes who we are. She writes in her autobiography of going out of her way to befriend the crankiest nun in her community, or choosing not to complain when she was falsely accused of an offense. Thérèse felt that it was a privilege to suffer for Christ who suffered so greatly for mankind. Like John the Baptist, who said of Jesus, "He must increase, I must decrease," Thérèse of Lisieux accepted her littleness without bitterness and found peace within it.

Many see Christianity as a religion of hypocrites. From this perspective, Christians are people who think they have all the answers, people who go around and try to "save" others.

St. Thérèse reminds us that the Christian path is more about submitting to grace and getting one's own house in order, and then, not with arguments, but with one's life, being a force for good in the lives of others.

It was her wisdom, not her scholarship, that led Pope John Paul II to name her a Doctor of the Church on her feast day in 1997. He wrote:

> This young Carmelite, without any particular theological training but illumined by the light of the Gospel . . . feels that the words of Scripture are fulfilled in her: "Whoever is a little one, let him come to me. . . . For to him that is little, mercy shall be shown" . . . and she knows she is being instructed in the science of love, hidden from the wise and prudent, which the divine Teacher deigned to reveal to her, as to babes.

When we are struggling to love those who are hard to love, we can look to St. Thérèse and pray that we, too, might learn "the little way." After all, she promised before her death that she would pass her time in "heaven doing good on earth."

## COOKING WITH EDIBLE FLOWERS

Thérèse is known as the "Little Flower," so if you are celebrating the name day of another Thérèse or Theresa today, consider using edible flowers, like roses, nasturtiums, or pansies, in a salad or to decorate a cake. Check with your grocery store and inquire as to what edible flowers they sell. If you use flowers from your garden, make sure they are pesticide free.

## ST. THÉRÈSE'S MORNING OFFERING

O my God, I offer you all my actions this day for the intentions and for the glory of the Sacred Heart of Jesus. I desire to sanctify every beat of my heart, my every thought, my simplest works, by uniting them to His infinite merits; and I wish to make reparation for my sins by casting them into the furnace of His merciful love.

O my God, I ask of you for myself and for those whom I hold dear, the grace to fulfill perfectly Your holy will, to accept for love of You the joys and sorrows of this passing life, so that we may one day be united together in heaven for all eternity. Amen.

# 55

~~~~~~~~~~~~~~~~~~~~~~~~~~~~~~~~~~~~~~

## DIA DE LOS MUERTOS AND
## ALL SOULS' DAY

It is a holy and wholesome thought to pray for the dead.

-2 MACCABEES 12:46, DOUAY-RHEIMS AMERICAN EDITION

The devotion to the memory of the dead is one of the most
beautiful expressions of the Catholic spirit.

-POPE JOHN XXIII

Madeleine L'Engle writes, "The death of a beloved is an amputation."
Even Jesus, who conquered death in the resurrection, stood and wept
at the grave of his friend Lazarus. We often act as if death does not
exist, but anyone who has lost someone knows that we have a need to
mourn and remember, and to recall the promises of Christ.

On November 1, Catholics celebrate All Saints' Day, a day marked
on the church calendar as one of only six holy days of obligation.
We attend Mass and say prayers of thanksgiving for both the well
and little-known saints, some of them, perhaps even from our own
communities, people who have inspired us and who, we believe, are
interceding for us in heaven.

On November 2, Catholics celebrate All Souls' Day. On this day
we remember all of the dead and pray for the souls in purgatory. It
might be as simple as praying, "Lord have mercy on them." Purgatory
is the stage after death where most of us will spend time, undoing the
damage we've done to ourselves and getting ready for heaven. And

who wouldn't want a chance to clean up and shower and change clothes before meeting God? In the second century, Tertullian spoke of purgatory. We also find it in the writings of Origen, St. Cyprian, and St. John Chrysostom, who said, "Let us not hesitate to help those who have died and to offer prayers for them."

In Mexico and elsewhere, these first two days of November are a national holiday called Dia de los Muertos or the "Day of the Dead." People use their time to remember their loved ones who have passed away. They visit graves and clean and decorate them. Others build small shrines in their homes with pictures, letters, mementos, or other reminders of those they have lost. Some place these pictures and mementos on a shelf, or surround them by candles, a cross, or a picture of the Blessed Virgin. Gravesites are often adorned with marigolds, a Marian flower. Some people prepare the favorite foods of their loved ones who have died and have a picnic. Families might also say a prayer or sing a song for the deceased. Others bake "soul cakes," sweet bread in a circular shape to symbolize the infinite nature of heaven.

These Day of the Dead celebrations vary from place to place. In Brazil, Mexico, and Spain there are parades featuring Catrina figures, small wooden skeletons, dressed as they would have dressed in life. In parts of Brazil people fly kites. In Haiti there are all-night celebrations involving loud music and drums.

At some Catholic churches in the United States, there are All Souls' Day processions, after which people write prayers for the dead on slips of paper and burn them. In San Diego there is a two-day celebration, which culminates in a candlelight vigil in the cemetery. In the Philippines, as in Mexico, tombs are cleaned and repainted, candles are lit, and gravesites are decorated with flowers. Then, entire families camp out for several nights, playing cards, eating, drinking, and celebrating.

Most Americans would not feel comfortable sleeping in a cemetery. For one thing, it might be against the law, but there's no reason that American Catholics can't carve out a small space in their home to place mementos of loved ones who have died, or, similarly, to visit a cemetery and say a prayer at the graves of those they have lost. When you have a picture of someone you admire who has passed away looking down at you from the wall, it is a reminder to honor that person with your life.

There are, in fact, many activities that people could engage in during this time of remembering. Older children might interview a parent or grandparent about a relative who has passed away. Ask a parent or grandparent about their parents' favorite foods, the biggest fight they ever had, how they reconciled, or what their family traditions were. What was their wedding like? Who was there?

Young children can also help bake soul cakes. Giving and receiving soul cakes door-to-door was the basis of the American practice of trick-or-treating.

Some Christians may be distressed by the fact that the Day of the Dead has many pre-Christian parallels, for example, Aztec festivals honoring the dead and worshiping the goddess of the underworld. Yet this should not be reason for concern, as we worship the Trinity, not other gods. Yes, there are many points of connection between Christianity and other religions, both ancient and modern. Christianity does not obliterate the unique cultural heritage of a people. Rather, the Church takes what is good and true in a culture and re-interprets it in light of the Christian story, that is, the Gospel. This is known as inculturation. For example, many of the Gospel writers used pre-existing Greek philosophical concepts, such as the Logos (the Word), to help their Hellenistic audiences come to a deeper understanding of Christ. Yes, there are festivals honoring the dead in every religion, but Catholics see these points of connection as evidence that throughout all of human history people have had a need for reverence, an intuition of an afterlife, and a longing for the one true God.

### Eternal Rest Prayer

Eternal rest grant unto them, O Lord, and let perpetual light shine upon them. And may the souls of all the faithful departed, through the mercy of God, rest in peace. Amen.

### Prayer at the Gravesite

*ALL MAKE THE SIGN OF THE CROSS.*

Praise be to God our Father who raised Jesus from the dead. Blessed be God forever.
*R./ Blessed be God forever.*

Pick a reading from Scripture:

### 2 Corinthians 5:1

*FOR WE KNOW THAT IF OUR EARTHLY DWELLING, A TENT, SHOULD BE DESTROYED, WE HAVE A BUILDING FROM GOD, A DWELLING NOT MADE WITH HANDS, ETERNAL IN HEAVEN.*

### Romans 8:38-39

For I am convinced that neither death, nor life, nor angels, nor principalities, nor present things, nor future things, nor powers, nor height, nor depth, nor any other creature will be able to separate us from the love of God in Christ Jesus our Lord.

After a time of silence all join in prayers of intercession or in a Litany of the Saints of the beloved dead asking them to pray for us. Everyone then says the Lord's Prayer.

*Our Father who art in heaven, etc.*

Then a prayer:

> Lord God, whose days are without end
> and whose mercies beyond counting,
> keep us mindful
> that life is short and the hour of death unknown.
> Let your Spirit guide our days on earth
> in the ways of holiness and justice,
> that we may serve you
> in union with the whole Church,
> sure in faith, strong in hope, perfected in love.
> And when our earthly journey is ended,
> lead us rejoicing into your Kingdom,
> where you live forever and ever.
>
> Amen.

Eternal rest grant unto them, O Lord. And let perpetual light shine upon them. May they rest in peace. Amen. May their souls and the souls of all the faithful departed, through the mercy of God, rest in peace. Amen. (All make the sign of the cross.)

May the peace of God, which is beyond all understanding, keep our hearts and minds in the knowledge of the love of God, and of his son, our Lord Jesus Christ. Amen.

# 56

# MARTINMAS AND LANTERN WALKS

I am a soldier of Christ and it is not lawful for me to fight.

–ST. MARTIN OF TOURS

November 11 is the Feast of St. Martin of Tours, also known as Martinmas. Like his father before him, Martin of Tours was a soldier, and an honorable one. He longed to be a monk, but the law demanded that sons of soldiers become soldiers themselves, so Martin went to serve the Roman emperor. The tradition holds that St. Martin, when he was still a catechumen, came upon a beggar shivering with cold. Moved to pity, Martin took off his fine wool officer's cloak and tore it in half, giving one half to the freezing man. Later that night, in a dream, Christ appeared to St. Martin, wrapped in Martin's cloak and saying, "See! This is the mantle that Martin, yet a catechumen, gave me." Martin woke and decided to be baptized.

After his baptism, he experienced a crisis of conscience. He knew in his heart that he could not serve two masters and said, "I am a soldier of Christ and it is not lawful for me to fight." So St. Martin became a "conscientious objector" and was thrown in prison for refusing to serve in the army of the Roman emperor. He told his emperor, Julian, "Put me in the front of the army, without weapons or armor; but I will not draw sword again." Enraged, Julian told Martin he would have his wish; he would be sent into the thick of the battle unarmed. Until the battle began he would be a prisoner of the emperor. Miraculously, the other side sued for peace and Martin's life was spared.

After he was released from prison, Martin became a Benedictine monk and eventually the bishop of Tours, a large city in what is now France. His compassion and generosity, along with his humble service to the poor, brought many people to the Church. As Martin was dying, members of his flock wept and begged him not to leave them. Bishop Martin became one of the first non-martyrs to be canonized.

Martinmas is a lesser-known feast, so feel free to celebrate it with friends or children on any day in November, and no one will likely be the wiser.

For some Catholics, Martinmas is like a little Mardi Gras, since it comes before the penitential season of Advent and signals the beginning of winter.

There are many traditions associated with St. Martin's feast. One is baking sugar cookies in the shape of horseshoes for St. Martin's horse.

## MARTINMAS RECIPES

Roll sugar cookie dough out flat with a rolling pin. Then cut it into long strips and curve them into horseshoes. If you have a child who loves to play knights, tell her the story of St. Martin of Tours while your cookies bake.

Then prepare a traditional St. Martin's day treat for the grown-ups such as a mulled wine.

## CLEAN OUT YOUR CLOSET

Since St. Martin is famous for following Jesus's command to clothe the naked, clean out a closet, basement, or attic, and donate your unused coats to a shelter in his name or call your local shelter and ask them what they need.

## LANTERN WALKS

Another tradition is to make lanterns and walk with them in the evening around your neighborhood or church, perhaps bringing banana bread or soup to a neighbor's house as a way of honoring St. Martin.

As winter approaches, the days are getting shorter and the nights are getting longer, so this is an excellent time to start praying with candles or to make lanterns and meditate on Jesus and the saints, who bring light into the world with their sacrificial love.

## TIN CAN LANTERNS

Making tin can lanterns is easy and inexpensive. This is a good craft for adults or children age six and older. Simply empty and wash a tin can (removing any labels). Fill it with water and put it in the freezer. Carefully, placing the frozen can on a towel, use a hammer and nail to pound holes through the can (freezing the can beforehand makes it less likely that you will crush the can). After the can has dried, paint it with bright colors and attach a bit of wire hanger to make a handle.

## PAPIER-MÂCHÉ LANTERNS

You can also make lanterns by blowing up a balloon and then covering the bottom two-thirds of the balloon with bits of colored tissue paper dipped in a flour and water mixture (which acts as a glue). Hang the balloons on a clothesline until they dry completely. Once they are dry, take them down and cut off the end where the balloon had been tied. Poke a hole in either side of the tissue paper and tie a piece of yarn or string across the opening to make a handle. This handle can be hung from a stick. Insert your votive into the opening.

## GLASS JAR LANTERNS

Mason jars with handles make beautiful lanterns, no decoration required. Before you light the votives placed in your lanterns, turn off the lights. You might sing a hymn like "O Radiant Light, O Sun Divine" or, if you have young children, "This Little Light of Mine." Or you could say a prayer such as this one:

> Jesus Christ is the Light of the World.
> R/ A Light no darkness can extinguish.

Then go for a walk outside with your lanterns and bring a neighbor something good to eat. When you come back home you can enjoy apple cider, or spiced wine and cookies, perhaps sharing stories about the people who have been the light of Christ in your life.

〜〜〜〜〜〜〜〜〜〜〜〜〜〜〜〜〜〜

# 57

# THE FEAST OF
# ST. FRANCIS OF ASSISI

St. Francis is the man of poverty, the man of peace, the man
who loves and protects creation.

–POPE FRANCIS

October 4 is the feast of St. Francis of Assisi, one of the best known
and most loved of all Catholic saints. St. Francis was canonized just
two years after his death, in 1228. Pope Francis chose him as his
namesake at the start of his papacy in 2013.

St. Francis lived several lives. Born in 1182 in Umbria, Italy, he
was the privileged son of a wealthy cloth merchant. As a teenager, he
wore fine clothes, traveled with his father on business trips, and got
drunk with his friends. He lived a worldly twelfth-century life.

At the age of twenty-one, at the beginning of the thirteenth century, his world began to change. At the height of the Crusades, he
went off to become a knight. In a battle between Assisi and Perugia,
Francis was captured and imprisoned. He was held in a dark cell for a
year before his father was able to obtain his ransom. After his release,
he became ill and experienced a spiritual crisis and conversion. He
spent long days praying alone in a tiny abandoned church outside the
city walls. Francis's life embodies what G. K. Chesterton once said:

"There are saints indeed in my religion, but a saint only means a man who really knows he is a sinner."

Prior to his conversion, Francis had always been repulsed by lepers and the poor and had gone out of his way to avoid them. At the time, lepers were so feared that they were forced to carry a bell wherever they went, announcing that they were unclean.

One day, when riding on his horse, Francis saw a leper. Moved by God, he gave the man his cloak and kissed his face. Francis wrote in his "Testament" shortly before his death, "God allowed me to begin my repentance in this way: when I lived in sin, seeing lepers was a very bitter experience for me. God himself guided me into their midst and among them I performed acts of charity. What appeared bitter to me became sweetness of the soul and body."

After this encounter, in prayer before a crucifix, Francis heard a voice telling him, "Repair my church which, as you can see, is falling into ruins." At first, he took this calling literally and began repairing the village church. Later he came to understand this to be a calling to repair the Church in the broadest sense.

Francis sought to imitate Jesus, who chose to live in solidarity with mankind—the poor and violent sinners—even to the point of death on a cross. Francis rejected his formerly materialistic ways and began to give away his possessions, indeed, his very life, in service of God and neighbor.

This troubled Francis's father, because Francis was set to inherit his father's cloth business. To prevent everything he had worked for from being given away, his father took Francis to court. At the trial, in a wild and transgressive act, Francis stripped off his clothes until he was naked, and returned them to his father, declaring that from this point forward he would serve only his Father in heaven. He was then covered with a peasant's cloak, which he marked with a cross.

Francis set out to live a life of prophetic Christian witness. The Franciscan rule was simple: "To follow the teachings of our Lord Jesus Christ and to walk in his footsteps."

Some thought Francis was crazy, others beat him, and still others threw dirt on him, but Francis's kindness and cheerfulness also attracted followers. By 1208, twelve people had renounced their possessions and come to share in his way of life. They would become the first Franciscans.

They owned nothing, not even shoes, and spent their days preaching, praying, repairing churches, helping poor farmers, and tending to lepers and outcasts. They accepted food in exchange for their labor but stored nothing. Franciscans embraced that belief that freedom from disordered attachments, even an excessive attachment to one's own life, was the path to deep and abiding joy. As Jesus says, "Whoever seeks to preserve his life will lose it, but whoever loses it will save it" (Luke 17:33).

In 1210, Pope Innocent III formally recognized Francis's order, after meeting with Francis, and having a dream in which he saw him holding up the church of St. John Lateran, the parish church of all Christians. Francis was tonsured by Cardinal Colonna and made a deacon.

## ST. CLARE OF ASSISI

Women were also among Francis's early followers. St. Clare of Assisi was a rich young woman when she heard Francis preach. Her heart was moved, and she decided to pursue a life of voluntary poverty. Clare's family wanted her to marry a rich young man and bring wealth and power to the family. But she refused, sneaking out of the house at night to meet her guide and friend. She traded her fine clothes for rough sackcloth and offered her jewels for Francis to give to those in need.

When her family discovered that Clare was missing, they suspected that she had run off to join Francis, and dragged her back. But she would not relent. She cut her hair and persisted in wearing the same kind of rough garment as Francis and his followers. Finally, they let her go, and she become one of Francis's first companions. Thousands would follow her example, including her sister, Agnes, who was also canonized.

Clare eventually served as the abbess to her female companions who lived in a house near the church of San Damiano in Assisi. Like Francis, she was known for performing the lowliest tasks on behalf of others. When her sisters returned from a journey, Clare knelt and washed their feet. Because they were discalced, that is, they did not wear shoes, this was an arduous and messy task. She also served at table, though there was seldom much to eat.

People tried to give Clare and her sisters gifts of land and live-stock, but they would own nothing. They called themselves the Poor Ladies. Clare said, "They say that we are too poor, but can a heart which possesses the infinite God be truly called poor?" Her order, like Francis's, lives on. Today they are called the Poor Clares.

## FRANCIS'S IMPACT ON THE CHURCH AND THE WORLD

Francis had a profound impact on thirteenth-century life in general, and on the life of the Church and of the world. In his book *St. Francis of Assisi*, G. K. Chesterton writes that Francis was, like all saints, an antidote to his age. When Muslims and Christians were killing one another over territory, Francis chose to own nothing, so there would be nothing to fight over. He embraced being called a fool for Christ. Chesterton writes, "The conversion of St. Francis . . . involved his being in some sense flung suddenly from a horse. . . . There was not a rag of him left that was not ridiculous. Everybody knew that at the best he had made a fool of himself. . . . [But] the word 'fool' itself began to shine and change."

The mendicant orders are often credited with saving the Church, by bringing the Church's focus back to the example of Christ. In an age of violence and excess, Francis was committed to Gospel nonviolence and a radical poverty. He obeyed Jesus's command to love all, especially enemies, and taught that it was blasphemous to take the life of a human being, created in the image and likeness of God. Francis lived the Gospel in all its strangeness, and was fearless in his commitment. He even went so far as to attempt to convert the sultan of Egypt to Christianity, not by violence, but by encounter. He jumped on a ship to Egypt and spoke to him face-to-face.

## THE SPIRITUALITY OF DETACHMENT

It might seem strange to us that, despite living in extreme thirteenth-century poverty, Francis was known for his joy. Many of the spiritual masters—St. John of the Cross, St. Augustine, and St. Ignatius Loyola—warn Christians about unhealthy attachments to possessions, power, or the opinions of others. Material things or wanting to be well liked are not bad in and of themselves, but true happiness can never come from possessions or status, and our unhealthy attachments can easily become addictions. Social scientists speak of the hedonic treadmill: once we acquire something we thought would make us happy, a new car, for instance, the happiness is only temporary, and we soon want an even nicer one. We are never contented, never free.

St. Francis's life demonstrates that true freedom comes from finding our self-identity in God. When we are looking to God and allowing God to do the work of forming us into who we are supposed to be, we are not as attached to the status that comes with possessions or the opinions of others. Because St. Francis was not attached, he was free to go where the Spirit led, and free to experience a kind of childlike joy in the birds of the air, the moon, and the stars. Jesus said,

> *"Blessed are you who are poor,*
> *for the kingdom of God is yours.*
> *Blessed are you when people hate you,*
> *and when they exclude you and insult you,*
> *and denounce your name as evil*
> *on account of the Son of Man"* (LUKE 6:20, 22).

Fr. Robert Barron suggests that in this passage Jesus is saying, "How blessed you are if you are not attached to material things. . . . How lucky you are, how happy and blessed you are if you're not addicted to good feelings." You are free.

Francis was free, and in his freedom he chose to praise. He was devoted to the Church, especially Jesus in the Blessed Sacrament, and he loved the natural world. In nature he saw a reflection of God's love. He is the patron saint of animals and the environment.

There are many legends involving St. Francis and his ability to communicate with animals. When he preached, the birds seemed to gather and listen, and when a wolf was terrorizing a village, the villagers credited Francis with convincing the wolf to leave the townspeople alone.

Because of his association with animals, some Catholic parishes offer a blessing for pets on Francis's feast day. The blessing of the animals often takes place after Mass and is a favorite event among children. People bring dogs and cats, but also hamsters and fish. In rural communities, it's not uncommon to see horses, llamas, or cows. The blessing of the animals is a way of acknowledging that all of creation belongs to God and is under God's hand.

In the same way that Francis followed Jesus's example to give the shirt off his back to the man in need, we can follow his example and cultivate in our prayer lives a sense of detachment and a willingness to follow God's will. Too often prayer is used in public life to explain what we did, or defend what we want to do. Inspired by St. Francis we can learn to pray, "Thy will be done."

As St. Francis said on his deathbed, "I have done what was mine to do. May Christ teach you what you are to do."

### St. Francis's Prayer in Praise of God, Given to Brother Leo

You are holy, Lord, the only God, and Your deeds are wonderful.

You are strong.

You are great.

You are the Most High.

You are Almighty.

You, Holy Father, are King of heaven and earth.

You are Three and One, Lord God, all Good.

You are Good, all Good, supreme Good, Lord God, living and true.

You are love.

You are wisdom.

You are humility.

You are endurance.

You are rest.

You are peace.

You are joy and gladness.

You are justice and moderation.

You are all our riches, and You suffice for us.

You are beauty.

You are gentleness.

You are our protector.

You are our guardian and defender.

You are our courage.

You are our haven and our hope.

You are our faith, our great consolation.

You are our eternal life, Great and Wonderful Lord, God Almighty, Merciful Savior. Amen.

### St. Francis's Prayer Before the Blessed Sacrament

We adore You,

O Lord Jesus Christ,

in this Church and all the Churches of the world,

and we bless You,

because,
by Your holy Cross You have redeemed the world. Amen.

### St. Francis's Meditation Prayer
My God and my All!

### St. Francis's Blessing to Brother Leo
The Lord bless you and keep you;
May He show His face to you and have mercy.
May He turn His countenance to you and give you peace . . . Amen.

# 58

# THE FEAST OF MARY'S PRESENTATION IN THE TEMPLE

Today she who will receive the Holy of Holies . . . is . . . placed
in the Holy of Holies with holiness and majesty.

–ST. GERMANUS OF CONSTANTINOPLE (PATRIARCH OF CONSTANTINOPLE,
715-730), FROM THE FIRST HOMILY ON THE PRESENTATION

This November 21 feast comes from an ancient story, recorded in the seventh chapter of the *Protoevangelium of James*, an apocryphal work that scholars believe was written before the year AD 200. ("Apocrypha" is a Greek word meaning "hidden things." Apocryphal books are Christian books that tell of the life of Jesus. They are not included in Scripture, that is, they are not canonical, and the Church has formally rejected some of them. The *Protoevangelium of James* is not one of the formally condemned books. It is an early popular work that enlarges upon apostolic teaching, in this case, about Mary.)

The *Protoevangelium of James* includes a story about Joachim and Anne, Mary's parents, bringing their three-year-old daughter to the Temple in Jerusalem to dedicate her life to God's service. Why did they wait until Mary was three? The story says that Anne was afraid that if they brought Mary at a younger age, she would miss her parents too much. It is a sweet moment, and it rings true, especially when we consider how long Joachim and Anne waited for a child.

Mary was their only one, and we can understand how reluctant they were to let her go.

The writer of this early account tells us that Joachim and Anne invited other young girls in the town to accompany Mary on her way. The girls were given lit torches to carry as they walked. The fire so captivated Mary's attention that she did not cry at the prospect of leaving her parents. It is the kind of protective gesture that every parent can imagine making. The ancient story goes that when Mary entered the Temple, the priest cried, "The Lord has magnified your name in all generations. In you ... the Lord will manifest His redemption to the sons of Israel" (7.7).

It is said that Mary's parents gave her to the priest, who took the little girl into the Sanctuary, the Holy of Holies. Her parents, who could not follow her there, left the Temple, rejoicing *and* grieving, one imagines, as Mary began the preparation for her role as the Mother of God. Mary's entrance into a period of prayer and preparation is why, in the Eastern Rite, this feast is classified as one of anticipation. Mary's entrance into the Temple anticipates Jesus's entrance into her womb and, from her womb, into the world.

In the sanctuary she was placed on the third step of the altar and there she danced for joy. The Temple sanctuary was to be her home for the next nine years, after which time she was betrothed to Joseph. The Scriptures, which are mostly silent about Jesus's childhood, are completely silent about Mary's life before the annunciation. But it is worth noting that Christians early on accepted the stories recorded in the *Protoevangelium of James* as true, both to the testimony of the apostles and true to their own experience and understanding of Mary. The Roman emperor Justinian built a church in the Temple area of Jerusalem and dedicated it to Mary. It was consecrated in 543, and it is from the date of the consecration that we get the date of the feast.

If you are a Roman Catholic, you may not be familiar with this November 21 feast, which came to the West from the East in the fifteenth century. But if you are part of the Eastern Church, where this feast has been celebrated since the early days, chances are this is an important day for you. The Feast of the Presentation of Mary is one of the twelve major liturgical feasts of the Eastern Rite year, feasts that are together known as the Dodecaorton. (The Dodecaorton is made of six feasts of Christ: Nativity, Baptism, Presentation in the Temple, Entry into Jerusalem, Transfiguration, Ascension; four feasts of the Virgin: Nativity, Presentation in the Temple, Annunciation, Dormition; and the eleventh and twelfth: Pentecost and Elevation of the Cross.)

In the east the day is called "Entrance of the Mother of God into the Temple." Mary will herself become the Temple, the sanctuary where God dwells. Through baptism and the Eucharist, we too are invited to become temples where God has a home.

Rejoice in this commemoration that falls so near the beginning of the season of Advent. Mary and Joseph search for a place where God may be born. The search goes on, in each of our hearts and in each of our lives, for a place where God may be born and grow.

## PRAISE OF MARY

> *A virgin's womb becomes the shrine*
> *That holds the Lord of heaven and earth,*
> *Through stainless maid, by grace divine,*
> *The God-child hath his wondrous birth.*
>
> *Her modest breast is made his home,*
> *The temple of her God is she;*
> *Enshrined in Mary's spotless womb,*
> *He comes the world from doom to free.*

—SEDULIUS, FIFTH-CENTURY POET AND
CONVERT TO CHRISTIANITY

# 59

# THE FEAST OF THE CONCEPTION OF JOHN THE BAPTIST

St. John Apostle of the Lord,
Lead us to Jesus.

-FROM THE LITANY TO ST. JOHN THE EVANGELIST

On June 24, both the Eastern and Western Catholic Church celebrate the birth of John the Baptist. On September 23, the Eastern
Rite churches celebrate his conception. (Count nine months from
September 23 and you'll be right at the feast of John's birth on June
24.) John and Jesus are repeatedly linked in Scripture and in the remembrances and practices of the universal Church, but we find them
emphasized most strongly in the east. For instance, on January 7, the
day immediately following the Feast of the Epiphany, the Eastern Orthodox Church keeps the Commemoration of St. John the Forerunner. John is not the Lord, but he is the precursor, or forerunner, of the
Lord. Jesus describes John in this way: "among those born of women
there has been none greater than John the Baptist" (Matthew 11:11a).

In the fourth and fifth centuries, St. Jerome preached on the conception of John in his Homily 87, on John 1:1-4:

But this man has been sent from God, "whose name was
John," and whose name corresponds to his calling. The name

"Ioannes" is interpreted as the grace of the Lord, for "io" means Lord and "anna" means grace. And so John is called the grace of the Lord. His mission as messenger he receives from the Lord.

John's parents, Elizabeth and Zechariah, are in a line of stories told in Scripture about faithful couples who ask God for a child but cannot conceive. Like Sarah and Abraham (Genesis 18:9-15), they are elderly. Like Hannah and Elkanah (1 Samuel 1:4-11), they have prayed for a child. Like Manoah and his wife (Judges 13:2-5), they will, after long years of waiting, bear a son who is to be dedicated to God from the womb. Elizabeth and Zechariah's son, John, will join the company of these holy ones—Isaac, Samuel, and Samson—whose life is given to serving God.

The angel of the Lord comes to Zechariah and tells him they will have a son, whose name will be John, and "he will be great in the sight of the Lord" (Luke 1:15). This news is so surprising that Zechariah is struck mute and remains silent until after his child's birth. (You can read this story in Luke 1:5-25.)

After John's birth, Zechariah's tongue is freed once he has bestowed on his son the name the angel gave him. After his long fast from speech, Zechariah proclaims a hymn of praise to God. This hymn, called the Benedictus, is part of the Morning Prayer of the Roman Church. "Benedictus" means "blessed," and "Blessed be the God of Israel" is the first line of the song, or canticle. (The Magnificat, or Mary's hymn of praise, is sung as part of Evening Prayer.)

Although the Feast of the Conception of John the Baptist is not in the Roman calendar, there is no reason that all Catholics, east and west, cannot join in honoring John's conception today. In an age when unborn children are regularly aborted, it is a gift to stop and reflect on the truth the Church proclaims: God knows us before we are born. We exist from the moment of conception, and God has a purpose for our lives.

## JOHN IS THE PATRON OF SHEPHERDS

John the Baptist, he who proclaimed Jesus the Lamb of God (John 1:29b), is the patron of shepherds. Most of us don't know any sheep-herders, but most of us do know people who are called to shepherd children. Not all of these shepherds are parents. Some are priests and nuns, teachers and coaches, aunts and uncles. Some are the shepherds of the disabled and ill of all ages. Consider helping one of these good shepherds in their work today. Ask the patron of the shepherds to help them, too.

> St. John, you are the Evangelist,
> Teach us to know and serve the Lord.

## JOHN IS THE PATRON OF MASONS, THOSE WHO BUILD OR WORK IN STONE

John the Baptist, who, quoting the prophet Isaiah, said of himself,

> I am the voice of one crying out in the desert,
> Make straight the way of the Lord.

Because of this self-description, John the Baptist is also the patron of masons, those who build or work in stone. Masons, or bricklayers, make straight ways. Consider straightening something in your life that has become twisted. It may be a relationship or a daily practice or a habit of thought. Ask the patron of masons to help you.

> St. John, Beloved of Jesus,
> Help us to love Jesus.

## JOHN IS THE PATRON OF TAILORS

Because John the Baptist fashioned his own garments out of animal skins when he lived in the desert, he is also the patron of tailors. What in your life is ripped or torn? What needs to be repaired, sewn together, or mended? Ask the patron of tailors to help you.

St. John, you did not abandon the Lord in Calvary,
Strengthen us in our faith in God.

## THE BENEDICTUS

Sing or say the Benedictus, Zechariah's song, in your Morning Prayer today. The version below, from the Lutheran hymnal *With One Voice* (Augsburg Fortress Publishing House, 1995), is set to the English folk tune "Forest Green." Because "Forest Green" is a common meter doubled hymn, it can be sung to other common meter hymns, like "Amazing Grace." You'll just sing that familiar tune twice ("doubled") on each of the stanzas.

> *Blessed be the God of Israel who comes to set us free*
> *And raises up new hope for us: a branch from David's tree.*
> *So have the prophets long declared that with a mighty arm*
> *God would turn back our enemies and all who wish us harm.*
>
> *With promised mercy will God still the covenant recall,*
> *The oath once sworn to Abraham, from foes to save us all:*
> *That we might worship without fear and offer lives of praise,*
> *In holiness and righteousness to serve God all our days.*
>
> *My child as prophet of the Lord you will prepare the way,*
> *To tell God's people they are saved from sin's eternal sway.*
> *Then shall God's mercy from on high shine forth and never*
> *   cease*
> *To drive away the gloom of death and lead us into peace.*

~~~~~~~~~~~~~~~~~~~~~~~~~~~~~~~~~~~~~~~~~~~~~~~~~~~

# 60

# TWO MARIAN FEASTS IN SEPTEMBER

She reaches out her hand to the poor,
and extends her arms to the needy.

–PROVERBS 31:20

Two important days in the Church calendar are observed one week apart: the Feast of the Nativity of the Blessed Virgin Mary on September 8 and the Memorial of Our Lady of Sorrows on September 15. The link between the joy of Mary's birth and the pain she will know throughout her life reminds us of that other week, stretching from Palm Sunday to Easter Sunday, in which joy and pain meet. Like Mary, we weep and we rejoice. We know sorrow and succor, and all of it in the way and the will of God, all of it in faith and hope.

## THE FEAST OF THE NATIVITY OF THE BLESSED VIRGIN MARY

One traditional Marian image is the Mother of God as a fruitful field. Christ is the great harvest, the blessed fruit, of her womb. It seems fitting, then, that the feast of Mary's birth is celebrated on September 8, as the harvest is drawing to a close and the days of thanksgiving begin. (If you count, you will see that September 8 falls nine months after December 8, which is the Feast of the Immaculate Conception.)

We don't know from either Scripture or tradition where or when Mary was born, but her nativity has been celebrated since the early days of the Church. Sometime in the 500s, St. Romanos the Melodist, an Eastern Christian hymnist, composed a hymn for the feast. That suggests the feast was known even earlier than the sixth century. The feast spread from the east to the west in the seventh century.

Traditionally, wine growers brought the grape harvest to church to be blessed on this day. Farmers traditionally brought harvested crops and winter seeds to be blessed. It is a day for all who sow seeds of faith and charity to pray that they may bear and reap a rich harvest.

Bake a birthday cake today and share it with friends and family. Sing your favorite Marian hymn, something simple and easily sung like "Immaculate Mary." Or tell this story from the thirteenth-century *Legends of Mary*:

> A hermit had on a certain night for many years heard music in the heavens. When he asked the cause an angel answered, "The Virgin was born this night, and what is ignored on earth is being celebrated by angels."

## MEMORIAL OF OUR LADY OF SORROWS

When we think of the sorrows of Mary, we usually think only of the cross. But the Church speaks of the Seven Sorrows, or Dolors, which cover her entire life. This feast dates from at least the twelfth, and possibly, the eleventh, century. Pope Pius X fixed the current date of the feast in 1913.

There are Seven Sorrows: the prophecy of Simeon that a sword would pierce Mary's heart (Luke 2:33-35); the flight of the Holy Family into Egypt (Matthew 2:13-15); the loss and finding of the Child Jesus in the Temple (Luke 2:41-52); Mary meeting Jesus on the way to Calvary (from the ancient tradition); Mary standing at the foot of the Cross as

Jesus is crucified (John 19:25); and the burial of Jesus (Matthew 27:57-61). Many of these sorrows are familiar to parents everywhere.

### THE FLIGHT INTO EGYPT

Refugee mothers and victims of domestic violence know Mary's fear as she fled her home and went hurriedly to Egypt. Could she let any of her family know she was leaving? Could she bring any keepsakes on the journey? Did they know anyone in Egypt to welcome the family and help find work for Joseph and a home for their baby?

### LOSING JESUS IN THE TEMPLE

What parent hasn't known the panic of losing a child? Mary and Joseph had set out on their journey home from the Temple in Jerusalem when they realized Jesus was not with them and the other pilgrims. How far had they walked when they had to turn back and search for their son? What worries did they share as they looked for Jesus? How could they understand his gentle rebuke of them as Jesus let them know he would have to be about his father's business? What parent hasn't sorrowed as a child leaves the refuge of home to go out into a world where joy but also danger and affliction await?

### STANDING VIGIL AS JESUS DIES

How many parents have watched a child suffer and die? How many mothers have cradled a dead child in their arms? In Mary's sorrows we have a companion and a guide in our own sorrows. As she received each new sorrow trusting in God, we can ask her to help us grow in trust and faith, in courage and hope. We can ask her to share her strength with us. We can cry out to her knowing that she understands, in her pierced flesh, the pain we bear. It's interesting that the name by which this feast was listed in the fifteenth century Roman Missal is "Our Lady of Compassion." The word "compassion" comes from two Latin roots: *cum* and *patior*, which together mean, "to suffer with." When someone we love is in pain, we feel that pain.

As Jesus's mother she had to suffer with him more than any other human being who ever lived. As our Blessed Mother, she suffers with us as we grieve and worry.

### THE DAILY CONCERNS OF RAISING A CHILD

Mary knows the daily difficulties of raising a child. We know that Jesus was human, just like us in all things except sin. That means he would have had the same energy and made the same clumsy mistakes as any small child. One of the readings for Mass on the Memorial of Our Lady of Sorrows is 1 Corinthians 11:17-26, 33. In this letter, St. Paul counsels the Christians in Corinth about coming together to "eat the Lord's supper." He chides them for bad manners, for eating while another goes hungry, for going ahead and eating without waiting for the rest of the community. Paul sounds like a mother here, and we can imagine that Mary cautioned the young Jesus not to gulp his food, not to come to the table without washing his hands first.

Are you sorrowing today? Go to Mary and ask for help. Blessed Teresa of Calcutta encouraged her sisters to pray, "Mary, please be a mother to me now." Do you know someone who is grieving? Consider what you can do to help. Take Mary at the cross as your example. She can't intervene or change the horror unfolding before her. But she can be present. She can bear witness. She can listen to the last words of her son. Just to be present to another's pain, to listen and not to look away, can be a gift and a source of comfort and peace.

Say the Memorare today. It is said to have been composed by the Franciscan St. Bernard of Clairvaux in the twelfth century:

> If the storms of temptation arise, if you crash against the rocks of tribulations, look to the star, call upon Mary. If you are tossed about on the waves of pride, of ambition, of slander, of hostility, look to the star, call upon Mary ... If you begin to be swallowed up by the abyss of depression and despair, think of Mary! In dangers, in anxiety, in doubt, think of Mary, call upon Mary.

# CHILDHOOD TO ADOLESCENCE

# 61

# HOW TO NAME A CHILD

For I am called by your name, O Lord, God of hosts.

–JEREMIAH 15:16B

Among a parent's first task is naming the newborn child. Catholic parents have an additional duty: to root the child in the tradition of the saints and angels, of Christian virtues, and of the holy men and women in whose footsteps we pray our children will walk. When we talk about the tradition we're not talking about a crowd from which we need to stand apart, but about a community we are called to stand within.

Think of the Catholic way of naming as both grounding and goal—this is where we plant our child and this is what we pray, that he or she grows in wisdom and in grace, like the holy ones who have gone before.

Naming roots the child in a tradition going back to Adam, who is named by God and who is tasked, in turn, with naming all the animals

(Genesis 1:19). Naming is revealed as a gift and a responsibility given by God to humankind. In the Scriptures, names are understood to disclose something of the nature of the person who bears them.

When the angel Gabriel comes to Mary to announce that she will conceive and bear the Son of God (Luke 1:26-38), the angel brings something else, the child's name. Mary is told, "You shall name him Jesus." In Hebrew, the name "Jesus" means "God saves." The name reveals both the child's identity and his mission.

When Jesus chooses Simon, son of Jonah, to be the rock upon which Jesus will build his church (Matthew 16:17-20a), he gives Simon a new name. "And so I say to you, you are Peter and upon this rock [petra] I will build my church." His new name is Petrus (though Paul calls him Cephas, from a Greek word meaning "stone"), and his new name reveals that he is to be just that, a rock upon which the Church will stand, a foundation stone for the Church that will arise.

It wasn't always the case that Gentile converts to the Christian faith took new names. Peter baptizes Cornelius, a Roman centurion (Acts 10:44b-49), and there is no record of Cornelius changing his name. Nevertheless, the custom of taking a Christian name (which, of course, Cornelius now is) began early. The first recorded case of a Christian changing his birth name to one that spoke of his faith is St. Ignatius of Antioch (died c. 110), who called himself Theophorus, "the God-bearer."

As the Church grew and spread throughout the world, local names, such as among the Celts in Ireland or the Slavs in what is now Bosnia, were kept by the newly baptized, but an effort was made to conform the old name to the new ways. The Celtic Diarmaid becomes the Latin Jeremias. The converted seventh-century Slav king Rudoslav names his son Petroslav. And he, in turn, names his son Paulimir. When converts, like Aethelwold of England or Deirdre of Ireland or Thekla of what is now Turkey, began to be recognized as saints, their names became Christian names. St. Charles Lwanga, the best known of the Ugandan Martyrs, has a traditional Christian first name and a traditional Ugandan surname.

By the fourteenth century, the common practice of giving saints' names to children at their baptism was codified in canon law.

Names are so important to Catholics that the very first question of the baptismal rite for infants and children is "What name do you give your child?" Each Catholic name is understood to be part of God's own name, as it is known in the lives of the saints and in the revealed nature of God. The name calls the child to honor God and those who have borne the name in ages past. That is why Catholic names often seem too big for their tiny bearers. The names John Paul or Wilhelmina may seem to weigh more than the eight-pound person who wears it. Don't worry. Rather, think of it the way you think of finding a piano for a beginner: You don't buy a plastic toy, even if that might seem more suitable to the child's current abilities. You look for a real piano in the hope of seeing the child become a real pianist. The hope with a child's name is that he will grow into his, that she will grow worthy of hers.

Children may be named after saints. A mother who, like Hannah, has wept and prayed to be given a child, might have turned to Hannah for help in the months and years of hoping. She might name a daughter after Hannah, or after Samuel, the child for whom Hannah prayed.

Parents may name a child after a saint to whom they have a particular devotion, such as Guadalupe, for the Virgin as she appeared to Juan Diego, or Michael, the guardian angel and patron of workers from police to grocers.

Parents may name a child after an aspect of God: Grace or Mercy. They may name a child after an attitude of thanksgiving, such as Adeodatus (God's gift), the name Augustine of Hippo chose for his son in the fourth century.

They may name a child after a Christian virtue: Hope or Faith (Fides or Fidelis) or Charity. Parents may wish to honor the lives of those family members or friends who have died, or whose living example is one to admire and imitate. This can be a way to connect the child to countries or peoples of origin, a Polish name for an immigrant Grandfather Stanislaw or a Haitian Creole name for a beloved Aunt Micheline. Both of these names are saint's names (Stanislaw was a bishop in eleventh century Poland, and Micheline is a variant of Michael), though perhaps not familiar to us.

What if the name of a beloved friend or relative is not a saint's name? It is a deeply Catholic impulse to honor another by giving her name to a child. Just pair it with the name of a saint or angel. So you might have a parent who bears as his first name a relative's last name, Logan or Rusk. The child could be named Joseph Logan or Joan Rusk. You might have a friend who is named after a season or a place, like Autumn or Madison, rather than after a Christian saint or Christian virtue. Simply combine the name of the beloved friend with a saint's name: Mary Autumn or Anthony Madison.

Parents can simply wait and see when a baby arrives, and name the child for the saint of the day. This is fairly uncomplicated if a child arrives on June 24, the Nativity of John the Baptist, whose name, in one form or another, both masculine and feminine, is known throughout the world. It is perhaps more complicated if a child is born on October 14 and is given the name Callistus, a currently uncommon name, both in its spelling and its sound. But for Catholic parents who desire to root their child in the tradition while finding an unusual and little known name, the daily Church calendar is a rich source. Americans often worry about giving a child a name that will be shared with five other students in the preschool. So they look for the different and the new. That can lead to names that, while unusual, are unanchored and unmoored. Be of good cheer: Your Abraham or Sernin or Perpetua may have to learn to spell that name slowly, and often, but chances are a Philippina will be the only one in her class, while also being part of our rich tradition of holiness and strength.

Parents often make lists of possible names during the months before a child is born. Take this time to read about the saints. Find someone whose life you would hope to emulate, someone whose life can be a guide and a goal for your child.

~~~~~~~~~~~~~~~~~~~~~~~~~~~~

# 62

# BAPTISM, GODPARENTS, AND CELEBRATIONS

In the birth that is from the water, let them
rejoice and be blessed!

–EPHRAIM SYRUS, FOURTH CENTURY

Baptism is the way in which Catholics receive members into the Body of Christ, the Church. And just as the Israelites crossed the Jordan River as they left their wandering in the wilderness for freedom under God's covenant, we come into the Church through water. Just as Jesus began his public ministry by undergoing baptism in the Jordan River, we acknowledge our new life as Christians by going down into the waters of baptism.

Like a wedding, a baptism is a public celebration of promises already made. A bride and groom go to the altar having pledged themselves to each other for life. At the wedding, they make those pledges in front of their community. Their pledges are witnessed by a priest on behalf of the community, both the one gathered at this time, in this place, and on behalf of the Church universal, bound through time and space by the love of Christ.

So the baptized are already offered to Christ—the child by his parents, the adult by her own will and action. Baptism is the public celebration of the grace that has brought these children and these adults to the font, where its blessed water is both the grave of sin and the life-giving womb of the church. Consider what the word "baptism" means. It is from a Greek word *baptizein*, which means to "plunge" or to "immerse." In baptism, we are plunged into the living waters of Christ, where all that is of God flourishes and grows, and all that is not of God withers and dies.

The Church teaches that in baptism we are marked with an indelible sign of faith. Nothing can erase this mark. Consider all the names by which we are called during our lifetimes. Consider how many of those names speak to our losses and our lacks. Consider how many of those names are meant to belittle us and dismiss us. But the Church tells us we carry in our flesh, wherever we go, our true names, the mark of our first and final belonging: Beloved of God, Sons and Daughters of the Most High. Our given names, then, should speak of our new lives and of our vocations.

Choosing godparents, like choosing a name, is a solemn act. If you are choosing them for an infant or child, think of the people best able to help form your child in faith. Who is ready and able to give a defense of the hope that is within us? (1 Peter 3:15) Who lives a life worthy of emulation? Who best conforms to St. Paul's exhortation to the Corinthians:

> Be on your guard, stand firm in the faith, be courageous, be strong. Your every act should be done with love (1 CORIN-THIANS 16:13).

Ask that person to stand as godparent.

The Church requires at least one godparent who is a practicing, confirmed Catholic age sixteen or older. There may be another person who is Christian but not Catholic, whom you wish to involve in your child's faith life. That person may be present at the baptism as a "Christian witness," but it is the Catholic godparent who will sign the baptismal certificate and go on record as the child's godparent.

The signs of baptism are water and the word. The priest pours holy water over the one to be baptized three times, saying, "(N.), I baptize you in the name of the Father, and of the Son, and of the Holy

Spirit." The bishop, priest, or deacon is the ordinary minister of baptism, but in an emergency any one person can baptize another using the trinitarian formula of Father, Son, and Holy Spirit. The one who performs this emergency baptism must intend what the Church intends in order for the sacrament to be valid. The Church makes such allowances because of the importance of the sacrament.

Happily, most baptisms are planned and scheduled and celebrated within the Church, where, because of its centrality to all Christian life, all sorts of wonderful smells and bells surround the central sign.

## WHAT TO EXPECT AT A BAPTISM

The child's name is given and the Church welcomes the child. The welcome is made flesh when the presider traces the sign of the cross on the child's forehead and invites the parents and godparents to do the same. (This sign is like an eternal tattoo or brand. We are marked as members of Christ's flock.) The Scriptures are proclaimed and, heartened by the accounts of God's faithfulness through the ages, we bring our prayers and petitions before God. A litany of the saints is added to the intercessions. (Talk to your pastor about including in the litany some saints important to you and your family. Your child is going to need help, and so are you. Don't be afraid to ask for help.)

Then we get to the part of the rite some people find confusing or troubling, the exorcism. Just the word makes people nervous. The Prayer of Exorcism in infant baptism is a strong and clear declaration of intent—to drown sin in the blessed waters of baptism—and a prayer for the child, for strength to continue to put sin to death.

> We pray for this child: set him (her) free from original sin,
> make him (her) a temple of your glory,
> and send your Holy Spirit to dwell with him (her).

The child will be anointed on his breast with oil, "the oil of salvation." In ancient Rome, athletes were rubbed down with oil before a contest. Catholics know, to use St. Paul's example, that the life of faith is a race, one we pray to run well, and so we keep this custom

(2 Timothy 4:7). The winner in a Roman race was crowned with the victor's laurel wreath, which is why martyred saints are shown in art with laurel wreaths.

Then the water in the font is blessed, after which the parents and godparents renounce sin and profess their faith. They model what they hope the child will one day declare and do for him- or herself.

Then the child is baptized and anointed for a second time, on the crown of her head, with the chrism of salvation. (When you hold your baby close, pay attention to the way the sweet aroma of the oil on her head lingers, sometimes for days. Inhale the fragrance, and give thanks.)

Finally, the child is clothed in a white garment, a sign of the new creation, and presented with a lit candle. A sign of Christ, the light no darkness can extinguish. At this part of the rite, the priest prays:

> May he (she) keep the flame alive in his (her) heart. When
> the Lord comes, may he (she) go out to meet him with all
> the saints in the heavenly kingdom.

You might want to add this prayer to your daily prayers for your child.

Then comes the prayer, called the Ephpheta (Mark 7:33-35), over the child's ears and mouth. When you think of the sounds and sights bombarding our children, the earbuds and smart phones awaiting them, the need for this prayer becomes very clear. We pray that their ears may be opened to hear God's word and their mouths opened to proclaim faith in God. You might add this part of the prayer to your daily prayers as well:

> May the Lord Jesus . . . touch your ears to receive his word,
> and your mouth to proclaim his faith, to the glory of God
> the Father.

The rite concludes with the Our Father and the blessings of the parents. Father Alexander Schmemann has written that to bless a person is to name that person rightly, as a gift from God. So when the Church blesses the parents, it names them rightly and gives them a name worthy of their new vocation, as "the first teachers of their child in the way of faith."

## CELEBRATIONS

If you are baptizing a child and have a family baptismal gown, use it. Or borrow an often-used gown from a friend. The blessed oil of many baptisms soaks into the fabric, as the smoke of votive candles soaks into the walls of a holy place. Or make the baptismal gown yourself from a simple pattern.

Throw a party in the church basement, in a park, or at home. Friends and family can bring dishes for a potluck. Consider foods connected to the name or names of the newly baptized. St. Dorothy's symbol, for example, is a basket of fruit and flowers. For a Madeline, consider making the madeleine cakes that bear her name. In Scotland, there is a tradition of serving St. Michael's bread, which is like a scone. For a David, make cutout cookies in the shape of crowns, or Stars of David. Almost any book of saints will give examples of symbols and attributes to spark ideas for dishes. But you don't need favors or candles or decorations or special table settings. All you need are the newly baptized, family, friends, food, and good cheer.

~~~~~~~~~~~~~~~~~~~~~~~~~~~~~~~~~~

# 63

# DAILY BREAD RECIPE AND LEARNING ABOUT THE BREAD OF LIFE

*A smell of fresh bread filled the house—this was comfort, security, peace, community.*

—DOROTHY DAY

This wheat bread recipe is easy to make on your own or with small children. It's healthy, makes your house smell great, and has only a handful of ingredients. I've made it with my kids and their friends. Flour gets everywhere, and they try to eat the dough raw, but they also enjoy kneading it, and they devour the rolls when they come out of the oven. So if you're in the mood, it's worth the mess.

Making bread together is a pleasantly sensual activity. Everyone gets to unplug, spread flour on a piece of parchment, sink their bare hands into warm dough, shape or braid it however they please, and watch as the dough goes into the oven. Thirty minutes later all the cooks can return to the table and feast on warm rolls.

Making and eating a meal together, whatever your stage in life, is good in itself, but the experience also makes it easier to understand why a loving God might have chosen to make his presence known in the world through food. In the wilderness, God provided manna, or "bread from heaven," for the children of Israel during their forty-year exile (Exodus 16). And in the New Testament, Jesus multiplies a few

fish and a few loaves, until the five thousand have had their fill (Matthew 14:13-21).

Bread has played an important role in the Church throughout the ages. There are countless examples of God showing his care for his people by providing them with food. Jesus tells us in John's Gospel, "I am the bread of life; he who comes to me will not hunger"; and we experience Jesus as "the bread of life" every Sunday in the Eucharist (John 6:35). After the resurrection, Jesus even cooks bread and fish for his disciples on the shore of the Sea of Galilee and tells them to "come, have breakfast" (John 21:12). What's more, Jesus commands his disciples to feed others, telling Peter, "Feed my sheep. Feed my lambs" (John 21:15-17). So baking bread links the little church that is the home to the larger Church, and it seems like a fitting Sunday afternoon activity.

If you're baking with young children, encourage them to shape the dough into stars and hearts, snakes and lizards, whatever they please. They can play with it, just like clay. While they work, you might consider asking them why they think Jesus calls himself the bread of life.

Share with them that in ancient times, and in the Bible, bread was the basic source of sustenance. People didn't get to eat as many different kinds of foods as we do today. Ask your children if they have ever been hungry and how it felt, and what it felt like when they finally got something to eat.

You might tell them that just as our bodies weaken when we don't feed them the right foods, so too do our hearts and minds need to be fed. When we don't go to Mass, or take time to pray, or treat one another with kindness, we sense that something is missing, and that something is Jesus, the bread of life, our teacher and our God. Just as food feeds our bodies, so, too, does the love of God feed our souls.

If you're baking alone, meditate on a God who chooses to come into our bodies as food.

Children learn by doing. Maria Montessori once said, "The preparation of the child for his full participation in the life of the Church is a much wider thing than the learning by heart of certain intellectual truths. It is a life in itself."

Baking bread together teaches without words. Your children are learning the importance of sharing a meal, and how giving food to the hungry can be an act of love, a gift of self. So even if baking bread doesn't spark a theological conversation between you and your baking partners, this recipe is a lovely way to spend a Sunday afternoon.

This recipe was adapted from *The Waldorf Book of Breads* and yields 12–24 rolls or about three loaves of bread:

2 tablespoons yeast
2½ cups warm water
3 tablespoons olive oil
2 teaspoons salt
3 tablespoons honey
3 cups whole wheat flour
3 cups white flour

Prepare the yeast by mixing it with the warm water (105–115 degrees Fahrenheit). Combine the oil, salt, and honey with the yeast and let rest for 5–10 minutes. The mixture should start to bubble up a bit; sometimes the bubbles are very small and rise to the top of the mixture, and sometimes there are larger bubbles. If your kitchen is cold you can set the bowl over a casserole dish filled with very hot water and cover the bowl with a towel.

After about 10 minutes begin adding the flour one cup at a time and stirring with a wooden spoon or spatula. After you have added about 4–5 cups of flour the dough will be easier to mix by hand either in the same bowl or on a board sprinkled with flour. Fold and knead the dough, adding the rest of the flour until the dough is damp but not sticky.

You can let the dough rest and rise if you like, or move right on to making buns, shapes, or loaves.

Bake in a preheated oven at 350 degrees for about 35 minutes for smaller rolls or shapes, and up to 45 minutes for loaves. You'll want the crust to be golden brown.

~~~~~~~~~~~~~~~~~~~~~~~~

# 64

# HOW TO BLESS A CHILD

I bless you, my child, in the Name of the Father, and of the
Son, and of the Holy Spirit. Amen.

—CATHOLIC BLESSING

A blessing realigns our world with heaven by acknowledging that
all is gift. Catholic parents have traditionally blessed their children.
The practice is rooted in Scripture. In the Old Testament,
the elder Tobias blesses his son before a journey saying, "May you have a good journey, may God be
with you in your way, and may His angel accompany you" (Tobit 5:21). In Genesis, Noah
blesses his sons Shem and Japheth (Genesis
9:26-27). Likewise, Isaac blesses his sons
Jacob and Esau (Genesis 27, 28:1–4; and
49). Jesus also blesses children in the
New Testament by embracing them, and
laying His hands on them (Mark 10:16).

Often what keeps parents from
blessing their children is the fear that
they will do it wrong, but a broad array of
prayers or gestures, even wordless prayers

of the heart, can be used. When I was a little girl my mother would tuck me in every night after reading a book and saying our prayers with the last line from the *Madeline* books. She would say, "'Good night little [girl]. Thank the Lord you are well. And now go to sleep,' said Miss Clavel." And I would reply, "And she turned out the light and closed the door and that's all there is, there isn't any more."

Bless your child before bed. It can be as simple as saying, "God bless you, sweet boy," or marking the child's forehead with the sign of the cross, using your thumb. The words and the gesture can feel like a blanket, a soft covering before the child goes into the darkness just before sleep. Start the day with a blessing. The world can be unkind. A blessing reminds us that we do not go out into the world alone. God goes with us.

As Catholics we mark ourselves with the sign of the cross many times at church, but this practice should also be kept in the home. Before Vatican II many families kept a holy water font in the house for this purpose.

Bless your child on his birthday or before the first day of school. Another good time to give a parental blessing is before travel. Some parents give their children a hug and a kiss before a trip, and then they mark them with the sign of the cross, or simply wave good-bye saying, "Go with God." My own parents always did both, and though there were times in adolescence when I found being physically blessed unnecessary or uncomfortable, especially when my friends were around, as a college student I came to expect my blessing, happily inclining my head to receive it, before jumping in my car and heading back to school.

Another time parents might want to bless their children is when they are sick or in the hospital or experiencing some kind of trial. They might place a hand on the child's head or shoulder and pray for them from their heart in the name of the Father, and of the Son, and of the Holy Spirit. These blessings leave an indelible mark on the child and should not cease when he or she is an adolescent. A parent might discreetly bless a teenager at home, before a trip, for example, without causing excessive embarrassment. And while in-person blessings carry the greatest weight, do not hesitate to write

"God bless you," or "I'm praying for you," to your child in letters, e-mails, or texts.

A parental blessing is a simple but profound reminder to the child that he is loved, and that his true identity comes from God. It is like a shield. The act of blessing one's child also reminds the parents of their awesome responsibility and allows them to pause for a moment and ask for God's grace. When a child is blessed it helps her realize that she ought to respect her parents, because her parents, however imperfect, love her and seek goodness for her. Likewise, it reminds the parent of the child's inherent dignity and individuality; she is a gift, not a possession.

When Pope Francis appeared publicly for the first time after his election, he asked the crowds to pray for him and for Pope Emeritus Benedict XVI, and then he led the people in the Our Father, the Hail Mary, and the Glory Be. These simple and familiar prayers are known to most Catholics and to many non-Catholics as well. Pope Francis invited us to join in simple prayers we know by heart. In so doing, he offered a model for prayer at home, and especially prayer with children.

As St. Ambrose says, "You may not be rich; you may be unable to bequeath any great possessions to your children; but one thing you can give them [is] the heritage of your blessing. And it is better to be blessed than to be rich."

# 65

# HOW TO CELEBRATE A NAME DAY

The things we love tell us what we are.

-ST. THOMAS AQUINAS

We know how to throw birthday parties, and we know how often birthday parties are about stuff. Parents dread the pricey toys received and therefore expected at the next child's party, as though the entire enterprise were just a form of barter.

Imagine, then, a simpler way to honor a child or a friend, or even yourself. This year, throw a name day party.

The name day is the feast of the saint whose name you have received at baptism. From very early in the history of humanity, people believed that knowing the name of a deity was the surest way to reach it. We know that when Moses approached the burning bush (Exodus 3:1-14) and heard God speaking from the fire, Moses asked God's name. The answer was a curious one: "I am who I am," and then "I AM." The Septuagint (the earliest known Greek translation of the Hebrew Bible) gives God's name as *ego eimi ho on*, or, "I am the One who is." This suggests the immensity and eternity of God. Using your saint's name is a humbler way to approach the One Who Is. By knowing a faithful servant of God—learning her story, asking for his help—we find a way to the Way.

Feast days typically commemorate the saint's death day, or entrance into heaven. This is surprising in a world that welcomes only certain kinds of births and pretends death doesn't exist. Simplicity and sugar, frugality and fun, rejoicing and reality—all found in one celebration.

Our inspiration for celebrating with a dessert party comes from *My Nameday: Come for Dessert* written by Helen McLoughlin and published in 1962 by The Liturgical Press. McLoughlin suggests a dessert party because, as she writes, "it is economical, festive and meaningful, and permits the family to splurge on a fabulous dessert without inflicting lasting wounds on the budget."

## ST. JOHN'S WINE

McLoughlin's book is filled with saints' names and recipes associated with or pertaining to each saint. For an adult John (or Juan, Sean, Jean, Hans) one might have a St. John's Wine party. St. John's Wine is a hot mulled wine, well suited to the December 27 feast day of the evangelist. Find a recipe you like and serve it. If your John's feast day falls in warmer months (and there are many holy men named John whose feast days fall throughout the year), consider making red sangria.

Sliced peaches + apples

berries

sliced oranges

1 bottle dry red wine

MIX

1/4 cup brandy

1/4 cup freshly squeezed oj

1/4 cup triple sec

In the Bible we read about three men who appeared at the tent of Abraham and Sarah. They brought the glad and surprising news that the elderly couple would conceive and bear a son. Abraham tells Sarah (Genesis 18:6), "Quick, three measures of bran flour! Knead it and make bread," all to welcome their guests. For a Sarah, the choice is plain: cake or a rich bread.

What if you don't know for which John an honoree is named, John of the Cross, say, or John Chrysostom? One clue is the proximity of the birthday to the saint's feast day. An Elizabeth born on or around November 17 probably has as her patron Elizabeth of Hungary, one of the rare married saints. If you can, ask the parents why they picked the child's name and in whose honor it was chosen. The parents may tell you it was Clement of Alexandria and not Clement of Rome, but they may also tell you the name primarily honors a member of the family or a beloved friend. If so, try to learn that story and tell it, or have someone tell it at the party.

Maybe no one knows, out of all the Thomases and Anns, which one is the patron saint. Consider asking various guests to tell the story of one saint who bore the honoree's name. A Gregory might come to the party just plain Gregory and leave as Gregory Nazianzen, or come as a plain Margaret and leave as Margaret of Scotland, with a whole new batch of stories to tell.

## CHOCOLATE CAKE

What if you've decided at the last minute to throw a name day dessert party? You aren't much of a cook and you don't have time to learn a tricky recipe. Here's a quick, easy, and always delicious chocolate cake recipe. It takes about as much time to mix as it would take to make a cake from a mix, but with better results. You'll need only one mixing bowl and one 13 x 9 sheet pan or a Bundt pan for this recipe.

*Mix in a large bowl:*
2 cups of flour
2 cups of sugar
½ cup of cocoa

2 teaspoons baking soda

¼ teaspoon salt

2 eggs

1 cup buttermilk *(You can "make" buttermilk by adding about 1 tablespoon white vinegar or lemon juice to a measuring cup. Fill the cup with milk up to the one-cup mark. Let the mixture sit and sour for a few minutes before using.)*

1 cup vegetable oil

*Beat well.*

*Add* 1 cup boiling water to the mix and beat it in.

*Add* 1 teaspoon pure vanilla extract

*Pour* the batter into a greased and floured cake pan and bake at 350 degrees for 35–40 minutes, until a knife inserted in the center of the cake comes out clean.

You can serve this cake with powdered sugar sprinkled on top. Or use your favorite icing or glaze.

What if you are an adult whose name day falls at a time when you are new in town, or recuperating and can't handle much company, or need some time alone? Don't let that keep you from marking the day. Treat yourself to a walk or a hike or an afternoon with a good book or a favorite meal. Perform an act of service in honor of your saint. Whatever you do, be glad and grateful for the saint who walked before you and shows you the way.

~~~~~~~~~~~~~~~~~~~~~~~~~~~~~~~~~~~~~~~~~~~~~

# 66

# FIRST COMMUNION AND FIRST COMMUNION GIFTS

*Receive the Jesus of peace and love.*

—ST. THÉRÈSE OF LISIEUX

We celebrate *First* Communions, not *only* Communions. That's because, unlike a college graduation, which is a once-in-a-lifetime event, the assumption about a First Communion is that it is a beginning. First Communion is the first step on a long journey, a journey we make with Christ.

Like baptism and Confirmation, one's First Communion is part of the sacraments of initiation. Until the thirteenth century, children received Communion, usually under the species of wine, on the day of baptism. In the Eastern Church, this is still the practice. Once baptized, Eastern Rite children are welcome to receive. But at the Lateran Council in 1215, the Roman (Western) Church gathered its bishops at the Church of St. John Lateran in Rome and decreed that baptized children would be brought to Communion once they reached the age of discretion. The trouble is that "the age of discretion" is a matter of debate. This has meant that at various times children were not allowed to receive until the age of fourteen. But in general, children receive First Communion during the Easter season around their second grade in school.

In 1910, Pope Pius X ruled that children should be able to receive as soon as they can distinguish the Bread of the Eucharist from ordinary bread. And, of course, that understanding varies from child to child. In the rules prescribed by the Congregation of the Sacraments, under Pope Pius X's guidance, the Church declared that a child doesn't need "a full and perfect understanding of Christian doctrine" in order to receive, but that it is the duty of parents and teachers to continue the study of the faith after the children have begun to receive Communion. Who, then, decides whether a child is ready to receive? According to the 1910 guidelines, that decision is up to the parents and the child's priest. Most parishes and parish schools have a "Communion class," made up of boys and girls of the same age and grade who will all receive together on the same Sunday in Easter, but this is not canonically required. Listen to your child. Watch your child. Talk to your child and your pastor and decide on the right time for your child's First Communion. Also check with your pastor as to the local norms of the order of the sacraments of first reconciliation and First Communion. In general, children now make their first confessions before receiving communion for the first time.

If your child is part of a First Communion class, the struggle is to keep the joyful reverence of the day. Hundreds of people taking photos is not an ideal introduction to the sacrament. Ask a single person to photograph or record a video of the event. After Mass, take all the pictures you want.

Children will want to be dressed nicely for the day, but there is no need to spend lots of money. You might set up a parish, or diocesan, network for lending gently used dresses, veils, and suits to upcoming communicants. Or ask among friends and relatives to see what is available. Some families embroider the names and dates of the First Communions celebrated by those who have worn the clothes, turning them into keepsakes.

## BUYING FIRST COMMUNION GIFTS

Three of the traditional First Communion gifts are Bibles, crosses, and rosaries. Those are good choices, because each is an item that children will continue to use as long as they live. The Bible is the story of the people of faith. It is our salvation history. In it we learn of the foolishness and fear and faithlessness of men and women in every

time and place. We are unfaithful, but God is ever faithful. We are inconstant, but God is unchanging. For both children and adults, all of us knowing our mistakes, our follies and our sins, this is good news, indeed. That St. Peter, the rock upon whom Christ builds the Church, can be weak and disloyal and still be used by Christ is both surprising and comforting. Look for a Bible, then, into which a child can grow, with worthy illustrations and good footnotes and study notes for when the child is ready. Keep the long view in mind. Consider an edition with pages to record sacraments and other milestones.

If you want a book that is more age-specific, consider giving a storybook now, with plans to give a Bible as a Confirmation gift later. A good place to begin the search for a storybook is with the lists of Newberry and Caldecott Award winners. Especially in the earlier years of the prizes, there are a number of books related to faith and Scripture. Helen Dean Fish and Dorothy P. Lathrop's *Animals of the Bible* won the first ever Caldecott Award when it was published in 1937. Approaching Bible stories through animals is an interesting and child-friendly take. The illustrations are more realistic than cartoonish and bear repeated examination. The text is from the King James Version.

Tomie dePaola has written a number of Bible story collections for children, such as *The Miracles of Jesus* and *Tomie dePaola's Book of Bible Stories*.

For a child whose reading skills are more advanced, you might buy the first volume, or the full set, of *The Chronicles of Narnia* by C. S. Lewis. This Christian allegory opens with an irresistible journey, from a coat closet found in a game of hide-and-seek (and what child doesn't love a hiding place) into a world where animals talk and four young children are called to reign as queens and kings.

When you buy a gift, you'll probably start at the church goods store (the best place to find a saint's medal), but don't be afraid to look beyond the church goods store. Looking for a cross as a First Communion gift? A museum shop is often a place to find something beautiful and unusual, such as a traditional southwestern straw appliqué cross. Other places to look are fair trade shops and online sites that offer handmade crosses and icons from artisans around the world.

If you give a child a rosary, look for something he or she will want to use as an adult. It's common to see adult Catholics still using their First Communion rosaries. Start with your local Catholic bookstore, but don't be afraid to broaden your search. Or maybe you have a rosary that belonged to a parent or grandparent or friend, a rosary you can pass on to the first communicant along with some stories about the person who used it.

A friend remembers going to visit his great-uncle as the good man lay dying. His uncle appeared to be unconscious as his nephew began quietly praying the Rosary. The nephew was surprised to see his uncle's eyes open and his hand emerge from under the blankets holding his well-used rosary. They finished the prayer together. Every family has stories like this one, and many have kept the devotional objects that are at the heart of the stories. Pass them along.

What if you don't have any money to spend on a gift? Consider the gift of presence. A gift certificate for a once-a-month hike, or an invitation for an afternoon of making cookies or gardening or playing basketball is a gift for both adult and child. The time to talk is time to grow in affection and understanding. Especially for a child with siblings, or whose parents work long hours, a child who knows what it is to struggle for attention in the family. Time alone with a trusted adult is a time to shine. Consider the child's interests. A commitment to attend every soccer game or recital is another way to show your love.

The Eucharist is a feast provided by God's own hand. Our gifts should mirror that generosity and care. Generosity doesn't equal money. Generosity means choosing, or making, a gift that is beautiful, meaningful, and helpful in leading a child to deeper faith.

When in doubt, talk to the child's parents. Ask them what might delight the heart of their first communicant. And think back to your own childhood. Remember a gift you treasure, or a gift you always wish someone had given you.

~~~~~~~~~~~~~~~~~~~~~~~

# 67

# FIRST RECONCILIATION

Lamb of God, you take away the sin of the world,
have mercy on us.

—AGNUS DEI

When my youngest child was three, he hit a friend who wouldn't hand over a toy. I called him aside and scolded him. I said, "Jesus didn't hit and he wants you to be like him."

My son looked me in the eye and said, "Well, Jesus didn't like to hit, but I do."

And there we have it. Jesus shares all aspects of our humanity, except sin, which, let's be honest, we often don't try very hard to avoid. Because we like to hit.

Sins are like weeds. If you don't keep after them, the yard or garden or field will be overtaken. Even small children can understand a weed, and they can understand how there might be weeds growing in the gardens of their hearts.

Children can also understand the Good News that Jesus is a gardener. Ask, and he will help you pull the weeds up, and cast them out. (You might read John 20:11-18 with your child. Mary Magdalene comes to the empty tomb after Jesus's resurrection. She finds a man standing outside the tomb and thinks he is the gardener. It is, in fact, the risen Christ, but Mary Magdalene gets it partly right. Christ has come to restore all of creation, which God created originally as a garden.)

But, as every gardener knows, pulling weeds means knowing weeds. It means being able to name wanted plants and distinguish them from the unwanted ones. St. Basil (fourth century) gave this definition of sin: "the misuse of powers given to us by God for doing good." Simple, true, and easy for us to understand, Basil's words are a sturdy guide for preparing children to make their first confession. What does Basil say? That all God has given us is good and is for the good. Eating, running, laughing, doing cartwheels, singing, reading, telling stories, bathing, riding a bike, hugging, drawing—all these are gifts of God to be used in God's service and to God's glory. (You might read the first chapter of Genesis with your child, paying special attention to God's pronouncement after each aspect of the world is created: "God saw that it was good.") But sometimes we take these good gifts and misuse them: Laughing in an unkind way at someone's differences or misfortunes, eating until we are sick or wasting food or being picky about what we eat—we can all think of ways we take a good plant and twist it into a weed.

That's why we use the word "reconciliation" for this sacrament. Reconciliation is a reunion, a bringing together of that or those who have been separated. It does not suggest difference so much as division, or separation, a separation of that which should be joined. (Look again at the first chapter of Genesis, where God creates us in his own image and after his likeness.) In the sacrament, God, and those who belong to God, are once again joined—the Creator and the created—together as God intended.

God is sovereign, that is, all-powerful, so why is our sinfulness a problem? Can't we just sit back and let God take care of everything?

God has chosen us to help Him in the work of holiness. We cooperate with God. We see the fruits of that cooperation on the altar. No human hands can make wheat or grapes, but human hands have the power to harvest wheat and grapes and turn them into bread and wine. So although we may not understand the reason, we know that God wants us to help in making the world as it was created to be, an abundant and life-giving garden. God wants us to pull weeds, something we can't do well if we have lost the ability to distinguish between weeds and flowers.

Talk to your child about his or her role, at home and in the world. She knows herself to be weak beside you. He knows himself to be too little to stay home alone or drive or do many of the adult jobs. Your children know you are stronger and more experienced and that you have authority over them. Still, asking your child to help, even from a young age, is important. Let them know how important it is by saying thank you: "I couldn't have gotten through the store if you hadn't been there to entertain the baby." Or "Thanks for putting away your toys [or clearing the table]." Here's a poem from Louisa May Alcott's novel *Little Men* for your children to memorize. It underscores the importance of their cooperation in all the works of goodness:

> *Little drops of water,*
> *Little grains of sand,*
> *Make a mighty ocean,*
> *And a pleasant land.*
>
> *Little words of kindness,*
> *Spoken every day,*
> *Make a home a heaven,*
> *And help us on our way.*

Once you've talked about the right use of gifts, talk about the misuse of those same gifts. Recall a car trip when you had to turn around and go back home because people were fighting. Ask your child to think about how it hurts to be hit or called a hateful name and how much it must hurt others when they are similarly mistreated. There are plenty of examples of people who love each other and care for each other being divided and driven apart by sin.

Sometimes siblings and friends stop speaking after an argument. What brings two people who are angry and apart back together? Someone has to admit fault, confess, and ask for forgiveness. Someone has to listen and forgive.

## PREPARING YOUR CHILD FOR THE
## SACRAMENT OF RECONCILIATION

1. The sign of the sacrament is confession. Your child may wonder why we confess to a priest. Does the priest forgive us, or does God forgive us? God forgives us, but God chooses to work with and through human beings. God chose to come to us as a man, and God chooses to be evident through "the work of human hands." When Jesus appears to the apostles after his resurrection, he gives them the work of binding and loosing sins. (John 20:19-23) Your child might understand this as naming the weeds and helping in the work of pulling them. Bishops and priests are descendants of the apostles, and they continue doing what Jesus asked of the first apostles.

2. Make sure your children see confession and forgiveness in their everyday lives. Ask your child's forgiveness when you lose your temper. Forgiving another means putting that offense away. It is not to be brought up again in a later argument. One of the meanings of the Old English word *forgiefan*, the origin of our modern word "forgive," is to "give up" or "surrender." We don't bank forgiven sins against the future; we erase them.

3. Make sure your children grow up hearing the words "Please forgive me," and "I'm sorry," and "I forgive you." We have a habit of dismissing others with "Let's just forget about it," or "It's okay" (when it clearly isn't), or "Well, don't do it again" (which suggests you will, and we'll be waiting). None of these expressions has the weight and power of the word "forgive."

4. Explain that although we don't forgive perfectly, God does. God is always waiting and ready to forgive, to reconcile, to heal, and to restore. Read the story of the Prodigal Son with your child in Luke 15:11-32. There's a lot that children won't, and don't need to, understand about dissipation and property rights and inheritance law. But even a small child

can picture the father watching and waiting for his lost son to come home, his joy at the sight of him.

5. Let your child see you going to confession. Children do what they see much more than what they are only told.

6. Rejoice with your child once he or she has confessed. Think of an everyday example, say, of how good clean sheets smell and feel, as a way to talk about how good it feels to be washed clean of our sins.

7. Respect the seal of the confessional. After you have helped your child prepare to make a confession, resist the urge to pry about what the priest and your child talked about. It is a good thing for your child to know that confessed sin would never be fodder for gossip, even of the most well-meaning sort.

# 68

# THE SACRAMENT OF CONFIRMATION AND CONFIRMATION GIFTS

> You who have been enlightened in the Father,
> in you the Holy Spirit will rejoice.
>
> —ARMENIAN RITE

> I think the Good News is about grace and hope and love
> and a relinquishing of self to God.
>
> —SUFJAN STEVENS

Originally, Catholics were baptized and confirmed before receiving Communion for the first time, and some dioceses in the United States have moved to restore the sacraments of initiation to their original order. In the Archdiocese of Denver, for example, third-graders are now confirmed.

Yet in most dioceses Confirmation continues to occur well after First Communion, during the final years of high school. This presents a challenge. At a time in an adolescent's life when she is least interested in what the adults around her have to say, at a time in an adolescent's life when his deepest connection is to his peer group, we ask that young woman or man to make an adult commitment to the Church.

Then again, the Church also asks first-time parents bringing their infants to the waters of baptism, "Do you clearly understand what you are undertaking?" when they clearly don't. The Church asks marrying couples, "Will you love and honor each other as husband and wife for the rest of your lives?" when doing so may involve suffering and sacrifice beyond their ability to imagine. And at Mass the Church asks us to receive the Body and Blood of Christ, and then go out carrying Christ within us.

The Church sets a high bar, knowing we will stumble and fall and fail to clear it. We will need to confess and ask forgiveness and try again. In the same way, the Church cuts our spiritual garments large and asks not that the sacraments shrink, but that we grow into them.

Confirmation is a part of the sacraments of initiation—baptism, Confirmation, and Eucharist. The sign of Confirmation is the laying on of hands and the sealing of the confirmand (a candidate for Confirmation) with blessed oil, or chrism. The bishop anoints the confirmand, and placing his hands on the person's head and addressing the person by name, says, "Be sealed with the Holy Spirit."

If you think of the sign of baptism, which is water, then the link between these two elements of the sacraments of initiation becomes clearer. Recall that the Church uses the language of "sealing" to describe Confirmation. Bathers are urged to rub oil into their still damp skin. The oil seals the moisture in. Confirmation is a sealing in of the waters of baptism into which we are plunged.

In the Rite of Christian Initiation for Adults (RCIA) it is customary for the unity of the sacraments of initiation to be restored in practice. At the Easter Vigil, adults who are to be baptized will receive all three sacraments at that liturgy.

Even when the sacraments of initiation are separated by some years, we honor their essential unity. One of the ways adults can help confirmands understand this unity is in the choice of a Confirmation name.

Adolescents in Confirmation classes often choose a new name as a sign of their mature acceptance of the baptismal promises adults made for them when they were babies. As Catholics, we understand how much names matter. At baptism, the Church will not accept a name that is hateful or hurtful or trivial, because the child of God is just that, a child of the Most High.

So it might be a good thing to encourage teens to keep their baptismal names and learn more about the name and all the saints who have borne it. What does it mean? Tell the story. Discovering the origins and inspiration behind one's name is another way of claiming it when you're an adult.

Some teens will still want to pick a new Confirmation name, especially if that is the local custom. Then you might encourage a name that is linked in some important way with the confirmand's baptismal name. An Anne might pick the name of another woman with direct ties to the nativity: Mary or Elizabeth. A Paul might pick the name of the apostle's missionary companion, Timothy. This is also a time when, as in religious life, the name is not based on gender, but holiness and charism. A Francis might pick the name of the saint of Assisi's friend, Clare. A Teresa might pick the name of the saint of Avila's friend, John of the Cross. A friend joined the Catholic Church following his marriage to a Catholic woman. As his confirmation name he took Ruth, a famous convert to Judaism whose story is told in the Old Testament (Ruth 1:16b-17). Or encourage the teen to pick the name of a saint whose story he or she finds inspiring.

## CONFIRMATION GIFTS AND PARTIES

There should certainly be a party for the newly confirmed, but let the young man or woman set the tone. Consider a seated dinner party with the parents and Confirmation sponsors cooking and serving the meal. If you decide on a family meal, invite people who were present at the newly confirmed person's baptism. Encourage them to tell what they remember and to share the stories they were told of their own baptisms and what they remember of their own confirmations. Place pictures around the room of grandparents and great-grandparents or devotional objects used by these ancestors in faith.

Some teens will just want to have a party with their friends—good music, good food, and good company. Remember, it's *their* party.

Since this is a time when the Church asks us to accept and claim as our own the promises made on our behalf at baptism, the party might be a party for others. Is there a family in the parish in need of a meal? Elderly friends or relatives who would enjoy sharing a meal at their nursing home or assisted living center? Is there a need for cooks and dishwashers at the local soup kitchen? Having a party might mean cooking together and taking the meal to others, either to drop off or to share.

If you are buying a gift for a teen confirmand, consider a medal bearing his or her saint's image and attribute. If the teen has a Bible with solid study notes, think about a biblical concordance (an alphabetical index of words found in the Bible along with the book and verse in which they are found) or a copy of *YOUCAT* (Youth Catechism of the Catholic Church) to go along with it. A rosary or crucifix, especially one that has been used reverently by an older relative or friend, will have both personal and spiritual resonance for the newly confirmed. But gifts don't have to be explicitly tied to this event; think about a good novel, like *The Brothers Karamazov*, by Fyodor Dostoevsky; or a collection of short stories, such as *A Good Man Is Hard to Find and Other Stories* or *Everything That Rises Must Converge: Stories*, both by Flannery O'Connor; or the epistolary novel by C. S. Lewis that features letters between a master devil and his subordinate as they seek to woo a man away from God: *The Screwtape Letters*.

Or consider giving music. Most teens orchestrate their lives with music, and here is a chance to introduce them to some worthy selections. It's not a preachy gift, but one that speaks to the vigor and variety of the Christian life. Carefully chosen music can also reinforce each adult Christian's duty: Not to flee the culture, but to seek in the culture all that affirms the good, the beautiful, and the true.

Make a mix or buy an album. Here's a list of albums to consider:

John Coltrane, *A Love Supreme*

Johnny Cash, *My Mother's Hymn Book*

Thad Cockrell, *To Be Loved*

Bruce Springsteen, *Greetings from Asbury Park*

Sister Rosetta Tharpe, *Up Above My Head*

Marvin Gaye, *What's Going On*

The Hold Steady, *Separation Sunday*

Joni Mitchell, *Blue*

Danielle Rose, *Mysteries and Defining Beauty*

Wilco, *Yankee Hotel Foxtrot*

Sufjan Stevens, *Seven Swans and Songs for Christmas*

Gaslight Anthem, *The '59 Sound*

The Innocence Mission, *We Walked in Song* and *Christ Is My Hope*

Belle and Sebastian, *The Ghost of Rock School*

Don Covay, *Mercy, Mercy*

*Benedicta: Marian Chant from Norcia*

Bob Marley, *Trenchtown Rock* and *Legend*

Paul Simon, *Graceland*

The Soul Stirrers, *Joy in My Soul: The Complete SAR Recordings*

The University of Notre Dame Folk Choir, *Prophets of Joy*

The Benedictines of Mary Queen of Apostles, *Angels and Saints at Ephesus*

Gillian Welch, *Revival*

Yo Yo Ma, *The Cello Suites* inspired by Bach

The Staple Singers, *The 25th Day of December*
Bach, *Christmas Oratorio*
Ben Harper, *Welcome to the Cruel World*
Ladysmith Black Mambazo, *Ultimate Collection*
Lauryn Hill, *The Miseducation of Lauryn Hill*

For more music, book, and movie ideas, visit our website: the catholiccatalogue.com.

# YOUNG ADULTHOOD

# 69

~~~~~~~~~~~~~~~~~~~~

# FINDING A PARISH

The Church is the traveler's inn where the
wounded are healed.

–ST. AUGUSTINE

When Catholics came to the United States in large numbers in the nineteenth century, they tended to immigrate to big cities like Philadelphia, New York, Chicago, and Boston, because that's where they found work. Each city had a number of ethnic Catholic enclaves, each with its own cultural and devotional practices (Polish, Lithuanian, Irish, Italian, Russian, or German). Every neighborhood had its own parish, and most of these parishes had their own schools. There, because of the large number of vocations before Vatican II (heroic nuns, brothers, and priests), working-class immigrant children could receive a free Catholic education.

In these tight-knit communities people strongly identified by their parish, even non-Catholics who lived in these neighborhoods would often say, "I live in St. Mark's [or St. Anthony's]." Parishes vied with one another for the glory of their side chapel repository or their annual May Day procession. Someone would die and the whole block would prepare for the funeral.

Parishioners went to church with their neighbors, co-workers, and extended family. People didn't move as frequently, so the parish was the village in which you got married, raised your children, and buried your dead. (Interestingly, the funeral rites of the Church still presume that the dead and the mourners are all in one place, so the prayers begin at the deathbed and go seamlessly to the grave. For many Catholics, worldwide, this remains the norm.) In fact, canon law still recommends that parishioners go to the parish in whose territory they live, unless there is a serious reason to do otherwise, for example, you worship in another rite (canon 518).

So there's something deeply Catholic about simply going to the church that's in your neighborhood, and if something isn't to your liking, seeing if you can either get involved and change it or learn to live with it. After all, priests don't pick their parish. They're assigned. Likewise lay Catholics have a history of, and a good reason for, not being too choosy: the Eucharist is the Eucharist, no matter who is saying the Mass.

If you go to your neighborhood church and feel like something is missing: you wish there were a Narcotics Anonymous meeting in the parish center, or that the music ministry were more robust, or that there was a group for moms, or young adults, or eucharistic adoration, speak to your pastor and see if you can get something started.

The Roman Catholic Church is big and various. It is—in fact—"catholic," which means "universal." So it touches every political party and ethnicity. But as much diversity as there is within the Body of Christ, there is also a great deal of unity. The *Catechism of the Catholic Church* puts it this way: "The Church is one: she acknowledges one Lord, confesses one faith, is born of one Baptism, forms only one Body, is given life by one Spirit, for the sake of one hope (cf *Eph* 4:3-5), at whose fulfillment all divisions will be overcome" (CCC, 866).

It's important to remember when picking a parish that the Church is not a club. We don't get to vote people in or out, just as we don't get to vote family members in or out. The Church is the Mystical Body of Christ. We are brothers and sisters. We didn't choose one another. God chose us for one another. Too often Catholics are divided along political, racial, or class lines, but when you celebrate the Eucharist with other Catholics, Sunday after Sunday, year after year, you become a community of people trying to live the faith. We are not all the same, but we are all members of the One, Holy, Catholic, and Apostolic Church.

The Church is one of the only places on earth where the homeless man and the wealthy housewife drink from a single cup. As St. Paul writes, "There is neither Jew nor Greek, there is neither slave nor free person, there is not male and female; for you are all one in Christ Jesus" (Galatians 3:28).

At Mass one Sunday, I saw a young mother wearing skinny jeans, with a sleeve of tattoos and bottle blonde hair, sitting next to a young mother wearing a modest black dress and a lace mantilla. (Their difference in dress may be because one grew up having never heard of a mantilla, and the other grew up covering her head, as a sign of respect, in church.) As they reverently participated in the liturgy, received the Eucharist, and smiled at each other's babies, these women were simply sisters in Christ.

So if you've moved to a new city, first try attending the Catholic Church that's closest to you. An online search for Mass times will provide you with a map of parishes in your area. It makes sense to worship with your neighbors if at all possible. It helps to create community if you also run into each other at the dog park, the grocery store, or the gym.

As Catholics we try to resist "spiritual tourism" or "church shopping." That is, we should avoid hopping from parish to parish, Sunday after Sunday, without ever putting down roots. Genuine community means making a commitment and joining a parish. Keep in mind that there's no such thing as the perfect church, or the perfect community. We're all sinners. So pick one and get involved, even if that means only attending on Sundays and visiting with people after Mass.

Still, it is a good thing to be in a parish where you are spiritually fed. Canon law states that Catholics have a right to worship in their preferred rite, to receive spiritual assistance from pastors, to form lay groups for the purposes of charity, and to receive Christian education (canons 212–217). So if the church nearest to you geographically is so lifeless that it will keep you from attending Mass, find another parish nearby and go there. Maybe you're African American and love to hear a Gospel choir at Mass, or you're Vietnamese and prefer to pray in your native tongue. Maybe you home school and want to attend a parish with a home school group, or you're an Eastern Catholic who prefers the Eastern Divine Liturgy. There are Spanish masses, Latin Rite masses, Catholic Charismatic communities, and Native American parishes. Each of these communities is picking up on different facets of the same two-thousand-year-old tradition.

There are a number of Catholic parishes within a few miles of my house, but I attend the one founded by the Congregation of Holy Cross, because Holy Cross founded both my last parish and the college I went to. I feel at home there, and I also get to meet lots of other people with connections to Holy Cross, South Bend, and Notre Dame.

Whichever parish you choose, the most important thing is that you attend. Catholics are obliged to attend Mass every week. What's more, if no one goes to Mass, churches will close, and there won't be any more Masses. As Tom Peterson writes in his book *Catholics Come Home*, "Since 1965, weekly Mass attendance has plummeted from 71 percent at its peak to a meager 17 percent in 2008." In other words, if we want to be members of vibrant spiritual communities we may have to reinvigorate them ourselves.

One of the best things about being Catholic is that any parish, anywhere in the world, can be what St. Augustine calls "a traveler's inn in which the wounded are healed." Even if you are in a city or country you've never visited before, you can walk into a Catholic Church and find the same Mass, the same Eucharist, the same readings, the same confession, and always a place to pray and be in the presence of God.

~~~~~~~~~~~~~~~~~~~~~~~~~

# 70

# HOW TO MAKE A RETREAT

Our hearts are restless till they find rest in You.

—ST. AUGUSTINE OF HIPPO

## JESUS WENT ON RETREAT

We call Matthew, Mark, and Luke the Synoptic Gospels because they see the story of Christ with a single eye, or a common view. John tends to be more theological, whereas the other three Gospels are more narrative in nature. A good way of understanding this is to read Matthew's or Luke's nativity story and compare it to the first chapter of John, in which Jesus is described, not as a baby in a manger, but as the Word, without whom "nothing came to be." Calling Jesus "the Word" does not deny the nativity story; rather it casts it within the framework of eternity, where the One who came to us as Jesus has no beginning and no end.

In the same way, we find a story about the prelude to Jesus's public ministry in the Synoptic Gospels that we do not find in John. The story is that after his baptism and before he began his public work, Jesus went on retreat (Matthew 4:1-11; Mark 1:12-3; Luke 4:1-13). And that is not the only time we see Jesus withdrawing from the crowds, and sometimes even from his disciples, to be alone with the Father

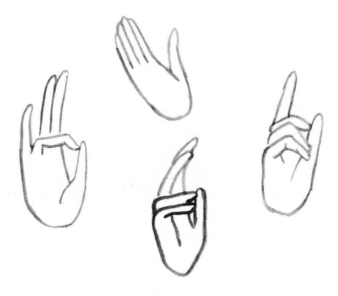

and pray. Matthew 14:23 gives us this description of Jesus, having dismissed the crowds and sent the disciples off in a boat:

> After doing so, he went up on the mountain by himself to pray. When it was evening he was there alone.

The Synoptic Gospels describe Jesus going to the Garden of Gethsemane to pray before his crucifixion. Taking time to be alone and pray is one of those things, like almsgiving and feeding the hungry, that we do in imitation of Jesus. We call such times apart "retreats," and it is instructive that the word has both a military and a religious meaning and use. When the military speaks of a retreat, they mean withdrawing from direct engagement with the enemy; moving back to friendly territory and away from the fighting. That meaning is not dissimilar from what the Church means by "retreat." The Jesuit priest Jean Daniélou would describe making a treat as disengaging "from the chains of our environment." We leave behind, for a while, whatever battles we have been waging and go to the friendly territory of the retreat, there to have quiet time with God and be refreshed.

The question, then, is how to find the right retreat, the right setting, and the right leader. Style and form matter, because an environment one person finds reverent sets another person's teeth on edge.

## DECIDE ON THE KIND OF RETREAT
## THAT IS RIGHT FOR YOU

Don't assume that you need to leave your town or parish to go on retreat. Many parishes sponsor one- or two-day retreats—often for men and women, separately—right in the building. This is a good way to meet other parishioners and to root yourself more deeply in the community. Talk to people you know and trust in the parish and learn more about the retreats offered there.

If you go to a retreat center, monastery, or convent, there are basically two kinds of retreats: individual directed or guided retreats (usually eight days long) and preached retreats (which vary in length). In a directed retreat, each person meets daily with a director for individual guidance in prayer. In a guided retreat, the whole group meets once daily with the director, but each person prays alone. In a preached retreat, prayer is ordered around the preaching and may be done before or after the preaching. There are also private retreats, where the retreatant and the director decide how to structure the time, or where the retreatant goes to a place, like an abbey or monastery, and decides, without a director, how, when, and where to pray.

Do you want daily Eucharist? Exposition of the Blessed Sacrament? Confession? If you are going to a house where the daily office is prayed in community, do you want to join in? Do you care if the leader is ordained, religious, or lay? A woman mourning the loss of a child or preparing to see her last child off to college may want to be directed by another woman (and this can be one of the sisters with a late vocation) who has been married and borne children. A military chaplain or veteran might best serve a person coming home from military service overseas. Don't assume a place will have what you want. Call or write and ask, or check the website.

## LOCATION

Be realistic. How quiet is too quiet? One retreat director tells of a woman who got up in the middle of the night and drove away from the convent because although she wanted quiet, she didn't want as much quiet as she found. Do you want to be in the mountains? Think about the effects of altitude and, at some elevations, the real possibility of altitude sickness. Do you want to be in the desert? Think about the heat and the dryness and how these elements might affect you. Do you want to be on the beach? Cost may well be a factor here, not to mention the real problem of distraction. (This can also be a problem with a city retreat.) Retreats and vacations have some, but not all, things in common.

Do you want to share a room? Be alone in a room? How about bathroom space: shared or single? I recall lying alone in my room in the darkness at St. Walburga's Abbey (mountains, high altitude, lots of silence) while the sisters sang Vigils. (Vigils is sung in the early hours of the morning, before the sun has risen. It comes between Compline, or Night Prayer, and Lauds, or Morning Prayer.) It was a moment of such peace. I was grateful for the solitude, but another person might have wished for someone with whom to share it. So think about what would work for you and make inquiries before you sign up.

## MEALS

Will you being eating alone or with a group? If you have dietary concerns or needs, can they be accommodated? Will you be expected to keep silence at meals? What is the policy on missing or skipping meals? Will you be expected to help cook meals or clean up after them? Find out.

## PACKING

Does the retreat center (or abbey or convent or monastery) have Internet access? If they do, or don't, will that be a problem for you? Might it be a good idea to unplug for a time? Or impossible? Do you need a Bible? What kind of shoes will you need to take a walk on the local terrain? Are there other physical activities planned? Is the facility air-conditioned?

## COSTS

Most communities use the revenue from retreats to support their life together. Find out what is required or recommended. If you have a lack of funds, talk to someone where you hope to go on retreat. They might have some options, such as helping in the kitchen in exchange for a reduced fee. Make sure you know the transportation required to get to the retreat. Find out the cost and see if you can get others to share the expenses. But don't let the cost keep you from making a retreat. If the place you have in mind doesn't work, ask for a recommendation to a similar place that is nearer, perhaps, or in other ways more affordable.

~~~~~~~~~~~~~~~~~~~~~~~~~~~~~~~

# 71

# FINDING A SPIRITUAL DIRECTOR AND DISCERNING A VOCATION

Everyone should get spiritual direction.

−THOMAS MERTON

The goal of spiritual direction is to become more self aware, which begins with becoming more aware of how God is working in your life. Most people vacillate between extremes of pride and despair. Sometimes the stories we tell ourselves simply aren't true: "I can never forgive my father." "I can only answer God's call to religious life when I find a community without flaws." "I'll never be able to stop panicking, or being unkind to my children, or dating the wrong people." "I don't know what my vocation is." A good spiritual director listens prayerfully to what a person is saying, and helps that person to discern what is real, and what is not, in a completely confidential setting. A spiritual director is a friend on the journey who helps people to see how "for God all things are possible" (Matthew 19:26).

Meeting with a spiritual director once a month keeps you accountable. It forces you to make room in your life for prayer, silence, introspection, and attentiveness; it helps you to check in with how you are living, or not living, your vocation. Spiritual direction helps you get unstuck and reconnect with God, whose will is your peace.

## THE ROOTS OF SPIRITUAL DIRECTION

The practice of spiritual direction has its roots in monasticism and the earliest days of the Church. In the third century, St. Anthony the Abbot obeyed Jesus's command to sell all he had and follow Him. He lived for ten years in the desert, fasting and praying and speaking only to the few other hermits who could teach him about seeking and finding God. People heard of his holiness and traveled to become his students in prayer. This settlement is widely considered to be the first Christian monastery, and St. Anthony is credited with beginning the movement that became the Desert Mothers and Fathers.

In the sixth century, St. Benedict (strongly influenced by the traditions of monasticism that began in the desert) wrote the Rule of St. Benedict. It was born out of his long and difficult experiences with monastic life. The experience was not always happy. Two different monks in his community tried to poison him. St. Benedict understood, as Dostoevsky once wrote that "love in action is a harsh and dreadful thing compared to love in dreams."

The Rule of St. Benedict was written, not to be read, but to be practiced. In his rule, Benedict lays out how to live a balanced Christian life with periods of work and prayer, rest and activity, speech and silence. He calls it "a little rule for beginners." In it he advises that the abbot of a monastery come to know each monk personally, to reflect upon each monk's talents, strengths, and weaknesses. He advises his monks to listen to their abbot's precepts, and to the teachings of Christ, with the "ear of [their] heart." Benedict is describing what we might now call spiritual direction.

St. Teresa of Ávila, who was herself a spiritual director, and who asked St. John of the Cross to become the spiritual director to her community of Carmelite nuns, once wrote, "Prayer is nothing else than being on terms of friendship with God."

But how do you learn how to become friends with God? How do you discern God's will in your life? It can help to have a wise and holy friend. Someone who helps you learn how to listen with the ear of your heart to what God is asking you to do. The Celtic monastic tradition calls the spiritual director an "Anam Cara" or "soul-friend."

Once reserved for priests and religious, spiritual direction is now available to anyone.

## MODELS

It is difficult to generalize about spiritual direction because the process is highly individual. There are many different models, the most famous of which was developed by St. Ignatius of Loyola, who founded the Jesuits.

Before he was a priest, Ignatius wrote a framework for spiritual direction called the Spiritual Exercises. It is one of the great works of Christian instruction in holiness. Like the Rule of St. Benedict it is meant not simply to be read, but to be experienced.

St. Ignatius taught his advisees to pay attention to what he termed "spirits of consolation" and "spirits of desolation." In other words, what in their lives made them feel more grateful, alive, and close to God? These spiritual consolations, he taught, were from God. For example, a spiritual director might ask, "When in your life have you felt yourself to be in the presence of God?" This question could help you discern your vocation.

On the other hand, "spiritual desolations," Ignatius taught, hold us back because they are not from God. People today might speak of envy, fear, or despair as desolations, and hope, sense of purpose, or peace as consolations. Ignatius also encouraged his retreatants to do an examination of conscience, or spiritual self-review.

Many people first encounter spiritual direction on an Ignatian retreat. On these retreats, people meet with their spiritual directors daily, usually for an hour. Such meetings might begin with prayer or a reading from Scripture. You might ask the Holy Spirit to help direct your conversation. Then your director might simply ask, "How are things?" After listening to you talk about your experiences on the retreat or in life, he might push you in certain areas, or give you a passage from Scripture to meditate on before your next meeting. Ignatian retreats tend to emphasize using your imagination to place yourself in the stories of the New Testament. Who do you sympathize with in the story? What is Jesus trying to say?

A woman who went on an Ignatian retreat in India told me that the style she encountered there was quite different. Her spiritual director, a Jesuit priest, instructed her to quiet her mind during the five periods of daily prayer. He repeatedly told her that she had "nowhere to be and nothing to achieve." She told me this priest helped her learn how to find rest in God, in silence, and in simply repeating the name of Jesus.

Other people seek spiritual direction in the midst of their daily lives. Perhaps they are going through a life change, struggling with a sin, like greed, or discerning a vocation to marriage.

Directees usually meet with their directors once a month for thirty minutes to an hour. This type of direction might cost anywhere from $50 to $90 a session. Some religious communities ask for a free will offering. A spiritual director doesn't tell her directees what to do. Rather she listens to the ebbs and flows of their life and helps them to discern for themselves how God might be calling them to live.

### FINDING A SPIRITUAL DIRECTOR

Spiritual Direction International maintains a global directory of registered directors, but you should also ask around. Do you know anyone in spiritual direction who could recommend a good person? Do you live near a monastery or convent, Catholic college, university, or retreat center? These are all good places to begin your search. Likewise, do you know a wise or holy person, a person of deep faith and prayer, or a gifted nun or priest in your community who might be willing to meet with you?

Finding a good fit is important for both the director and the directee. Look for someone you feel comfortable with, someone who is wise and experienced, but also blunt. A spiritual director should be someone who is a good listener, but who will also, when necessary, challenge you. Most spiritual directors recommend meeting for three or four sessions before deciding if it feels like a good fit. If it's not working out, they might be able to recommend someone else. Or if what you're looking for is more like psychotherapy, they might be able to point you in that direction.

All of us can benefit from a spiritual friendship that helps us reconnect with the God who loves us and who said, "If you love me, you will keep my commandments" (John 14: 15). Catholics believe in a God who wants to enter into a relationship with us, "For we are his handiwork, created in Christ Jesus for the good works that God has prepared in advance, that we should live in them" (Ephesians 2:10).

# 72

# SANT'EGIDIO, LAY GROUPS, SERVICE, AND SOCIAL JUSTICE

No one has a right to sit down and feel hopeless. There
is too much work to do.

—SERVANT OF GOD DOROTHY DAY

Imagine that you've just graduated from college and moved to a city for your first real job. How will you live your faith and find community? Or perhaps you've just started a family and want to raise your children around people living the faith. Or you're an empty nester and you find yourself with more free time on your hands and depressed by what you read in the news. How will you respond to the universal call to holiness? One way is to join a lay movement or association.

There are hundreds of lay movements and groups officially recognized by the Church. Groups like the Knights of Columbus, which has over 1.8 million members and is the world's largest Catholic fraternal service organization. St. John Paul II called it "the strong right arm of the Church" and praised its members for their brotherhood, and direct service to the poor and the marginalized. In 2013 the Knights of Columbus gave over $170 million to charity and performed over 70 million hours of direct service: from running blood and coat drives, to building homes, participating in disaster relief, and helping crisis pregnancy centers.

African American Catholics might consider the Knights and Ladies Auxiliary of St. Peter Claver, the largest historically African American lay organization in the United States. Groups like this one create community and participate in direct service to people on the peripheries, such as offering scholarships and serving the sick and disabled.

Perhaps you'd like to cook dinner for homeless people at a Catholic Worker house once a week. Catholic Workers are committed to nonviolence, doing the works of mercy, and protesting injustice. If you have a devotion to the Blessed Mother you might want to get involved with the Legion of Mary. If you have a heart for the disabled, you might want to check out a L'Arche community.

These and dozens of other lay groups and small faith communities demonstrate how laypeople share in the vocation of the original apostles, how they are called to serve their neighbors and witness to the love of God.

Too often there is a perceived tension in Christian circles between those members who focus on spirituality (prayer, the sacraments, Scripture, and the spiritual works of mercy) and those who focus on action (charity, social justice, and the corporeal works of mercy). This is unfortunate, because if we pray and take God's Word seriously, then we will want to care for the poor, the outcast, the unborn, and the elderly, and we will want to work for a more just and equitable world. Jesus himself chose poverty, and he repeatedly and explicitly calls for his disciples to care for the poor. In fact, in the Gospel of Matthew, this is Jesus's final word on entering the kingdom of heaven (Matthew 25:31-46). He says, "Whatever you did for one of these least brothers of mine, you did for me" and "what you did not do for one of these least ones, you did not do for me" (Matthew 25:40, 45).

## THE COMMUNITY OF SANT'EGIDIO

One of the lay groups that best models how a solid foundation in prayer and the Word of God bears fruit in good works is the Community of Sant'Egidio, which has been praised by the last three popes for its spirituality, ecumenism, and service to the poor.

In college, my best friend was a member of a Sant'Egidio community. She met with her group for Evening Prayer every Monday and visited a nursing home in a poor part of town every Friday. The day I broke up with my boyfriend I was depressed and didn't want to leave my house. I told her not to come over, that I just wanted to be alone. She came over anyway, and after doing my dishes and listening to me talk for a while she said, "C'mon let's go," and took me with her to visit the nursing home. Every part of me just wanted to stay home and watch movies, but doing something kind for someone else, and taking a break from feeling sorry for myself, actually made me feel a lot better.

In any major city in the United States you can find a Sant'Egidio community. Their Evening Prayer services are renowned for their beautiful a cappella singing and preaching. Even non-believers enjoy these services, and all are welcome, so it's a good place for seekers. Today there are 50,000 official members in seventy countries and many more who participate in the work of the community in an unofficial capacity.

Sant'Egidio was started in Rome in 1968 by a group of high school students who found themselves living in a secular post-Christian world. They rejected communism and fascism, and were troubled by the American bombings of civilians in Vietnam. They were inspired by the Scriptures and wondered what it would look like to live the Gospel in the world. They wanted to change the world by changing people's hearts.

The founders of Sant'Egidio were inspired by the example of St. Francis of Assisi, who made friends with the poor, spoke with Muslims during the Crusades, and who, like Jesus, rejected the other-as-enemy logic of the world.

These teenagers were also responding to the isolation of modern life. They wanted to go out on the streets and meet their neighbors.

They began by going to the poorest part of Rome and starting an after-school program. There they shared what they had learned in their classes with young people who could not afford to go to school.

From these humble beginnings the community has continued to grow and flourish. They've opened hospices for AIDS patients, held interfaith prayer services in the spirit of ecumenical dialogue, and opened restaurants where mentally and physically disabled persons can work. They've fed the homeless and hungry, worked for the abolition of the death penalty, and even ended wars. In 1992, Sant'Egidio peace negotiators brokered a peace deal that brought an end to a fifteen-year civil war in Mozambique that had cost over a million lives and displaced more than half a million people.

One of the key tenets of Catholic social teaching is "solidarity," the belief that individuals and nations have a special responsibility to provide for the poor and the outcast, the people Jesus calls "the least of these." The Church teaches that, despite our ethnic, religious, and ideological differences, we are all members of a single human family, and we are called to be our brothers' and sisters' keepers.

Laypeople live their baptism every day in a myriad of small and unseen acts. They give to the poor. They wipe children's noses and bottoms. They work two jobs to feed their families. They bring Communion to the sick and homebound. The work can be hard. It's good to have friends and acquaintances who encourage and support you along the way.

# 73

# CATHOLIC TATTOOS

For I bear the marks of Jesus on my body.
–ST. PAUL (GALATIANS 6:17)

Christians believe that baptism leaves an indelible mark on the soul. For some, tattoos can be an outward mark of that inward reality. According to the Pew Research Center, 36 percent of young Americans between the ages of eighteen and twenty-five have at least one tattoo. Some get tattoos as a sacramental, like a cross or a medal, that is permanent. In the West, many young Catholics have found that the crucifixes, rosaries, medals, icons, paintings, prayers, and saint attributes of Catholicism often translate well into tattoo art.

Catholics believe that the body is sacred and a temple of the Holy Spirit, as St. Thomas Aquinas wrote, "And so with the affection of charity with which we love God we should love our bodies too." So a tattoo must not disrespect the human person or the human family in any way. Likewise, a tattoo should not be motivated by vanity, self-hatred, or pride. If you are considering a tattoo, make sure you get it from a safe and reputable tattoo parlor. A year or two is not too long to consider this, or any, lifelong commitment. Is getting a tattoo divinely motivated or simply the glorification of self? Make sure you

consider both the image and its placement. Is the tattoo for you or for others? How visible should it be? Should it be in white or black ink? Is this a sign or a symbol you can live with as an employee, a spouse, a parent, a priest or religious?

Tattoos aren't for everyone. Many find them beautiful, others dislike how they look, but the Catholic Church does not forbid them. In fact, the Catholic Council of Northumberland in 786 deemed a Christian bearing a tattoo "for the sake of God" worthy of praise. Some even see the pain associated with the tattoo, which can be intense, as a kind of spiritual exercise.

In Egypt, the practice of Christian tattoos goes back thousands of years. A persecuted minority under Muslim rule, many Coptic Christians would get a small tattoo of a cross on their inner wrist, forehead, or temple, despite the consequences. Some Coptic children were forced to convert to Islam. As a result, many Copts would tattoo their children, wanting to mark them with the sign of the cross, come what may. Coptic Christians still suffer tremendous persecution, but their willingness to be different has made them a dauntless minority. They remain the largest Christian community in the Middle East, and the practice of Christian tattooing remains widespread in rural Egypt.

Flannery O'Connor's favorite short story of those she wrote is called "Parker's Back." In the story, O. E. Parker, a nonreligious and chronically dissatisfied man who is covered with meaningless tattoos, has a frightening experience: He is thrown from his tractor just before it crashes into a tree and bursts into flames. O'Connor writes, "If he had known how to cross himself he would have done it." After this experience, Parker rushes into the city to get "God" tattooed on his back. As he flips through the pages of the religious tattoo art, he rejects the comforting images of "The Smiling Jesus" and the "Physician's Friend" and instead chooses an image of a "Byzantine Christ with all demanding eyes." When he goes home to his fundamentalist Christian wife to show her the tattoo, thinking she will be moved by the change in him, she instead accuses him of idolatry and beats him "until she had nearly knocked him senseless and large welts had formed on the face of the tattooed Christ."

Many Christians still see the man with "God" tattooed on his back as a freak or an outcast, but perhaps this is in some way the goal. A follower of Christ ought to be a challenge to himself and others, someone difficult to classify, a stranger in a strange land. Someone who suffers, like O. E. Parker, who, at the end of "Parker's Back" is cast out into the night alone "crying like a baby." In one sense all Christians are O. E. Parker, claimed for the world by job titles, brand-name clothes, and other status symbols, and terrified of being claimed by God. For Parker and others like him, the religious tattoo is an outward sign of an inward conversion, and because of its permanence, a lifelong commitment.

There are many different types of Catholic tattoos. Some honor a beloved saint: an anchor for St. Clement of Rome, an ax for St. Thomas More, a heart for St. Teresa of Ávila, the tau cross of St. Francis. This attribute can be a reminder for those who wish to follow the way of the saint. One might also have a reproduction of a painting or icon of a saint turned into a tattoo.

## TYPES OF CATHOLIC TATTOOS

Tattoos can also be a sign of devotion to Christ, a sign of God's love, or a reminder to turn away from sin. Among the more common images are: a cross, a crucifix, a sacred heart, a line of Scripture, or a picture of Jesus.

Some get tattoos after celebrating the sacrament of marriage; for example, someone might get a tattoo of a spouse's name in a heart. This permanent mark is a sign of a permanent commitment. The spousal tattoo might be followed by a tattoo of a child's name, birthdate, or baptismal date, or a symbol associated with their child's or children's namesakes.

People who have overcome serious illnesses sometimes get tattoos as a sign of their endurance through the battle, or their gratitude to God. I know a young woman who was diagnosed with cancer when she was twenty-seven years old and thirty-two weeks pregnant. She prayed to the Holy Spirit during her time of trial and experienced incredible peace in the midst of her suffering. When she was declared cancer-free she got a tattoo of a white dove on her wrist as a reminder of the peace she found by "giving everything over to God."

Still others get tattoos as a way of keeping a loved one's memory alive. A Catholic hospice nurse I know prepared the body of a man who had died on her shift. She saw that he was covered with tattoos, each bearing a person's name and the words "Rest in peace." She said, "It made me glad to think that so many people were waiting for him."

If you're considering a tattoo, find a work of art and an artist whose work bears the weight of the mystery (this might mean traveling to another city or state). Then consult a spiritual advisor or trusted friend. Think and pray about it and take as much time as you need to feel certain that this is what you really want to do, and that this is not merely a passing interest. Too many people get tattoos that they later come to regret. Finally, frugality is a virtue, but not when it comes to tattoos. You get what you pay for, so save up for an artist whose work you admire.

Tattoos with religious themes remind us that the saints of today may look different from those of ages past. What remains the same is that the light of Christ shines through them all.

# ADULTHOOD

~~~~~~~~~~~~~~~~~~~~~~~~~~~~~~~~~~~~~~~~~~

# 74

# THE SACRAMENT OF MARRIAGE

My beloved is mine and I am his.

—THE SONG OF SONGS 2:16

American culture sets a high bar for weddings: a beautiful setting, a diamond ring, and an expensive dress. By contrast, all that you need for a wedding in the Catholic Church is the bride and the groom (one of whom must be a baptized Catholic), a priest or deacon, and two witnesses.

The Catholic Church sets a high bar when it comes to marriage. The sacrament of matrimony is to be entered into freely by adults who have undergone a period of discernment. Catholics who want to marry in the Church are asked to meet with a priest or deacon nine to twelve months before the ceremony for marriage prep, or Pre-Cana. In these meetings the priest or deacon might offer financial, emotional, or spiritual advice to the couple. The couple will discuss their personality types; their expectations, hopes, and fears; how to space children for reasons "appropriate to responsible parenthood" using Natural Family Planning; and anything else that might be relevant. The priest or deacon will make sure that both partners are entering into the marriage without reservation. Some couples choose

a priest or deacon who already knows them; others might do their Pre-Cana on an engaged couples retreat, or through a class at their church.

## MARRIAGE IS A VOCATION

The reason that a period of discernment is required is that Catholics believe that marriage is a vocation, or calling. Just like a priest or religious, a married person is committing him- or herself to a school for holiness. They are promising to be faithful to one person for the rest of their lives "in good times and bad, in sickness and in health."

They are promising themselves to a life of love, mutual service, and fidelity. They are surrendering their radical independence and becoming, as Jesus puts it, "one flesh." Catholics of childbearing age also promise to "accept children lovingly from God and bring them up according to the law of Christ." This prescription goes back to the Jewish idea that children are not primarily burdens but blessings. Traditionally, Jewish weddings took place outdoors as a sign that the marriage might be blessed with as many children as the stars of heaven (Genesis 15:5).

In short, marriage in the Catholic Church, as opposed to civil marriage, is a tall order, only possible with God's grace, a supportive community, and the total commitment of both spouses. Both spouses must be willing to work on themselves, to forgive, even to walk out into the snow naked for one another like St. Francis did for Christ and the Church.

## MARRIAGE IS A SACRAMENT

In addition to being a vocation, marriage is a sacrament in the Catholic Church. Since the thirteenth century, the Catholic Church has officially recognized marriage as a sacrament, as Jesus blessed marriage when he attended the wedding feast at Cana. A sacrament is a visible sign of God's invisible presence in the world. In marriage, the couple is called to become a source of grace and blessing to each other, to their community, and to their children, whom they are to teach by example in the home. The family home is rightly called "the domestic Church" and is a school for the virtues of love, endurance, joy, hard work, forgiveness, and self-gift.

Catholics believe with St. Paul that marriage is also a great *mystery*, and that by its fidelity, it ought to mirror the love Christ has for his people, the Church.

## THE WEDDING LITURGY

For the wedding ceremony, the engaged couple picks the readings: one from the Old Testament, one from the New Testament, a Gospel reading, and a responsorial psalm. They also pick the music. Planning the liturgy is a good way for couples to think about what they hope their life together will be about.

For our wedding my husband requested the Litany of the Saints. To him it seemed the honest way to begin: asking for help. We knew that marriage could be tough, and we figured we could use all the help we could get. So instead of the "Wedding March" or Pachelbel's *Canon*, we walked down the aisle, arm in arm, to a litany of the saints. In preparation we had made a long list of the names we hoped to include in our litany: the names of the saints we admired and the saints our family members had been named after or had chosen for their confirmations. With priestly permission, we bent the rules slightly at the Mass and at the end of the litany invoked a handful of deceased holy men and women who were dear to us—not yet canonized or beatified, but whom we nevertheless asked for prayers. As I heard the names chanted, I could imagine the beloved dead helping us on our way. All our family and friends, even those who had died, had gathered there to offer prayers and give blessings.

Whatever you choose to do, keep in mind that the wedding Mass is an opportunity to pick readings or hymns that you will return to again and again in your life together. At our wedding, a friend who was also a musician performed "Amazing Grace."

If you are a Catholic marrying a non-Catholic, ask the priest about having a word service instead of a Mass. A Catholic marrying a non-baptized person needs to receive a dispensation from the bishop in order for the marriage to go forward.

Interestingly, the sacrament of marriage is the only sacrament not administered by a priest. The bride and groom administer the sacrament of marriage to each other when they say "I do." The priest or deacon accepts, blesses, and pronounces the marriage.

## WHY MARRY?

It's easy to look at the sacrament of marriage as outdated or unlivable in today's world because it demands so much compromise from both husband and wife. Is it possible to be faithful to one person for a lifetime and actually be happy? Marriage is hard. People change. No one knows what the future holds.

In fact, some people who marry in the Catholic Church *are* granted annulments because the sacrament was in some way invalid. One spouse never intended to be faithful, was unable to give consent due to mental illness or familial pressure, or was abusive, for example.

And yet many married people say that being happily married for life is possible precisely because being married is not about perfection. Rather, marriage requires a radical acceptance and forgiveness of your own imperfection and the imperfection of your spouse. Marriage is an opportunity to grow in love, to grow in holiness, and to grow in forgiveness. It requires change.

Perhaps you will discover that you aren't as good a listener as you had previously thought, that you need to drink less, that you're impatient, that you've been pretty narcissistic most of your life, that you need to say "thank you" or "I love you," that a spouse's illness will mean changing your plans, or a child's struggle will mean that you will need to spend more time at home.

But what in life is worth doing that isn't hard? To become proficient at anything (a sport, an instrument, a craft, medicine, law, painting) requires years of dedication and sacrifice. And what in life do we truly appreciate that comes easily? The greatest blessings are often the ones that we've had to fight for. But who doesn't long to give their heart to something irrevocably, to be known for who they really are and loved anyway. Even though the people of God mess up time and again, God never stops loving them. In the same way, spouses are to love each other as Christ loves the Church, and a love like that changes everything.

# 75

# CONSECRATED VIRGINITY

*I belong to Him whom the angels serve.*

−ST. AGNES OF ROME

Since the apostolic age, Christians have understood that building the kingdom of God will require that some people remain single. These celibate people, free from the demands of marriage and family life, the need to make a living or raise children, are able to commit themselves in a unique way to God's service, and are free to go wherever the Spirit leads (CCC, 922).

As Paul writes in his First Letter to the Corinthians:

> I should like you to be free of anxieties. An unmarried man is anxious about the things of the Lord, how he may please the Lord. But a married man is anxious about the affairs of the world, how he may please his wife, and he is divided. An unmarried woman or a virgin is anxious about the things of the Lord, so that she may be holy in both body and spirit. . . . I am telling you this for your own benefit, . . . for the sake of propriety and adherence to the Lord without distraction (1 CORINTHIANS 7:32-35).

If you are a woman who does not feel called to marriage or to religious life, then you may have a vocation to consecrated virginity. To consecrate something is to bless it, or dedicate it to God's service, to name it as sacred. Both people and things can be consecrated. A church building is consecrated, for example, so too is the abbess of a monastery. Consecrated virgins are women who feel called to live in the world as single people and yet who desire to give themselves irrevocably to God alone.

Consecrated virginity is an ancient vocation, one that predates religious life. Before there were religious orders for women there were consecrated virgins. The tradition holds that St. Matthew the apostle was martyred for consecrating a virgin. St. Agnes, St. Lucy, and St. Cecilia, early Christian martyrs, were also consecrated virgins. Each had vowed her life to the service of Christ and refused her arranged marriage. Each was executed for being a Christian, but not before leading many others to Jesus and the Church. St. Cecilia, for example, was so certain of her calling that her intended husband, Valerian, wanted to know the source of her peace. Because of Cecilia, Valerian was baptized, even though he knew that practicing Christianity would lead to his death as a martyr.

The custom of blessing virgins to live independently in the world fell out of practice during the Middle Ages, when it was unsafe for a woman to live alone without the protection of a religious order, father, or husband.

*The Rite of Consecration to a Life of Virginity for Women Living in the World* was reintroduced at the Second Vatican Council and was approved by Blessed Pope Paul VI in 1970. At that time, it was not uncommon for women to run companies and countries and live on their own. It seemed like the right moment to reintroduce a blessed way of life from the early Church, wherein women could live independently and give glory to God through work and prayer.

Just as ordination is a vocation that is open only to men, since priests and bishops are said to represent Christ, the Bridegroom, consecrated virginity is a vocation that is open only to women. Members of the order of virgins are said to represent the Church, the Bride of Christ. Consecrated virgins also have a special devotion to the Virgin Mary, who was consecrated by the Holy Spirit at the annunciation.

Unlike women religious, who make vows to God, the consecration to a life of virginity is a blessing that a woman receives from her bishop. As such, consecrated virginity is the only irrevocable vocation in the Catholic Church. A priest, for example, can be released from his priestly duties and given permission to marry, though he is always considered a priest, but a consecrated virgin cannot be released from her blessing, just as the Eucharist cannot be unconsecrated. Neither can a person be un-baptized. A consecrated virgin is consecrated for life.

In 2014 there were between six and seven thousand consecrated virgins living in the world. These women are not usually hermits or anchorites, though some are. They work regular jobs, jobs not necessarily in the Church (though they do devote themselves to the service of their local diocese), and they wear regular clothes, not habits. They meet with their local bishop annually to discuss their spiritual life and service to the Church, but unlike diocesan priests or members of a religious order, they are free to discern independently where they would like to live and what kind of work they would like to do. Consecrated virgins are scholars and doctors, missionaries and firefighters. They work in dance studios, churches, and in social work. Wendy Beckett, a Sister of Notre Dame de Namur who left her convent in 1970 to become a consecrated virgin, went on to become a world-renowned art critic.

After Vatican II, many nuns left their convents and shed their habits to serve God and live independently in the world. Some of these women may have had vocations to consecrated virginity.

The life of a consecrated virgin is unfettered and, in many ways, uniquely liberated, and yet, as is the case with any kind of vocation, there are crosses particular to it. It can be a lonely life. A young woman considering consecration told me, "It can be difficult to find your self-identity in God alone. In some ways, a consecrated virgin is a lifelong pilgrim."

Members of a religious community often take a vow of stability and are duty-bound to care for one another. Likewise, parents and children are obligated to love one another. A life of consecrated virginity means forgoing that kind of support. For this reason, some consecrated virgins have formed themselves into associations for mutual support, like the United States Association of Consecrated Virgins.

Consecrated virgins are often asked, "Why don't you just live in the world as single women? Why take a vow?" One young woman told me, "I think everyone has a desire to give themselves irrevocably to something. This is a way of saying, 'This is who I am, and who God is calling me to be. It's not just a holding pattern. It's not that I haven't met the right person. Jesus is not a consolation prize.' For me, the attraction is to belong completely to the Lord, to recognize every moment of your life as giving glory to God, and to show the world that you can be a regular person that is totally dedicated to God."

Consecrated or not, the world needs single people to be good aunts and uncles, siblings and friends. Celibate people who live in the world are free to form deep and lasting friendships, as Jesus did, and to be present to people who are suffering in a way that monks who live in monasteries and people who are raising families may not be able to be. One consecrated virgin told me that people she has only just met often open up to her and tell her their problems. Consecrated virgins, nuns, priests, and single people may also be more willing to take risks, to travel to a foreign country as a missionary or relief worker, relying only on the hospitality of strangers, for example, or to take a homeless person into their homes.

In the Rite of Consecration of Virgins Living in the World, women wear a bridal veil and receive a ring as a symbol of their commitment to Christ. They are given a book of the Liturgy of the Hours (the Divine Office), which they are expected to pray daily for the needs of the Church and the world. Consecrated virgins also attend daily Mass.

Still, many bishops will not consecrate young women because they want young women to be sure that the desire for consecration is not merely a phase. And yet, if you have spoken to consecrated virgins, done your research, and are confident of your calling, one consecrated virgin told me, "Don't wait. Just as it's important for people to know young, talented, and good-looking priests who could have chosen money or marriage and chose God and service instead, it's good for the Church to see young women who could do anything, but who have chosen to dedicate their lives to Christ."

# 76

# MAKING A HOME ALTAR, SHRINE, OR PRAYER CORNER

*Catholicism is a matter of the body and the senses as much as it is a matter of the mind and the soul, precisely because the Word became flesh.*

–FR. ROBERT BARRON,
*Catholicism: A Journey to the Heart of the Faith*

Human beings are social by nature. We're interested in how other people order their lives. Part of the reason there are so many reality, home design, and renovation shows on television is that we're curious to see what the interiors of other people's houses look like. We want to know how these private spaces speak to what the people value, or don't. Watch one of these shows and you'll quickly discover that, at the moment, Americans are in love with stainless-steel appliances and open floor plans.

What you probably won't see on one of these shows is a home altar, shrine, or prayer corner. If the people who reside in these TV-ready houses are religious or spiritual, you wouldn't know it by looking around. Of course, many of the items in our homes are dictated by necessity, but others betray who we are and what we love. Beige rooms with mostly undecorated walls, in which technological gadgets are the visual focal point, have come to define contemporary living. This is unfortunate, because, as William G. Storey writes, in *A Catholic Book of Hours and Other Devotions*, "Long before Christians built churches for public prayer, they worshiped daily in their homes."

Before Vatican II, many Catholic homes had religious art and devotional items placed throughout. It wasn't uncommon to find a cross or a crucifix in every bedroom, a statue of St. Francis or the Blessed Virgin Mary in the garden, a picture of the Sacred Heart of Jesus or an icon of a patron saint in the cooking or living area, and of course a Bible and book of prayers, along with some candles, incense, or holy water, somewhere on a shelf.

Shortly after moving into a new house, apartment, or single room, Catholics would first bless their home, dedicating it to Jesus, and then begin putting away their things, which also meant finding places for crosses, rosaries, or other devotional items. Some of these devotional items, like a grandparent's sick call crucifix, would be passed down, one generation to the next.

The Orthodox tradition was similar, but more focused. After blessing the home many Orthodox Catholics would set up a prayer corner or small shrine, where an individual or family could gather for prayer, spiritual reading, or contemplation. Creating a more focused space for icons or sacred art, which can be gazed at or reverenced as an aid to prayer, for example, by kissing an icon of Jesus every night before bed, turns the images into liturgical items.

When we think about incorporating sacred art into our homes many of us feel uneasy and have no idea where to begin. Often we've never seen sacred art that wasn't poorly wrought or overly sentimental. As a result, many of us think that we don't like the way contemporary religious art looks. Or we might feel self-conscious about putting something so personal or profound on a wall for anyone to see. Then again, our faith *is* personal, but it *isn't* private. It's part of who we are. When I was a teenager, I gave my parents a hard time about all of the religious art in our home. It made me self-conscious.

Yet there's a valuable distinction to be made between religious art, which is merely decorative (hang it or don't hang it; it's up to you), and religious art, or sacramentals, that serve as liturgical objects because they are used to facilitate prayer. Sacramentals are works of art, objects, signs, symbols, or prayers, taken from ordinary life, that point us toward, and connect us with, the holy. Holy water, for example, is a sacrament that reminds a Christian of his or her baptism.

When I was growing up, I teased my parents about all of the religious art in our home, but I also loved standing around the Advent wreath and lighting candles in the darkness. For me, when we used candles or icons in family prayer, they ceased being merely decorative and started to become meaningful. As centerpieces go, our family Advent wreath wasn't particularly lovely, yet some of my most profound experiences of prayer as a child happened around it, that is, when we used the wreath not simply as a holiday decoration but to say Vespers and prepare our hearts for the birth of Christ. Gazing at lit candles in an otherwise dark room helped to orient my heart to Jesus "the Light of the World," and a light no darkness can extinguish.

The Scriptures tell us, "Rejoice always. Pray without ceasing" and "in all circumstances give thanks, for this is the will of God in Christ Jesus" (1 Thessalonians 5:16-18). How might our lives be different if we designated a small space in our homes for prayer, contemplation, or gratitude, just as we designate large spaces for watching television, making dinner, or folding laundry?

## HOW DO I MAKE A HOME ALTAR, SHRINE, OR PRAYER CORNER?

When it comes to private devotions, there are endless variations and formulations. Your prayer space can be as simple or as elaborate as you like. What's more, people's aesthetic sensibilities vary. For example, some dislike contemporary art, while others, like Pope Benedict XVI, who commissioned work from modern artists, appreciate classical as well as abstract and nonrepresentational artwork.

Here are some ideas to get you started.

## Creating a Set Space

The early Christians would hang an icon of Jesus, or a cross, on an eastern-facing wall, so that they could pray facing the east (as Catholics still do at church). This practice was in keeping with the Jewish tradition, "Look to the East, Jerusalem" (Baruch 4:36).

Praying facing the east is also rooted in the New Testament. The wise men found the Christ child in the east by consulting Scripture and following a star, and "the sign of the son of Man" is supposed to appear in the east upon Jesus's return. If you hang a cross or an icon of Jesus on an eastern-facing wall, consider praying before it.

Another idea is to turn a closet or small room into a "prayer closet" for individual prayer. In the business of life we all need reminders from time to time to "go to your inner room, close the door, and pray to your Father in secret" (Matthew 6:6). I know a mother who used to encourage her older children to go into the family prayer room with the readings of the day and meditate on them before making a big life decision, like where to go to college. Sometimes they would come out of the prayer space with no sense of what they should do, and so she would encourage them to return the next day, and the day after that, until they had peace.

Your prayer corner might be a place to hang a piece of religious art, such as an oil painting or an icon, or a shelf on which to keep a small spiritual library. My husband and I enjoy seasonal prayer with our children, but we are working to create a more permanent place for sacramentals in our home. We have a friend who's an artist and a monk, so we've asked him to do a painting for us of the Catholic Worker artist Ade Bethune, to whom we have a devotion, and we hope to put the painting in a future prayer space. Your prayer space might also be a place to keep family keepsakes: First Communion or baptismal photos, or the holy cards of loved ones who have died, or sacramentals like Palm Sunday crosses, incense, or a baptismal candle.

Others keep vigil lights or candles in their prayer corner. A burning candle can be a visible reminder of the promise of Christ that "where two or three are gathered together in my name, there am I in the midst of them" (Matthew 18:20). The lighting of a votive candle can also be an invitation to prayer, or a visual way of making one's needs known to God. After lighting a candle you might pray an invocation like this: "God be with me." "Come, Lord Jesus." Or "Come, Holy Spirit."

Do you prefer praying outdoors? Many Catholics like to pray while walking or running. Still others create wayside shrines in their yards or on roadsides. These are frequently seen in Europe, Mexico, and South America. They often spring up in the United States along highways at a place where someone has died, but they can show up anywhere. Outdoor shrines often feature a cross or a small statue of Jesus or the Blessed Virgin Mary in some kind of a wood or stone shelter.

### Creating a Space That Changes with the Seasons of the Church Year

Some items might stay in your prayer space year-round: the Bible, a cross, holy water, candles, a prayer book, such as *Catholic Household Blessings and Prayers*, or a rosary received at your First Communion. Other items might change with the liturgical season.

Clear off the top of a dresser, a mantel, or a bookshelf and make this a place to pray around the Advent wreath before Christmas. In Lent, use the candles and candle holder, unadorned, without the greenery. In addition, in Lent, you might put out an alms box. Similarly, the family might gather here to pray a Rosary, novena, Vespers, or a Chaplet of Divine Mercy for a special need.

If you have young children, involve them in changing your prayer space with the seasons. During Advent a purple cloth might appear.

In Ordinary Time you might use a green cloth, in Easter, white. May is Mary's month, so an image of the Blessed Virgin might appear, or fresh flowers in her honor. In November, Catholics remember the dead, so you might put out pictures of deceased relatives as a reminder to pray for them.

Likewise, experiment with different postures in personal and communal prayer. Catholics believe that the soul is enmeshed in the body, or that the body is the form of the soul. As such, what we do with our bodies matters.

Traditionally, Catholics praying in a group would stand for hymns and psalms, sit for readings and meditation, and kneel for intercessions and final prayers. Gestures might also be incorporated: the sign of the cross, bowing in reverence to the Holy Trinity, and extending your hands during the Lord's Prayer. In addition, a final kiss, hug, or handshake might be done for the sign of peace. Changes in posture aren't obligatory, of course, but they can help facilitate a sense of reverence. Try different postures and discover what happens when you approach God in prayer in different ways.

And if none of this works for you, that's fine, too. Catholics are required to attend Mass once a week. Popular devotional practices, like Evening Prayer, aren't obligatory. They're simply tools that can help turn our hearts and lives toward God.

In the end, we make space in our homes for things that are important, for things that need to be done. Of course, having a place for prayer isn't necessary in order to pray. God is ever-present, and prayer can happen anywhere and at any time. And yet, knowing God is present and perceiving God's presence in our daily lives are often two very different things. It might be worthwhile to try designating a small corner in our homes for contemplation.

Jesus said that we need to "turn and become like children" in order to enter the kingdom of heaven (Matthew 18:3). Young children aren't self-conscious. They love to light candles and sing hymns in the darkness. They love dipping their fingers in holy water and blessing a room. This might be part of why so many people love working out. Exercise classes like CrossFit give adults permission to be unself-conscious, to be like children, to climb ropes and balance on one foot and stand on their heads. I think there's an unself-conscious person in each of us, yearning to make space in our lives for encountering truth, goodness, and beauty, which Pope Benedict XVI said, "can become a path toward the transcendent, toward the ultimate Mystery, toward God."

~~~~~~~~~~~~~~~~~~~~~~

# 77

# CATHOLIC ROAD TRIPS AND PILGRIMAGES

We are wayfarers, pilgrims of the Absolute.

–POPE ST. JOHN PAUL II

We're all familiar with the errand. It's a trip from one place to another in pursuit of a specific goal. Going to the grocery store or the post office is an errand. It's one type of journey, and a pilgrimage is another. But the category "journey" is about what the two, errand and pilgrimage, share.

The word "pilgrim" is from the Latin *peregrinus*, a word that means "foreigner" or "stranger." Does that mean one must travel to a foreign land in order to be a pilgrim, to be one who goes on pilgrimage? No, there are holy sites near and far.

Still, many pilgrims do travel far from home, for example to the Sanctuary of Our Lady of Lourdes in France. Over 5 million pilgrims travel to this site every year to pray and ask God for healing. Others might visit Christ's burial cloth, the Shroud of Turin, in Italy; or the Holy Land, to see the places where Jesus lived, worked, and performed miracles. Pope Benedict XVI wrote, "The places of pilgrimage have marked a kind of geography of faith . . . that is, they make visible, almost tangible, how our forefathers encountered the living God, how He did not withdraw after creation or after the time of Jesus Christ, but is always present and works in them so that they were able to experience Him, follow in His footsteps, and see Him in the works He performed."

While you don't have to travel far from home to be a pilgrim, being a pilgrim does demand the attitude of a foreigner: curious, unsure, wondering, willing to be surprised. Foreigners expect new tastes, new sights, new smells, new sounds. They expect to be unsettled.

The one running an errand neither expects nor welcomes wonder. The whole point of an errand is speed and utility. The whole point of a pilgrimage is awe, however long that takes and wherever it leads.

A pilgrim journeys to a holy site with the hope of encountering the holy. Scripture includes many accounts of pilgrimage. One might even see Jesus's earthly life as a pilgrimage. He is conceived in Nazareth, in Israel, and born in Bethlehem, in Judah. In his flesh he knits up the divided kingdom. Jesus spends his earliest years on earth in exile in Egypt, hallowing this foreign land with his presence, just as he will do in Samaria near the end of his life on earth. Jesus *is* the holy site, the sacred place, and as he journeys, wherever he journeys, he brings blessing.

A pilgrim journeys to the sacred place. One might see the Samaritan woman at the well as a pilgrim (John 4:4-42). She thinks she has gone on an errand to draw water from the local well. When she encounters Jesus there, she is suddenly plunged into a foreign land. The water he offers is not water she has ever imagined. Who is this man? How can he, a Jew and a male, speak to her, a Samaritan and a woman? How does he know those hidden parts of her heart? How can she become an evangelist, the one of whom John writes, "Many of the Samaritans of that town began to believe in him because of the word of the woman who testified."

We pilgrims hope to be changed as the Samaritan woman was changed. As Pope Benedict XVI wrote:

> It is from this inner encounter with the Lord that there originated the places and images of pilgrimage in which we, so to

speak, can participate in what they saw, in what their faith provided for them.

There are many pilgrimage sites in the United States. Some of them are dedicated to native saints. Consider visiting one or more of them:

The Shrine of St. Elizabeth Ann Seton—Emmitsburg, Maryland

The Shrine of St. Katharine Drexel—Bensalem, Pennsylvania

The Shrine of St. John Neumann—Philadelphia, Pennsylvania

The Shrine of St. Kateri Tekakwitha—Fonda, New York

The Shrine of the North American Martyrs—Auriesville, New York

The Shrine of St. Mother Marianne Cope—Syracuse, New York

The Shrine of St. Damien of Molokai—Kaunakakai, Hawaii

The Shrine of Blessed Francis Xavier Seelos—New Orleans, Louisiana

The Shrine of Venerable Fr. Solanus Casey—Detroit, Michigan

The Shrine of St. Rose Philippine Duchesne—St. Charles, Missouri

The National Shrine of St. Frances Xavier Cabrini, Chicago, Illinois

The Shrine of Our Lady of Le Leche—St. Augustine, Florida

## THE SOUTHWEST

New Mexico is also a rich site for pilgrimage. El Santuario do Chimayo is often called the Lourdes of America. Located in a small village in northern New Mexico, the church is an old adobe structure, filled with native art and the letters and pictures from pilgrims who have found healing there. Pilgrims go to a little room off the main body of the church to el Pocito, a hole in the ground, from which they scoop the healing earth. Some anoint themselves with soil from el Pocito. Others take it home to anoint their bed-bound ill.

In nearby Santa Fe, pilgrims visit the Loretto Chapel, which is no longer a church, but was built by the Sisters of Loretto in 1873. In the midst of the construction they realized that they had a choir loft, but no stairs leading up to it. The remaining space did not allow for stairs to be built. They would have to use a ladder.

The sisters knew the dangers of using a ladder in full habit. They started a novena to St. Joseph. On the ninth day of the novena, an elderly carpenter showed up and offered to build a staircase at no charge. They expected him to do an errand, but he led them on a very different kind of journey.

The carpenter worked, using only a hammer, a T square, and a saw. He built a circular stairway of thirty-three steps that makes two 360-degree turns. It is built with no central supports, no nails, and no glue. The whole thing is connected with wooden pegs.

After the carpenter finished, he disappeared. The sisters tried to find him to thank him. They checked with the local lumberyard, only to discover he had made no purchases there. Further investigation revealed that the wood he used was not native to New Mexico and was not available for sale in the area in 1873.

The sisters came to believe that the carpenter was St. Joseph, come to help them as he has helped so many others.

## ROAD TRIPS

Summer is a natural time to take a Catholic road trip or pilgrimage. You can even go on pilgrimage without ever entering a church. Go to Kearney, Nebraska, to see the annual migration of the Sandhill cranes, or hike the Maroon Bells in Colorado, twin 14,000 foot peaks. Learn how to stand in prayerful silence before the grandeur of what God has made. As it says in Psalm 148:

> *Praise Him, sun*
> *and moon;*
> *praise him, all*
> *shining stars.*

*Praise him, highest heavens.* . . .
*For he commanded and they were created* (PSALM 148:3-4, 5).

Or, if you're already heading to an American city rich in Catholic history, take some time out of your trip to light a candle at one of these historic sites:

New Orleans, Louisiana: The first Catholic Mass in Louisiana was celebrated in New Orleans in 1699 on Mardi Gras. Visit the oldest continually functioning cathedral in the United States, the Cathedral of St. Louis, in Jackson Square, built in 1789.

St. Louis, Missouri: The "Old Cathedral," or the Basilica of St. Louis, is the oldest cathedral west of the Mississippi River. You can also visit the adoration chapel of the Holy Spirit Adoration Sisters, who have been in perpetual adoration for over eighty-five years.

San Antonio, Texas: The San Antonio Missions to the Native Americans are preserved in San Antonio as a National Historic Park. You can bike or walk the ten-mile mission trail, or visit the San Fernando Cathedral, founded in 1731.

Pittsburgh, Pennsylvania: St. Anthony's Chapel is home to over five thousand relics including a piece of Jesus's crown of thorns and a piece of St. Joseph's cloak. If you love beautiful iconography, visit St. John the Baptist Byzantine Catholic Cathedral while you're in town.

Los Angeles, California: There are over 4.2 million Catholics in the diocese of Los Angeles. Attend Mass at the modern cathedral, Our Lady of the Angels, home to a piece of St. Juan Diego's tilma. In addition, there are many historic Franciscan missions along the coast such as the San Gabriel Arcángel Mission, founded in 1771 and the Mission San Fernando Rey de España, founded in 1797.

As the world has become more affluent and travel has become easier, more people than ever before are going on pilgrimage. These people are leaving behind their noisy lives, if only for a moment, to listen for the still small voice of God.

# 78

# DOMESTIC, PRIESTLY, AND APOSTOLIC BLESSINGS

I can with one eye squinted take it all as a blessing.

—FLANNERY O'CONNOR

When we think of blessings, we usually mean "something I wanted," or "something I understand to be good," like health or wealth or safety. We all say, "Oh, what a blessing," when a healthy child is born, and the birth of a healthy child *is* a blessing. But if you look at the *Book of Blessings: The Roman Ritual*, you will find blessings for joyful times—the blessing of a mother before and after childbirth—and sad times—the blessing of parents after a miscarriage or stillbirth. There are blessings for crime victims and blessings for addicts, as well as blessings for the Advent wreath and blessings for a new home. Blessings for times when the word "blessing" does not come to mind cause us to ask, What is a blessing? Can we be blessed—and can we bless—in all circumstances? This is a way of thinking about blessing that may be unfamiliar to us, so let's begin by asking some questions.

## WHAT DOES IT MEAN TO BLESS?

The Church holds that all of life is under the hand and, so, the blessing of God. The late Father Alexander Schmemann, an Orthodox priest, put it this way,

> God blessed the world, blessed man, blessed the seventh day (that is, time), and this means that He filled all that exists with His love and goodness. . . . So the only *natural* (and not "supernatural") reaction of man, to whom God gave this blessed and sanctified world, is to bless God in return, to thank Him, to *see* the world as God sees it and—in this act of gratitude and adoration—to know, name and possess the world.

The act of blessing, then, is threefold: knowing, naming, and possessing the world. If we know the world, we acknowledge that all of it, even our enemies, belongs to God. Consider what Jesus tells his disciples: "love your enemies, do good to those who hate you," and, further, he says, "bless those who curse you, pray for those who mistreat you" (Luke 6:27-28). Our enemies, like us, are created, known, and loved by God. To acknowledge that truth is to bless them. To bless one's enemies is not the same as liking one's enemies, or even, at least at the beginning of the journey, forgiving them. It means blessing them: knowing and naming them rightly. A wise priest once told me that if I could not forgive someone I hated, I should begin by simply picturing that person held in God's hand, knowing that person as belonging to God, and naming a belonging I could not yet recognize.

When we speak these truths in blessing, we name what we must know. To bless a child is to name him or her as known and loved by God, as a child of God. To bless a meal is to say, "This meal is a gift from God." To bless in the midst of trouble is to name this, too, as under the hand of God.

And then we come to this idea, that to bless is to "possess the world." The word "possess" evokes images of a thing bought and sold, the antithesis of the freely given gifts of God. Listen to God's promise to Israel:

*Your people will all be just;*
*for all time they will possess the land;*
*They are the shoot that I planted,*
*the work of my hands, that I might be glorified.* (ISAIAH 60:21)

Possession here is in the context of God's sovereignty, and it is key to understanding blessing. One cannot say, "Well, this child belongs to God. Let God feed her." All creation does belong to God, who hands it over to us to possess as stewards. We possess the world as farmers possess the land; the wise ones know that others will come after them, to plant and to sow. Their job is to work wisely and well, as long as it is given them to work. They do not control the rain or the drought. They cannot control the winds or the sun. But they can, and must, weed and water and sow and reap. Holy possession also helps us withstand difficulties. It is terrifying to be helpless, out of control, swept along by events we can neither understand nor direct. But, in right possession, we understand that here, too, we are, in St. John Paul II's words, "call(ed) to share in the unfolding of God's plan of creation." In bearing patiently, in prayer, in hope, in continuing to care for others, in refusing to despair, we possess the land of our lives.

## HOW DO WE LEARN TO BLESS?

We learn this skill as we learn any other, by doing it. We should be asking and giving blessings. We should be blessing in the fallow seasons and the full. We should be blessing in joy and in sorrow, in laughter and in tears, at birth beds and deathbeds. In feasting and in fasting. In our homes and at church. People and objects, for all are part of the created world, as named and known and possessed by God, who entrusts us to name, know, and possess in turn.

We call these blessings sacramentals, because, as we read in the *Catechism of the Catholic Church*, they prepare us to receive the grace of the sacraments and dispose us to cooperate with [grace] (CCC, 1670). *Sacramentals have the power to help us know, name, and possess rightly.*

The Church makes a distinction between blessings that are offered by a priest or deacon and blessings that are offered by any baptized person. Parents, who have a special office because of their care and oversight of children, bless their children, for example, but they do not bless a new altar or a religious medal, blessings which are reserved to the ordained. Again, from the *Catechism*, "the more a blessing concerns ecclesial and sacramental life, the more is its administration reserved to the ordained ministry" (CCC 1669).

## DOMESTIC BLESSINGS

Begin by reciting a blessing before meals and before bed. Then add a blessing for waking, for noontime (the traditional time for the Angelus prayer in Mary's honor), and so on throughout the day and throughout one's daily activities. These blessings do not have to be long. Here's a blessing before bed from *Catholic Household Blessings and Prayers*:

> Visit this house, we beg you, Lord,
> and banish from it
> the deadly power of the evil one.
> May your holy angels dwell here
> to keep us in peace,
> and may your blessing be always upon us.
> We ask this through Christ our Lord. Amen.

If you like to sing, pray this old hymn by Thomas Ken. It can be sung to any common meter tune, such as "Tallis' Canon," or "O God, Our Help in Ages Past."

> All praise to thee, my God, this night,
> For all the blessings of the light;
> Keep me, O keep me, King of kings,
> Beneath Thine own almighty wings.
>
> Forgive me, Lord, for Thy dear Son,
> The sin that I this day have done,

That with the world, myself and Thee,
I, before sleep, at peace may be.

Teach me to live that I may dread
The grave as little as my bed;
Teach me to die that so I may
Rise glorious on that final day.

Here's a prayer to be offered over a child's bed, one to which a parent or caretaker could add soothing gestures, touching the child's hand or foot, at the appropriate time during the blessing:

Christ is shepherd over you,
Enfolding you on every side.
Christ will not forsake you, hand or foot,
Nor let evil come near you.

All three of these prayers are taken from a longer order of prayer before bed. As you grow in the practice of daily blessings, you may want to add more Scripture and Gospel canticles. (Gospel canticles are songs from the Gospels. Traditionally, the Song of Zechariah is sung at Morning Prayer; the Magnificat, or Song of Mary, is sung at Evening Prayer; and the Song of Simeon is sung at Night Prayer.) As you and your child look forward to the final blessing, your child may want to add prayers for friends or siblings or grandparents or for needs in the world. We name, know, and possess the needs of our families and friends and those of brothers and sisters we will never meet, but who are linked to us in God's love.

## CHURCH BLESSINGS

Other blessings are reserved to the ordained. When you move into a new apartment or house, ask your parish priest to come and bless the house. Prepare a meal to share with him and others. Bring religious medals, rosaries, or crucifixes to the parish and ask that they be blessed. Ask your priest about other opportunities for priestly blessings. I was once at a gas station in rural New Mexico when a priest drove up. Two young men in a battered pickup asked him to come and bless the truck they use for their work. It was a good example of blessing: The men knew their work, and its implements, to be gifts. By asking for a blessing, they named this truth and then set off to work, possessing in fullness what they had been given. It was a moment of grace in the midst of a long journey.

## PAPAL BLESSINGS

Consider obtaining a papal (or apostolic) blessing for friends celebrating their marriage or anniversary. You can also request a papal blessing for baptism, First Communion, confirmation, priestly ordination, religious profession, secular consecration, ordinations of permanent deacons, and birthdays. This makes a lovely and lasting gift, and the proceeds go to charity.

The blessing will be printed on parchment and can be obtained by sending a request (by regular post or fax, but not e-mail) to the Elemosineria Apostolica, Office of Papal Charities. You can get more information online. The donation for the parchment, which is hand-lettered by one of approximately twenty-nine calligraphers, is just that, a donation that goes toward the care of the poor. You will be asked to pay for cost of the parchment, as well as the cost of packaging and mailing it. It will take at least a month from the time the request is submitted for the parchment to be written and delivered.

Our circumstances change. We are strong and then weak, at peace and then cast into raging seas. But when we seek to see the world as God sees it, when we seek to know, name, and possess the world as God would have us so to do, we are, in all ways, blessed.

# 79

# CATHOLIC SOCIAL TEACHING

There is no other case of one continuous intelligent institution
that has been thinking about thinking for two thousand years.

–G. K. CHESTERTON, *The Thing: Why I Am Catholic*

The social teachings of the Church are an essential part of the faith,
yet many people are unaware that they exist. Since the earliest days of
Christianity, letters and documents of religious instruction have
been circulated, and people like St. Augustine and St. Thomas Aquinas have been ruminating on the social gospel, and asking, "What
should we do as followers of Jesus?"

In the modern era, Catholic social teaching began to be laid out in a formal way by Pope Leo XIII. This era began when he wrote *Rerum Novarum* (On Capital and Labor) in 1891. Since then, popes have written more than a dozen encyclicals, or letters, addressed to the entire world, and "all people of goodwill," on matters of social justice, human dignity, the environment, and peacemaking. In addition, local bishops write pastoral letters on social issues such as the importance of family, the rights of workers, wise stewardship of creation, welcoming immigrants, questions of war and peace, and caring for the poor. Laypeople and scholars also play an important behind-the-scenes role in the creation of these documents.

Two virtues central to Catholic social teaching are charity and justice. These themes are not new to Catholicism. They are essential elements of the faith, going back to the Acts of the Apostles. And yet the Church clearly felt the need to restate her teachings on charity and justice, and think through their application to contemporary circumstances, in light of the Industrial Revolution, the rise of Communism, and the transformation and secularization of European society in the nineteenth century. For example, Karl Marx, the author of *The Communist Manifesto*, famously described religion as "the opium of the people," a pie-in-the-sky delusion of a poor and exploited people, waiting passively to die and go to heaven, where they would finally experience justice and peace.

The social encyclicals of the Church rebuked this idea of a passive Christianity that has nothing to say to subjugated peoples or their subjugators. Catholic social teaching reminds Christians that our life on earth is supposed to be a foretaste of the kingdom, and that we are to witness to "new heavens and a new earth, in which righteousness dwells" (2 Peter 3:13). In this vein, the early encyclicals speak of the need for "social reconstruction," or organizing our individual and communal lives around Gospel values.

Catholic social teaching is also responding to the rise in the nineteenth century of social Darwinism and *laissez-faire* capitalism, which viewed people as commodities, to be disposed of, or devalued, when they were no longer economically viable or productive.

In their speeches and writings, contemporary popes echo Catholic social teaching. For example, when Pope John Paul II spoke about the failures of both communism and capitalism, saying, "I myself, after the historical failure of communism, did not hesitate to raise serious doubts on the validity of capitalism, if by this expression one means not simply the 'market economy' but 'a system in which freedom in the economic sector is not circumscribed within a strong juridical framework which places it at the service of human freedom in its totality.'" Or, for example, when Pope Benedict XVI spoke about the need for immigration reform in the United States, saying, "[Immigration reform] is thus of profound concern to the church, since it involves ensuring the just treatment, and the defense of the human dignity of immigrants." Or, when Pope Francis speaks of abortion and euthanasia as products of a "throwaway culture." He said, "the widespread mentality of profit, the throwaway culture, which has today enslaved the hearts and minds of so many . . . calls for the elimination of human beings, above all if they are physically or socially weaker. Our response to that mentality is a decisive and unhesitating 'yes' to life."

Of course, the best way to learn about Catholic social teaching is to read and reflect on the pertinent documents, from *Rerum Novarum* to *Laudato Si*. When we read the documents, which draw heavily on Scripture and the natural law tradition, certain key themes emerge:

1. **Human dignity.** Every human being is created in the image and likeness of God and is sacred, regardless of race, class, gender, ethnicity, sexual orientation, age, or ability. Catholics believe in a seamless garment of life from conception to natural death. We are all members of one human family, and are called to be our brothers' and sisters' keepers.

2. **Family and community.** The Church rejects the myth of self-authorship. We are communal and interdependent by nature. We are born into families and communities. As a result, we have a duty to protect and promote those institutions, like marriage and schools, which encourage human flourishing.

3. **The dignity of work and the rights of workers.** Work is an

essential part of human life, and workers have a right to a fair wage, safe working conditions, and collective bargaining. The Catholic Church teaches that economics should serve human relationships, not the other way around.

4. **Solidarity.** Jesus instructs his disciples to put the needs of the poor and the vulnerable first (Matthew 25:31-46). Solidarity means committing ourselves to the good of all and standing up for our brothers and sisters, especially the voiceless, people Jesus calls "the least of these."

5. **Stewardship of creation and the universal destination of goods.** We have been entrusted with caring for creation. God has given us many gifts, from the environment and natural resources, which are common goods, to our individual talents. People have a right to own private property. And yet these gifts are not to be squandered, or used only to our own advantage. Rather we must use the gifts we have received wisely and with grateful hearts.

6. **Subsidiary.** Governments have a tendency to become excessively bureaucratic, in some cases becoming totalitarian, where individuals lack basic freedoms, such as religious freedom. To counter this authoritarian tendency, laws should be passed at the local or grassroots level whenever possible. Issues that can be addressed locally should be.

7. **Peace.** It is not permissible to take an innocent human life to solve a social problem. Jesus taught the nonviolent love of friends and enemies and said, "Blessed are the peacemakers." Christians are called to pursue peace and reconciliation and to avoid war and violence, such as capital punishment, whenever possible. War is permissible only if it meets all of the criteria of just war theory. For example, nuclear weapons and other forms of modern warfare, which intentionally target noncombatants, or don't meet other criteria, such as proportionality, are outside the scope of a just war, and may never be used.

Of course, the principles of Catholic social teaching can often seem lofty and removed from the busy lives of ordinary Catholics. Like many people, my husband and I have student loan debt, young children, a small business, and a mortgage. Just keeping up with the bills, creating a loving home, and getting dinner on the table is enough to keep us occupied most of the time. When every dollar is allocated and every hour accounted for, how are the Church's social teachings relevant to our daily lives? Loving God and our family is our first task, but do we need to do more? I think the answer is that we need to do something, but we need not feel burdened by thinking that we have to do it all. In fact, thinking that we need to do it all can become a kind of pride.

As Pope Benedict XVI wrote in *Deus Caritas Est*:

> There are times when the burden of need and our own limitations might tempt us to become discouraged. But precisely then we are helped by the knowledge that, in the end, we are only instruments in the Lord's hands; and this knowledge frees us from the presumption of thinking that we alone are personally responsible for building a better world. In all humility we will do what we can, and in all humility we will entrust the rest to the Lord. It is God who governs the world, not we.

The Catechism gives three main reasons for the existence of Catholic social teaching: to propose principles for reflection, to provide criteria for judgment, and to give guidelines for action (CCC, 2423).

In the middle of the twentieth century, groups like the Christian Family Movement took this three-part instruction to heart and formed small groups or "cells" of lay Catholics who met weekly to discuss social issues, decide what needed to be done in their local communities in light of the Gospel, and then act on their deliberations. Their goal was to "Be doers of the word and not merely hearers" (James 1:22).

I am fortunate to know many doers. For years my in-laws cooked meals at a soup kitchen once a week. A close friend of mine started a free summer camp for poor kids in her neighborhood with nothing to do. When I met him, my husband lived with homeless people in a Catholic Worker community. I have friends and family members who have taken birth mothers and elderly family members into their homes and cared for them, adopted children from orphanages, reduced their companies' carbon footprint, faithfully visited people in nursing homes, brought life-saving medicine to Iraq when doing so was illegal under U.S. sanctions, started nonprofits in Haiti, taught marriage prep classes at church, given free legal aid or medical care to people who couldn't afford it, or who have cooked meals for people who are sick or have a new baby. We don't need to do everything, but we do need to do something. It starts with the person right in front of us, as Blessed Teresa of Calcutta said: "If I look at the mass I will never act. If I look at the one, I will."

Too often we suffer from a lack of imagination when it comes to what our daily lives could look like. In the busyness of life, it is easy to lose sight of the ordinary people, of extraordinary faith, who have changed the world by their actions. In our own time, church communities have often been agents of social change. For example, civil rights for African Americans and the civil rights movement in the United States were born out of American Baptist churches and the Southern Christian Leadership Conference.

In the same way, Catholic social teaching asks all people of goodwill to think about what we might be able to change in our communities by living lives rooted in the love of Jesus Christ. As Pope Benedict XVI wrote, "Love is the light—and in the end, the only light—that can always illuminate a world grown dim and give us the courage needed to keep living and working. Love is possible, and we are able to practice it because we are created in the image of God."

~~~~~~~~~~~~~~~~~~~~~~~~~~~~~~~~~~

# 80

# SICKNESS AND SUFFERING

The Lord has truly borne our sufferings;
he has carried all our sorrows.

Jesus doesn't explain why there is suffering, illness, and death
in the world. He brings healing and hope. He doesn't allow
the problem of evil to be the subject of a seminar. He
allows evil to do its worst to him. He exhausts it,
drains its power, and emerges with new life.

-N. T. WRIGHT, *Simply Good News*

There is no suffering we can know that Christ has not known first.
I remember as a teenager thinking of the traditional three hours we
keep, from noon to three, on Good Friday. It did not seem so bad to
me, Christ in agony on the cross for three hours. Other people I knew
suffered for years. As long as I knew her, my maternal grandmother
suffered with open, weeping sores on her legs, the result of vascular
insufficiency. She walked and stood in pain, always in pain.

As I grew, I came to realize that in those hours on the cross,
Christ knew every moment of pain—my grandmother's pain and the
pain of all the grandmothers who ever lived. Christ knew every blow,
every gunshot, every moment of despair, every moment of fear, and
every pang of loss ever suffered. He knew every phone call with bad
news, every door opening onto the state troopers with their terrible

tidings, every doctor walking out of surgery shaking her head. He felt the terror of the scalded and beaten child. All the suffering that ever was or ever will be, Christ took upon, and into, himself. There is nothing we can know or face or fear or bear that he has not known and faced and feared and borne first.

So we suffer, but we suffer in the sure and certain knowledge that we are not alone. The grace we know in suffering comes from keeping company with Christ, who keeps company with us. And the grace comes, in the words of a patristic teaching, that, "What Christ assumes, Christ redeems." In some way that is, admittedly, hard to understand or accept, the Church teaches that Christ makes holy all that he takes on, which is our full humanity. Christ became human, like us in all things but sin. He grieved. He feared. He suffered, and not just his own losses and injuries, but those of each one of us. Each one. No one's pain is unknown to the crucified Christ.

In the post-Christian West, sickness is often seen as a personal failure or as a personal option that can be avoided through the right combination of diet, exercise, and healthy thinking. The first questions most of us ask when we hear of someone's dire diagnosis are meant to reassure not the ill, but the worried well, that is, ourselves.

"Didn't he smoke?" we ask, because we don't smoke and are thus secure. Right?

"She had put on a lot of weight," we say, because we are fit and are thus protected. Right?

In our culture, the sick bear not only the burden of their illness, but also a burden of shame, the accusation (whether spoken or unspoken) that if they had only taken more vitamin D or walked farther or given up red meat, they would be well. But we recall Jesus's words in the Gospel of Matthew, when he says of the heavenly Father, "For he makes his sun rise on the bad and the good, and causes rain to fall on the just and the unjust" (Matthew 5:45). Sickness and suffering are not the lot of some people, but of all people. It is part of the human condition.

This attitude of blame and fear makes us shun the ill, but the Church teaches that caring for the sick is one of the corporal works of mercy. It is a work we are given as part of the Body of Christ, which has suffered, and continues to suffer, in its Head and in its members. To be present to the sick and suffering is a Christian duty.

## WHAT CAN WE DO?

Just as you encourage the sick in your care to receive medical care and treatment, encourage them to receive Communion. We know from a letter that St. Justin Martyr wrote around AD 155 to the pagan emperor Antonius Pius, explaining what Christians do on Sundays. He writes of the conclusion of the liturgy:

> When he who presides has given thanks and the people have responded, those whom we call deacons give to those present the "eucharisted" bread, wine and water and take them to those who are absent.

St. Justin is speaking of the sick, those who are not able to join the assembly. This concern has been constant from St. Justin's day to our own. Check with your parish to see which Extraordinary Ministers of Holy Communion (laypeople who are trained and sent out on behalf of the community to take Communion to the sick and housebound) are available to visit the patient.

Do not hesitate to take or accompany a sick person to receive the Sacrament of the Sick, the prayer and anointing by which a priest commends the ailing to God. It re-members us to the suffering Christ, who is present to every human need. (Call your parish to find out when the sacrament will be offered. Of course, if the patient is too ill to leave the home or hospital or nursing facility, you can make arrangements for a priest to come and administer the sacrament.) Too many Catholics continue to believe that the Sacrament of the Sick is reserved for those in immediate danger of death, but it is available to all the seriously ill or those facing surgery or hospitalization.

Perhaps the patient in your care faces a long-term illness and requires long-term spiritual care. In addition to requesting visits by your parish priest, ask if your parish has a Stephen's Ministry program. These laypeople, named after the first deacon, St. Stephen, undergo intensive training to befriend the sick and the homebound. They are not pastors, therapists, or medical professionals. They are friends and listeners who can be a great help not only to the patient but also to family caregivers. They operate under rules of strict confidentiality, and you can be sure your needs and struggles, and those of your sick friend or family member, will be held in confidence.

Always pray for the ill. Ask first, of course, if you want to pray with the patient, and make sure this is what the patient also wants. Be mindful, as well, of the patient's pain and need to rest. The seriously ill have small reserves of strength. Fortunately, God hears even the briefest, plainest prayers. These are sometimes called aspirations, and they are helpful when emotions are too intense for words, or time or strength are short. One of the best known and loved of these simple prayers is called the Jesus Prayer:

Lord Jesus Christ, Son of the Living God, have mercy on me, a sinner.

Another is this familiar prayer from the Rosary:

Pray for us, holy Mother of God,
That we may become worthy of the promises of Christ.

Sometimes people are reluctant to suggest prayer because they don't know what to say. There are many good prayer aids and sources. *Catholic Household Blessings and Prayers* has a section on blessing the sick. Other good resources for the sick, and those who care for them, are *A Ritual for Laypersons: Rites for Holy Communion and Pastoral Care of the Sick and Dying*, published by Liturgical Press; *Communion of the Sick*, also published by Liturgical Press; and *Pastoral Care of the Sick*, published by Catholic Book Publishing Corporation, and published in bilingual editions.

It is important for us to remember, as the book of Wisdom says, "God did not make death, nor does he rejoice in the destruction of the living" (Wisdom 1:13). St. Paul, in his letter to the church at

Corinth, writes, "The last enemy to be destroyed is death" (1 Corinthians 15:26).

We have to understand that sickness and death do not enter the world through God's will or God's design. There is no sickness or death in God, who is wholeness and life eternal. Sickness and death come as a result of sin, which entered the world and spread—spreads—like a virus, a virus that has plagued us since the Garden.

We are accustomed to action, to work, to solutions, and often all we can do in the presence of human suffering is to be present to it. This is difficult for Westerners, who often equate quiet companionship with failure or impotence, just as people in Jesus's day equated his death on the cross with failure and impotence. Christians know the power in suffering. We know that in and through Christ's suffering, death itself has been defeated. There will be an end to sickness and death, and it is this assurance that allows us to pray, with the sick, and when we are sick, "Lord Jesus, I hope in you."

# 81

# THE SACRAMENT OF THE SICK AND VIATICUM

*Though the mountains fall away*
*and the hills be shaken,*
*My love shall never fall away from you,*
*nor my covenant of peace be shaken,*
*says the Lord, who has mercy on you.*

—ISAIAH 54:10

The current debate about "death with dignity" is often framed by two poles: death with, presumably, no dignity, in which one either dies in intractable pain, tubed and masked and medicalized, attended by gowned and masked strangers; or, death with dignity, in which one dies in a place and at a time and in the manner of one's choosing, a favorite album playing and invited friends and family gathered round as the sufferer takes a handful of pills and ends the suffering. In reality, "death with dignity" has become another term for suicide.

But the Church offers a third way: an ancient tradition of prayers at the deathbed, of anointings and blessings, coupled with a modern approach to pain management. The Church allows pain medication sufficient to ease the suffering of the dying, even when that medication has unintended side effects, which may hasten death. But, and this matters, *the intention* is to ease suffering in one actively dying, not to kill the patient (CCC, 2279). The Church understands its role, and the role of its members, is to be present with the dying, to accompany the dying on their journey, and to assure that the dying are not alone. The Church invites us to see what death with dignity actually looks like: It looks like the Sacrament of the Sick and the Mass of Christian Burial. It looks like Christ walking the way to Calvary, Christ hanging on the cross. It looks like Christ, who suffered and died as one of us, the people who must also suffer and die.

My mother did not die at home, where she had lived for years with my husband and me. That was a sorrow for her, and for me. Her last months were spent in the memory care unit of a nursing home, and it was a hard time for her and for all of us who loved her. But she was never abandoned or forgotten. Stephen's Ministers brought her Holy Communion. Her parish priest visited each week. Her hospice nurses were gentle and faithful in their care. We talked to her and sang to her and held her hands. We stroked her cheeks and brushed her hair. My sisters took turns coming from long distances. My grown children brought their children to visit, bringing light and laughter to her rooms. My pregnant daughter encouraged her grandmother to touch her growing belly and to feel the kicks of this unborn great-grandchild. Another daughter brought her infant son and laid him on my mother's breast. And when she died, my mother was not alone. She went from our loving arms into the loving arms of God.

Catholics often speak of last rites when referring to the Sacrament of the Sick, and there is some confusion about the meaning of these terms. Before the reforms of the Second Vatican Council, the Sacrament of the Sick was known as extreme unction; since that time, it is known as the Sacrament of the Sick, and it is one of the seven sacraments of the Church. The popular term for Extreme Unction, "last rites," suggests that the sacrament is received only at the point of death. (And, in earlier times, most serious illness *did* lead to death.)

Because of Vatican II's Constitution on the Sacred Liturgy (*Sacrosanctum Concilium*), the sacrament is not reserved just for the dying, but is for the service of the seriously ill at any age. The sacrament has three signs: the offering of the prayer of faith, the laying on of hands by a priest, and the anointing of the sick with blessed oil. A person may receive this sacrament as often as necessary, such as in the case of serious illness, before serious surgery, or, for the elderly, when the person weakens or fails, even if no illness is present. In its fullest form, the anointing of the sick will be preceded by the celebration of penance and followed by the celebration of Mass.

Like all sacraments, this one is communal. It is right and fitting for the church to gather with the sick, to support them in prayer, and to encourage them in faith. This gathering may occur in a church, a home, a hospital or care center, wherever there is need.

What of those who are not only sick, but dying? From its earliest days, the Church has acknowledged that, within the broader question of the care of the sick, the dying have particular needs. So in addition to the Sacrament of the Sick, the Church always offers Holy Communion to the dying. This final Communion is a rite reserved for the time of death and is called viaticum, a word that means "food for the journey." Death is surely a journey for which we need the strength and sustenance only the bread of heaven can provide. This is a position the Church has maintained since its earliest days.

At the Council of Nicaea in AD 325 the Church declared Holy

Communion given to the dying "the last and most necessary viaticum."

At the Second Vatican Council the Church held that

> Communion received as viaticum should be considered a special sign of participation in the mystery, which is celebrated in the Eucharist: the mystery of the death of the Lord and his passage to the Father.

Indeed, so important is this sign that the Council cautions the dying and their priests and families against delay, so "that the faithful are nourished by it while still in full possession of their faculties."

The ordinary place of reception is within the Mass, and the dying are encouraged to receive both the Body and the Blood of Christ. They are also invited and encouraged to renew the faith professed by them, or for them, at baptism. It is good to be reminded that they are the adopted children of God and the coheirs of eternal life. And though we often hear the expression "You can't take it with you," the Church teaches that the eternal can pass with us from life into death. Indeed, all that we *can* take is all that we *need* take on the final journey. In viaticum, in the reception of Holy Communion, the Body and Blood of Christ go with us. As food and drink, as companion and guide, as Lord and Savior, Jesus Christ goes with us.

What if no priest is available? A deacon or an Extraordinary Minister of Holy Communion may bring viaticum.

Do not hesitate to call your local parish or to contact the hospital chaplain if you or someone you know is in need of the sacrament. Even if the hospital is not Catholic the chaplaincy staff will be able to contact a priest.

There is a core unity between the three sacraments of baptism, Confirmation, and Eucharist. Together they constitute the sacraments of initiation. Just so, within the Sacrament of the Sick there is a unity of elements: penance, anointing, and viaticum.

But the formal reception of the sacrament need not be the end of our provisioning a dying brother or sister for the final journey. In the Benedictine tradition, once it is clear that a member of the community is dying and after the final anointing, the whole community is summoned and gathers round the deathbed to pray psalms, litanies, and other familiar prayers. For families and friends, this might take the form of singing well-loved hymns or lullabies, such as "Abide with Me," or "The King of Love My Shepherd Is," or "All Through the Night." You might pray the Rosary together, or a litany, such as the Litany of St. Joseph (found on pages 219–221), because he is the patron of the dying.

There is this simple, and lovely, traditional Catholic prayer:

> Jesus, Mary, and Joseph,
> I give you my heart and my soul.
> Jesus, Mary, and Joseph,
> Assist me in the hour of my death.
> Jesus, Mary, and Joseph,
> May I die and rest in peace with you.

Or this prayer, written by Blessed Cardinal John Henry Newman:

> May God support us all the day long till the shades lengthen
> and the evening comes and the busy world is hushed and
> the fever of life is over and our work is done. Then in mercy
> may God give us a safe lodging and a holy rest and peace at
> the last.

Once death has come, do not feel that you have to immediately leave your loved one's body. Linger awhile if you wish and are able, and continue to pray or sing or sit quietly. Do not be afraid to touch or caress the hands and face of the dead. Pray with the body. Praying for the dead is one of the spiritual works of mercy. This prayer is known by many Catholics and should be known by us all:

> Eternal rest grant unto (Name), O Lord,
> R/. And let perpetual light shine upon (him/her)

May (he/she) rest in peace.
R/. Amen.

May (his/her) soul, and the souls of all the faithful departed, through the mercy of God, rest in peace.

R/. Amen.

~~~~~~~~~~~~~~~~~~

# 82

# THE FUNERAL LITURGY: WAKE, FUNERAL, AND COMMITTAL

*All we go down to the dust;*
*and weeping over the grave, we make our song:*
*Alleluia, alleluia, alleluia.*

—FROM THE ORTHODOX LITURGY, THIRTEENTH CENTURY

Her absence is like the sky, spread over everything.

—C. S. LEWIS, *A Grief Observed*

We are created to live forever with God. So death is a parting, but not an end. We believe that those who have died with Christ in baptism, even though they are hidden from our sight, are alive in Christ. That is why we continue to pray for the dead. For not even death, as St. Paul reminds us, can separate us from the love of God in Christ our Lord (Romans 8:38-39). God's love reaches beyond the grave. God's mercy is mightier than death. So we grieve, but we do not, as St. Paul puts it, "grieve like the rest, who have no hope" (1 Thessalonians 4:13). The same hope that infuses each Mass infuses our funeral rites.

Just as the Church understands the funeral liturgy to be linked with each Christian liturgy, in which we, always and everywhere, proclaim the crucified and risen Christ, so the three parts of the funeral liturgy are linked as one. All of these elements, from the vigil to the gravesite, are movements in a single composition. Like the Triduum, which flows from sunset on Holy Thursday through Good Friday to the Easter Vigil on Holy Saturday night, the movement from death to burial is one. You will notice a seamless quality to the prayers and gestures and readings, as many of them recur. You will also notice that the focus is on Christ. When many memorial services are celebrations of the life of the deceased, the Catholic funeral rites, while never ignoring the deceased, focus on Christ.

Consider the wisdom at work here. "Celebrations of life" often focus on pictures of the deceased skiing or vacationing, playing, laughing, and having fun. What of the sad, the poor, the mourners, the ill, the scorned, people whose lives are not photo-ready? People who have no record of successes and awards to display? Are they not also loved? The Catholic Church gives full respect and solemnity to each death, in part, by focusing not on personal achievements or position—which some have in abundance and some not at all—but on the single hope we all share: Christ's victory over death.

When a member of our parish hanged himself, the newspapers were filled with stories of his conviction for sex crimes and his incarceration. That is all anyone knew about him from the media. Then we arrived at the parish for his funeral, where the priest began, simply, "In the waters of baptism John died with Christ and rose with him to new life. May he now share with him eternal glory." The focus was on Christ's saving work, not on one man's failure in following Christ. My daughter turned to me and said, "The Church has given him back his name."

In baptism we receive our true names: daughter of God, son of God, names given to us in baptism, names that can be neither bought nor earned nor manufactured nor seized. They can only be given, by God, the author and finisher of all life, and they go with us, from the baptismal font to the grave. Nothing can strip us of those names.

## THE FUNERAL VIGIL

The funeral vigil, perhaps better known as the wake, has its own rhythms and ways. One of the good works young people can accomplish is to bring back the wake. When we keep the wake in its fullness, we give each aspect of the journey its due.

Most of us believe the wake must be held at the funeral home, and most of us have only had the experience of a funeral home wake, but, in an older tradition—predating the modern funeral home by centuries—people were waked at home. You should talk to your pastor and the staff at a local funeral home if you plan to be waked, or to wake others, at home. It helps to have this conversation well in advance of the wake, as you will need to make plans to have the body transferred from the funeral home to the house and then to the church. I experienced this with my mother's death. She did not want to be embalmed, nor did she want to be waked in a funeral home, but in our dining room, the site of so many gatherings and meals. We made the decision to embalm her, since, as is the case with so many families, there were family members who wanted to see her and say good-bye, but who would not be able to be at the deathbed. They traveled a long way to the funeral, and we wanted to accommodate their needs. So she went first from her deathbed to the funeral home.

Talk about this with your family and with the ill and the elderly in your care. Make your own wishes known to your spouse or children or close friends. Understand that fulfilling your wishes may, or may not, be possible. It may help to have a number of suggestions, or to have your plans ranked in order of importance to you.

We placed my mother's coffin by the west windows in our dining room, and we kept vigil all through the day and night before her funeral. The coffin was kept open for most of the day and into the evening, so that friends and family members could see and touch her one last time. Late in the evening, we gathered and sang the litany of the saints as her coffin was closed and sealed, to be opened again only on the last day. Most of the mourners left then, but I stayed on the couch nearby, dozing and waking, and remembering and giving thanks.

The vigil service can take the form of a Word service, with Scripture readings and prayers, or it can be taken from the Office of the Dead from the Liturgy of the Hours. Many elderly Catholics, who remember this custom from their youth, will request that a Rosary be said at the vigil. For all of these decisions you'll need to talk with your parish priest.

Don't hesitate to surround the rites of the Church with food and drink, with stories and songs and memories. This is the time for personal recollections, for eulogies, that is, "good speech," about the dead. Probably not all of the recollections will be solemn. The wake is the time to laugh *and* cry. Its purpose is to keep watch with those who mourn, as they keep watch with the beloved dead. The Church's wisdom is to allow this time for genuine human emotion and personal reflection, time to focus on the one who has died.

So, if you want to set out pictures, or sing favorite songs, or bake a cake you associate with the dead, or put out the deceased's artwork or record collection, the wake is the time to do that. You'll find that a place other than the funeral home is better suited to the personal nature of the wake. What if you don't have enough room at your house? Is there a club room at your apartment complex, a gathering space in your parish basement? Ask and see if you can find a space large enough to host the wake. But don't be afraid of crowding. It can be a comfort to have people close in times of grief, and people should feel free to come and go during the wake.

## THE FUNERAL MASS

The funeral Mass is an action by the Church for the Church. It is, as the bishops of the United States put it, "an act of worship, and not merely an expression of grief." All who wish to come are welcome, not just family and friends. We gather to give thanks and praise to God, who has conquered sin and death. We cover the coffin with the white pall, or cloth, which recalls our baptismal garment. We commend the deceased to God's tender mercy and compassion. We draw strength from the celebration of the Eucharist and from the faith as it has been handed down from one generation to the next for over two thousand years. So stick with the rite. The wake is the place to sing "Take Me Out to the Ballgame," and remember how Dave loved the Cubs. The funeral is the time to sing "The Strife Is Over" and recall Christ's resurrection.

Many families are mixed in their religious practices. The local bishop has the authority to allow a non-Catholic to proclaim the Scripture or read the intercessory prayers at a funeral Mass.

Baptized Catholics, catechumens, and infants who died before their parents could have them baptized all receive a Catholic funeral. The local bishop has the authority, in certain instances, to allow a non-Catholic to receive Catholic funeral rites (canon 1176).

## RITE OF COMMITTAL

The committal is the final movement of the funeral rites, the final act of caring done by the community for its deceased member. This brief service speaks to the hope with which we gather, the hope in which we live, that the deceased, along with all the faithful departed, will share in the glory of Christ's resurrection. If possible, the Rite of Committal should be celebrated at the place of burial or entombment. Most of us have to drive from the church to the cemetery for this rite. If you can walk from one place to the next, consider it a blessing. But the long, slow drive can also be a goodness and a source of grace. In 2007, my father-in-law was buried in the town where he was born. As the long line of cars set out from his parish church to the cemetery, we began to see a wondrous thing: drivers pulling off the road and waiting respectfully until we had passed, pedestrians stopping and removing their hats or bowing their heads, a group of city workers kneeling as we passed by. None of these people knew the man we buried that day, but they displayed a respect for human dignity that has stayed with all of us who witnessed it.

## BURIAL OR CREMATION?

Burial of the dead remains the normative and preferred practice of the Church, but since 1997, cremation has been, and is, allowed, "unless it was chosen for reasons contrary to Christian doctrine" (canon 1176.3). Later that year, the bishops confirmed the special texts and ritual directives for cremation, which were then published as an appendix to the *Order of Christian Funerals*. It states, "Although cremation is now permitted by the Church, it does not enjoy the same value as burial of the body. The Church clearly prefers and urges that the body of the deceased be present for the funeral rites, since the presence of the human body better expresses the values which the Church affirms in those rites (no. 413)."

Some desire cremation because, in general, it costs less than full body burial. This is a legitimate concern, but there are ways to reduce funeral costs and still have a full body burial. Talk to your parish priest and see what funeral societies operate in your area. Many of them offer low-cost options, such as plain, locally built, pine boxes, which can significantly reduce costs, or contact the Trappist monks of New Melleray Abbey. These monks make their living by crafting simple, affordable and sustainable wooden caskets from the trees on their property. They view each casket as a work of mercy, and offer a Mass in remembrance for each person buried in one. If you make plans well in advance of the funeral, it is helpful to check and see what the laws and regulations are in your area. People often assume a service offered by the funeral home is required by law when it is not.

Whatever is decided, the Church asks us always to keep the sanctity of the body in mind. Therefore the Church does not allow cremated remains to be scattered or made into jewelry or kept in urns at home. All of these practices are open to the abuse of the remains, and it is no more allowed than it would be allowed for a mourner to take a part of the body of the deceased to keep at home. The Church requires that cremated remains be placed in a respectful vessel and treated just as a body in a casket is treated. Since the human body has an eternal destiny, no matter in what form, the cremated remains must be treated like an intact body, to be entombed or buried immediately after the funeral. The Church does allow burial at sea, providing that the cremated remains of the body are buried in a heavy container and are not scattered.

# *Coda*

～～～～～～～～～～～～～～～～～～

And this is the journey of life: walking onward to meet Jesus.

–POPE FRANCIS

This book ends with our earthly lives, with a funeral and burial. And yet, for Christians death is not an ending but a beginning, as those who have died are born into eternal life. As we profess in the Nicene Creed, "We look forward to the resurrection of the dead, and the life of the world to come."

A central feature of the Catholic life is the ongoing connection between the living and the dead. After the burial of a community member, though we return to our lives, the dead are not forgotten. They join the "great cloud of witnesses" of whom St. Paul writes (Hebrews 12:1-2). We continue pray for them, and ask those in Heaven to pray for us.

When we go to Mass, when we visit the sick, when we participate in the liturgy, and say the same words that the early Christians spoke in the first centuries of the Church, we are connected to those who have gone before us in faith. As G. K. Chesterton wrote in *Orthodoxy*, "Tradition means giving votes to the most obscure of all classes, our ancestors. It is the democracy of the dead. Tradition refuses to submit to the small and arrogant oligarchy of those who merely happen to be walking about."

From the first century to the twenty-first, men and women have been gathering on Sunday to sing and pray, listen and speak, to bless and break bread, to bless and drink wine.

From the earliest days of the Church, Christians have been eating together, going on pilgrimage, and observing days and seasons. When we discover, or rediscover, some of the lost practices of our cultural and spiritual heritage, we strengthen the connection with our great-grandparents in faith.

When we begin, or continue, to sing litanies and make Advent wreaths and pray in the darkness before sleep, when we cook together, and tell stories, and learn Marian prayers, when our children grow up in homes where people show hospitality, our ancestors are never forgotten. Our lives continue where theirs left off.

Pope Francis describes the Christian life as a journey, "walking onward to meet Jesus." We come from God, and our hope is that, in the fullness of time, we will return to him.

It is to this hope—of life, abundant and eternal in Christ—that we pray our book calls all who read it. The ancient practices described here are meant to create space in our daily lives for an encounter with the goodness that is God, as St. Augustine wrote, that our lives might "be His Praise."

—Anna Keating
Memorial of St. Benedict, Abbot
July 11, 2015

# Acknowledgments

~~~~~~~~~~~~~~~~~~~

I haven't space to thank all the people who have helped form me in faith. I include in that blessed number the parishioners of St. Mary's Cathedral in Colorado Springs, where my husband and I have worshipped for the last thirty years. We are grateful for the saints there, living and dead, who have taught us, as G. K. Chesterton writes, "to walk gaily in the dark."

I would like to thank Father Andrew D. Ciferni, O. Praem, and Sister Genevieve Glenn, OSB, for their help and counsel. They are generous teachers. Thanks, too, to Gabe Huck, who, many years ago, planted the seed that grew and flowered into this book. My friendship with these good people is a gift and a grace in my life.

Always, always, I thank Abraham, Elisabeth, Mary Margaret, Anna Cate, Andrew, and now, their children. I learn from them even as I teach them, and I will be forever grateful to have been given that holy work. And, of course, love and thanks to Martin, whose holy work this also was, and is.

—Melissa Musick

This book was written and revised in the nine months after my daughter Ruth was born. I would not have been able to complete it without the help of my in-laws Ceci and Mike Keating, who graciously watched my children so that I could write. Words cannot express my gratitude.

I would also like to thank my husband, Geoffrey, my first and best reader, as well as my dear friend Cassie, for her encouragement, not only on this project, but over many years.

It was important to me from the beginning that the book express something of the beauty of the life. We couldn't have achieved that without the help of our illustrator and my friend Chau Nguyen.

I am supremely grateful to our agent, Greg Daniel, and editor, Gary Jansen, and everyone at Image. Thank you for all your work.

Before *The Catholic Catalogue* was a manuscript, it was a website. Many thanks to everyone at The Heads of State, especially Woody Harrington and Sean Brodbeck, for their brilliant site design.

Thanks to my parents, for raising me in the faith, and many thanks to my mother and coauthor, Melissa.

I am indebted to everyone whom I interviewed for this book, especially Michael Baxter, Meg Hunter-Kilmer, and Fr. Andrew Ciferni.

Finally, thanks to Claire Kelley for her insights, and everyone who wrote for, interned at, or otherwise supported *The Catholic Catalogue* website, especially Beth Kelleher, Kelci Schmidt, and Claire Fyrqvist.

—Anna Keating

# Permission Credits

Grateful acknowledgment is made to the following: